Teaching History with Film
Strategies for Secondary Social Studies

Alan S. Marcus

Scott Alan Metzger

Richard J. Paxton

Jeremy D. Stoddard

 Routledge
Taylor & Francis Group

NEW YORK AND LONDON

First published 2010
by Routledge
270 Madison Avenue, New York, NY 10016

Simultaneously published in the UK
by Routledge
2 Park Square, Milton Park, Abingdon, Oxon OX14 4RN

Routledge is an imprint of the Taylor & Francis Group, an informa business

Typeset in Bembo and Helvetica Neue by Prepress Projects Ltd, Perth, UK
Printed and bound in the United States of America on acid-free paper by
Edwards Brothers, Inc.

Library of Congress Cataloging in Publication Data
Teaching history with film : strategies for secondary social studies / Alan S.
Marcus ... [et al.].
p. cm.
Includes bibliographical references and index.
ISBN 978-0-415-99954-0 (hb : alk. paper) -- ISBN 978-0-415-99956-4 (pb
: alk. paper) -- ISBN 978-0-203-86299-5 (ebook) 1. History--Study and
teaching (Secondary)–Audio-visual aids. 2. Motion pictures in education. I.
Marcus, Alan S.
D16.255.A8T44 2010
907.1'2--dc22
2009027949

British Library Cataloguing in Publication Data
A catalogue record for this book is available from the British Library

ISBN 10: 0–415–99954–5 (hbk)
ISBN 10: 0–415–99956–1 (pbk)
ISBN 10: 0–203–86299–6 (ebk)

ISBN 13: 978–0–415–99954–0 (hbk)
ISBN 13: 978–0–415–99956–4 (pbk)
ISBN 13: 978–0–203–86299–5 (ebk)

To my son Samuel, whose passion for life and belly laughs are contagious; and to my daughter Sophie, whose positive outlook on life is inspirational and whose snuggles are like a daily vitamin.—Alan

To David and Sandra Metzger, for all the love and support a son could ever want; and to Jennifer, for all the faith and love a husband could ever need.—Scott

To Kelly, Noah and Lili, and all the houses we have built.—Rich

To Kim, who is always supportive and puts up with my comments when we watch a movie. In memory of Steve, who I wish was still around so that I could force him to watch Patton *one more time.—Jeremy*

Contents

Acknowledgements   xi

Part I   **Using Film to Teach History**   **1**

  1   Introduction   3
  2   Issues in Using Film to Teach History   17

Part II   **Using Film to Develop Empathy**   **27**

  3   Empathy for Caring   31
  4   Using Film to Develop Empathy as Perspective Recognition   51

Part III   **Using Film to Develop Analytical or Interpretive Skills**   **69**

  5   Movies as Primary Documents   73
  6   Using Film as a Secondary Source   91

Part IV   **Using Film to Teach about Controversial Issues**   **109**

  7   Using Film to Teach about Contemporary
    Controversial Issues   113
  8   Using Film to Teach Controversial Issues in History   135

Part V   **Using Film to Visualize the Past and Film as
               Historical Narrative**   **155**

  9   Using Film to Visualize the Past   159
  10 Using Film as Historical Narrative   175

Figure Permissions and Credits   191
Notes   193
References   193
Index   196

Acknowledgements

First and foremost we express appreciation to all of the wonderful and dedicated teachers who let us into their classrooms and shared their practices, their students, and their passion. Without them this book would not exist. We also extend our gratitude to our editors at Routledge, Catherine and Heather, for their guidance and patience. It was a pleasure to work with them. We are grateful to Tom Levine at the University of Connecticut, who read various versions of the manuscript and offered valuable feedback and advice. We would also like to thank the Thomas S. Thompson Distinguished Professorship at Pacific University and The College of William and Mary for financial support in completing this project.

Using Film to Teach History

CHAPTER 1

Introduction

Figure 1.1 Forrest Gump (1994). An intellectually challenged man (Tom Hanks) experiences major historical events of the 1960s and 1970s.

Visit any school in the United States on any given day of the school year and you are likely to find at least one teacher showing a movie about the past. Second perhaps only to the textbook, films are one of the most prominent teaching resources in the history classroom (Marcus & Stoddard, 2007; Marcus, Paxton, & Meyerson, 2006). It is not only in school that children and teenagers encounter film versions of history. Young people today are immersed in visual representations of the past seen in movie theaters, on television and computer screens, and now on portable DVD players and even cell phones. In fact, we would not be the first to suggest that a great deal of what students "know" about the past comes not from textbooks or teachers but from "Hollywood" movies (Briley, 2002; Pultorak, 1992; Wineburg, 2000). Yet, when social studies teachers look for models of the effective use of motion pictures in history classrooms—techniques that will not only "cover" historical topics but also teach something about the work of "doing" history or historical interpretation—the cupboard is surprisingly bare.

The goal of this book is to provide educators with models that illustrate powerful history teaching using motion pictures. These "cases" of real practice—close descriptions of teachers practicing their craft along with reproductions of supporting materials—are designed to provide educators with ideas and skills for implementing effective film-based lessons. They are also presented to give teachers a deeper understanding of the thorny issues involved in using film to teach history. We hope these stories of working teachers and their students will encourage readers to consider how movies color the way people think about the past. Furthermore, we hope these lessons can be adapted and tailored to many other classrooms in ways that will make students think deeply about movies not just as entertainment but as historical accounts and interpretations to be examined, questioned, and discussed.

This book aims to provide educators with helpful ideas inspired by actual practice. All four authors are former classroom teachers who now work as educational researchers and teacher educators training the next generation of social studies teachers. Our field-work with classroom teachers drew us to examine two questions: (1) Why use history movies in the classroom? (2) How can history movies be used effectively in the classroom? The examples described in the chapters that follow will explore these issues in depth. But, before turning to these real-world examples, it is worth the time to consider some background behind these important questions.

BACKGROUND ON FILM AND HISTORY EDUCATION

Teachers have long been comfortable using certain kinds of films in the history classroom. A perennial favorite is the *historical documentary film*. Broadcast outlets such as PBS and the BBC and cable networks such as A&E, the Discovery Channel, and the History Channel have aired thousands of titles. Often less than an hour in length and available affordably on VHS and DVD, documentary videos are a natural fit for social studies teachers. For almost any topic that needs to be covered in a history classroom, there is a documentary out there that narrates—sometimes even dramatizes—the topic in detail. Documentary videos are often produced specifically with an educational market in mind. They can readily be used in the classroom much in the same way any "document" can be used to cover information. Certainly there are tensions and concerns revolving around the educational impact of documentary videos. Popular documentaries favor certain topics such as wars and famous figures over others that may be less well known but more challenging. Documentaries can take on the veneer of neutral objectivity even though they are constructed and interpretive, and young people may uncritically accept authoritative documentaries in the same light as their unquestioned textbooks (Marcus & Stoddard, in press; Paxton, 1999; Stoddard, 2009). Nonetheless, the narrative, factual structure of most documentary videos may explain why so many teachers use them in the classroom easily and comfortably.

By contrast, *historical feature films*—full-length commercial movies set in the past, made for a popular audience, and marketed through the mass media—can give many teachers pause. Children and especially teenagers are frequently quite familiar with "Hollywood" movies and may be excited to watch a big-budget epic starring popular celebrities with impressive sets, costumes, and special effects. Teachers may be drawn to bringing movies into their lessons as a way to tap into youth popular culture and increase student attention and motivation.

On the other hand, history movies are explicitly dramatized and fictionalized accounts of the past. Whereas most teachers are comfortable trusting the factual accuracy of documentary videos, accuracy is a much more problematic issue for feature films. Almost all people recognize that Hollywood movies "make things up" about the past, but recognizing exactly which parts are invented and which are accurate can be quite difficult. Investigating the accuracy of a history movie can require expert subject-matter knowledge and many hours of study. As a result, showing a history movie in the classroom can seem a little ambiguous or intimidating to teachers. Exactly what knowledge are the students supposed to glean from watching the movie? How are they supposed to think or feel about the past after watching it? What if something in the movie inspires students to ask really hard questions to which the teacher might not know the answer?

Factual accuracy is not the only issue at stake, of course. There are a host of very practical concerns. Movies can be long and require a great deal of class time. Saving time by showing select short clips requires the teacher to carefully watch the film in advance to pick out which clips to use. Movies often contain objectionable violence, language, and sexual content. As if these aren't enough, there are also serious intellectual and academic concerns. If "doing" history should involve more than just passively watching a story about the past, what should students do before, during, and after a movie to tap into its educational value? If movies tell only one "side" of a complex historical event or issue, what should teachers do to help students recognize multiple perspectives (particularly those that might be missing)? If most movies contain interpretive or moral messages about the past, how should teachers get students to reflect on the meaning of the film? However, these concerns are problems only when they are ignored or neglected. When handled thoughtfully and skillfully, these questions can become useful means for inspiring powerful historical thinking in the classroom. In Chapter 2 we specifically address these issues and offer strategies for dealing with the challenges of teaching with film.

WHY USE HISTORY MOVIES?

Extraordinary claims are made about the power of motion pictures to teach history—that "Hollywood" movies have the capacity to lift students to "a higher level of inquiry" (Sabato, 1992, p. 84), to "preserve details of life that may not be communicated or appreciated in writing" (Johnson and Vargas, 1994, p. 109), and to help history "come alive to students" (Dobbs, 1987, p. 16). Numerous books and articles already advocate the use of feature films in the history classroom (Briley, 2002; Kraig, 1983; Maynard, 1971; Paris, 1997; Toplin, 2002). Indeed, the power of movies to motivate student learning about history shouldn't be underestimated. Movies are part of youth culture—students are exposed to them far beyond the walls of their schools and even before formal schooling begins. Students often bring to class personal interest in, and sometimes prior knowledge about, movies set in the past. Young people may get more excited about lessons using popular media than about instruction only using official school materials such as textbooks, primary documents, or worksheets. Scholarship on history education suggests that movies have considerable potential to contribute to a variety of competencies of historical literacy (Marcus, 2005; Metzger, 2007b).

In their "storytelling" role movies can help students recognize and analyze different narratives about the past and examine the constructed nature of historical interpretations—a key component of effective historical thinking. Teachers accomplished in film-based instruction take advantage of movies as widely viewed historical "documents" not only to teach about a particular time period or event but also to teach *historical film literacy*—that is, skills and dispositions that empower students to look at movies set in the past critically as historical documents, not just entertainment (Marcus, 2005, 2007).

Although movies can serve as motivating tools for history teaching, they also hold potential risks (Metzger, 2005, 2007a; Metzger & Suh, 2008). Movies frequently portray imagined characters and events right next to or interspersed among real historical people and events. Consider the blockbuster film *The Patriot* (2000), which climaxes in a dramatic battle incorporating some authentic elements from the actual battles at Cowpens and Guilford Courthouse and a fictionalized hero (played by Mel Gibson) alongside real historical figures such as Nathanael Greene and Lord Cornwallis. Many movies engage in *presentism*—a mode of historical thought in which present-day ideas and attitudes are anachronistically introduced into depictions of the past or are used to evaluate or judge what happened in the past. For example, *Kingdom of Heaven* (2005), set during the Crusades, features a religiously tolerant hero (played by Orlando Bloom) who proclaims before the battle over Jerusalem that neither Christians, Jews, nor Muslims have sole right to the Holy Land—an attitude perfectly comfortable to modern-day audiences but utterly alien to medieval mentalities. Teachers may become overwhelmed by the difficulty of sorting out these kinds of complex issues and may settle for using movies in rather uncritical ways. Difficult or controversial issues raised by movies may be glossed over or ignored altogether.

Underlying all these difficulties is the unavoidable reality that history movies are their own kind of historical document (Rosenstone, 2002, 2004; Toplin, 1996). Perhaps they are more akin to historical-fiction novels than scholarly works, but even this comparison sells short the diversity of history movies. Many play fast and loose with the historical record, for instance the Roman epic *Gladiator* (2000). Others endeavor to be as historically accurate as possible, as does the recent version of *The Alamo* (2004). Yet others strive to be fastidiously accurate about known details while using imagination to fill in unknown blanks or uncertain motivations, such as *Marie Antoinette* (2006) or *Alexander* (2004). Some history movies have a message to convey and adapt or fictionalize the past to support that tale, such as *The Last Samurai* (2003), which portrays the final rebellion of Japanese samurai as a critique of the hollowness of Western culture and capitalism. All of these movies to different degrees blend authentic and imagined elements, realism and creativity, to produce a special mode of historical storytelling (Rosenstone, 1995; Toplin, 2002, 2007).

Hazards abound for educators who presume that history movies are only entertainment or that they can be used just to "cover" historical facts. Despite these undoubted challenges, we believe that the promise of motion pictures in the history classroom outweighs the drawbacks. This book aims to help teachers overcome potential problems by offering strategies informed by research on history teaching and learning and drawn from effective classroom practice.

HOW CAN HISTORY MOVIES BE USED?

There seems to be little doubt that movies are among the most powerful art forms developed in the twentieth century, with considerable influence over many forms of thought, including historical. Given this influence, it is reasonable and appropriate for social studies teachers to want to use movies to motivate and facilitate student learning. More people encounter history through movies than through any other form, including textbooks. Even a "flop" Hollywood history movie is seen by more people than read all but the most successful historical books. Consider the recent remake of *The Alamo* (2004), which had a production budget of more than $100 million but grossed barely over $20 million at the box office. This historically detailed film was considered a disastrous failure in the film industry—yet, based on the average ticket price in 2004 of just under $6.50, more than 3 million people saw *The Alamo* in theaters (and more have seen it since on cable television or home video). Educators are deceiving themselves if they think history movies are of trivial importance. Teachers who bring history movies into the classroom recognize that these films are widely influential in informing how people today think about the past.

So how can history teachers use movies in critical and powerful ways? One important notion cuts across all considerations of how movies can be used effectively for educational ends: Films function as "texts" that can be analyzed, questioned, and discussed just like any other kind of historical document. Just because the "vocabulary" of film is audio-visual rather than print-based doesn't make movies less of a human statement of meaning with social, cultural, and political messages open to interpretation and interrogation.

In the memorable phrase of John O'Connor, films are "moving image documents" that can be examined for the content they contain, the forces behind their production, and the reception they received in the broader culture (O'Connor, 2007). Some films, like most textbooks, obscure authorship and make it seem as if there is no one person behind the message. On the other hand, many films trumpet their director. For example, Oliver Stone, Martin Scorsese, and Spike Lee are history moviemakers whose role as director is often as well known as the stars of their pictures. A director may or may not be involved in writing the screenplay but still exerts influence over how the script is enacted. Some both write and direct a film, as Sofia Coppola did for *Marie Antoinette* (2006). This is not to say that all film-based history lessons must focus attention on directors and writers, but the first step to historical film literacy is to help young people recognize that movies are made by people for particular reasons and that the messages they contain are neither neutral nor accidental.

In other words, just like print novels or stories, movies have *purposes* (intentions) and *themes* (messages). Historical film literacy revolves around empowering young people to recognize, describe, question, and analyze a film's purposes and themes. Why is a history movie telling a story about an era or event in a particular way? Why are certain perspectives emphasized and others de-emphasized or ignored? Whom does the movie want the audience to cheer for or against? What perspectives on the past does the movie encourage the audience to empathize with and why? What moral reactions about the past does the movie aim to evoke, or provoke, in viewers? For example, the movie *300* (2007) about the ancient battle of Thermopylae between Greeks and Persians was made and released during U.S. military actions in Iraq and Afghanistan. Greek Spartans are classroom but how and to what ends. When confronted with a critic of teachers' heavy reliance on videos in the classroom, Stanford educational researcher Sam Wineburg responded that "rather than do away with popular culture . . . we might try instead to understand how these forces shape historical consciousness, and how they might be used . . . to advance students' historical understanding" (Wineburg, 2001, p. 250). Wineburg and his colleagues have noted the cultural influence of the movie *Forrest Gump* (1994) on how people across generations think about the 1960s and which elements are collectively remembered or forgotten (Wineburg, Mosborg, Porat, & Duncan, 2007). Their observation only adds to a sense that history education needs to include historical film literacy and cannot ignore the cultural influence of movies on how people come to understand the past.

In the end, powerful film-based instruction is purposeful and knowledgeable. Teachers must model for students how to recognize, describe, question, and analyze the historical interpretive elements of many kinds of historical documents, including movies whether in full or even just short scene clips. Paving the way for historical film literacy requires teachers to be purposeful about their educational goals in bringing movies into the classroom. Purposeful goals should include not only considerations of subject-matter knowledge but also historical thinking and understanding.

WHAT'S TO COME IN THIS BOOK

A great deal of knowledge about good teaching never makes its way into the professional literature, remaining instead in the minds, or behind the classroom doors, of innovative teachers. This book aims to describe, reflect on, and share innovative educational practices using history films. The chapters in this book chronicle working teachers who use movies to do more than simply cover a particular person, event, or period of time. Rather, each section focuses on how a teacher attempts to use film to support the development of students' historical film literacy and engage students in powerful and authentic examinations of the past and persistent historical and contemporary issues. The book is divided into five parts organized around broad educational outcomes in social studies. Parts II through to V contain eight chapters that explore specific themes in history education using film. The reader will witness teachers and their students as they attempt to distinguish fact from fiction, recognize multiple perspectives and missing perspectives, and evaluate film as evidence. Other chapters describe lessons devoted to the use of movies to develop historical empathy, as a means for analyzing or discussing essential issues or historical controversies, to develop analytical or interpretive skills using film as a historical source, and to help students visualize the past.

This is a curriculum book designed for working teachers, teachers-in-training, and teacher educators. The idea is to illustrate strategies for smart, skillful uses of movies in the history classroom: examples that are provocative, educative, and capable of being recreated in other classrooms. Those of us who have stood in front of groups of middle and high school students trying to interest them in the study of history know that the work isn't easy. We make no claims that the teachers described in this book are perfect, but we are grateful to them for allowing us to peek into their classrooms, think about their teaching techniques, and learn from their experience.

Part I: Using Film to Teach History

In this chapter we have offered a rationale for why feature films are an important resource for secondary social studies teachers and laid out a vision for how film can be used effectively to develop students' historical understanding. Chapter 2 describes practical challenges that educators may face in teaching with feature films, discusses implications for history teaching and learning, and offers some practical strategies for dealing with them.

Part II: Using Film to Develop Empathy

The second part of our book explores the educational value of historical empathy through "caring" and "perspective recognition" (Barton & Levstik, 2004). Chapter 3 examines how film can be used to help students care about the historical experiences of people. History movies can be particularly powerful ways to develop empathy, especially for groups of people who have been marginalized historically. The case looks at Mr. O'Brian's unit on the history and anthropology of the Hmong people. He faced a considerable challenge in getting his Oregon teenagers to care about the Hmong experience. His unit began with *Gran Torino* (2008), a highly praised Clint Eastwood drama that depicts a clash of cultures between a retired Korean War veteran and his immigrant Hmong neighbors. After exploring Hmong history and culture through portions of documentary films and reading an ethnographic book about the Hmong, the class returned to *Gran Torino* as Mr. O'Brian pushed students to deconstruct the film, and in particular the Hmong characters depicted in it, from their more knowledgeable and empathetic perspective.

Chapter 4 illustrates the potential for using film to engage students in historical empathy as perspective recognition. Although feature films often fictionalize or embellish aspects of the historical record for dramatic purposes, they can also be a powerful medium for helping students recognize the decision making and experiences of people from the past. In addition to altering or fictionalizing the historical story being told, films also position their audiences to see the story from particular viewpoints. This chapter looks at empathy to promote perspective recognition through the case of Mrs. Johnson's unit on the rise of totalitarianism and the Holocaust using four films: *The Wave* (1981), *In Memory of Millions* (1994), *Swing Kids* (1993), and *America and the Holocaust: Deceit and Indifference* (1994). Mrs. Johnson began with *The Wave* (1981), a made-for-television movie about a classroom teacher whose simulation of how young people were drawn into the Nazi Youth goes awry, to get students to consider how totalitarianism can become established in a society through the power of group think. She then had students look at the perspectives of Holocaust perpetrators, victims, survivors, bystanders, and non-Nazi Germans who resisted, while watching *Swing Kids* (1993) and the documentary *In Memory of Millions* (1994) and through reading primary and secondary accounts. She concluded the unit with a critical look at the perspective of many Americans during the Holocaust and what the United States did and did not do by watching the documentary *America and the Holocaust: Deceit and Indifference* (1994).

Part III: Using Film to Develop Analytical or Interpretive Skills

Movies can be effectively used as primary and secondary "texts" to be analyzed in conjunction with other kinds of documents, such as print readings. All films are primary sources that can be analyzed and interpreted as artifacts from the time period in which they were made. Films can reflect the prevailing values and norms of society of the time in which they are created—or dissenting or critical reactions against prevailing values and norms. Chapter 5 examines how films used as primary sources can help students better interpret movies as historical artifacts as well as improve their ability to examine other historical documents. This chapter presents the case of Ron Briley's lessons for his Modern American History class on the 1960s using a diverse series of movies. His unit began with two fundamentally different takes on the Vietnam War: *The Green Berets* (1968) and *Platoon* (1986). Next, students viewed *Bonnie and Clyde* (1968)—ostensibly a movie about the Depression Era bank robbers, used here as a primary historical document reflecting a particular perspective on the cultural conflicts and social changes of the tumultuous 1960s when it was made. Extensive discussion of the film and its theme was followed by viewing *The Graduate* (1967), a movie about a young man estranged from the 1960s society in which he is coming of age. Finally, students watched *Easy Rider* (1969), the iconic cross-country motorcycle road trip of hippie soul-searching. Mr. Briley's film-based unit concluded with a synthesis essay that asked students to use historical documents to reflect on and assess the counterculture movement.

Film also can be used as a secondary source to be evaluated by comparing film to primary sources from the time period represented in the film. Chapter 6 investigates the potential of film to be used as a secondary account and interpretation of historical events. This chapter presents the case of Mr. Hector's unit on Westward Expansion using the recent version of *The Alamo* (2004) as a secondary source to complement other secondary accounts and primary documents. His goals were for students to understand "what happened at the Alamo" including the basic sequence of events, the people involved, and, to the extent possible, the "reality" of the Alamo. He accomplished this goal by focusing students on the information they could learn from the film and reinforcing that information with readings and discussion. Building upon this understanding of what happened at the Alamo, he also asked students to interpret a primary source using what they had learned. This application of students' knowledge served to assess their learning and ability to analyze multiple sources.

Part IV: Using Film to Teach about Controversial Issues

Films implicitly and explicitly address contemporary controversial issues. Movies made in previous eras can be used to offer historical context about a contemporary controversial issue, connecting the present to the past. History classes are a natural place to include lessons on controversial social and political issues.

Chapter 7 examines a unit in which film is used effectively to introduce a controversial issue and to "scaffold" classroom discussion and activities that explore it in depth. This chapter looks at the case of Mr. Clark's use of *The Jazz Singer* (1927) and portions of *Norbit* (2007) and *Soulman* (1986), as well as other examples from popular culture, to explore issues of race and identity in the 1920s and today. His unit on the 1920s began with activities exploring theories of blackface and with viewing *The Jazz Singer*. During and after the film, he asked his students to consider the ways in which identity conflict is shown in the film, including musical, racial, religious, and generation identity, and to consider how the film connects to historical trends such as the great migration, the Harlem Renaissance, and the media industry. Finally, students examined the ways in which the film celebrates and/or demeans African-American culture. Other examples or parodies of blackface in popular culture past and present were also shown and analyzed, and students discussed the similarities and differences between the historic and modern examples. The modern examples were then used as a mechanism for exploring racial attitudes and issues today, in particular a local debate over the school board's consideration of a request from African-American parents to ban Mark Twain's *The Adventures of Huckleberry Finn* from the curriculum.

Film also can work as a tool to explore important historical issues, connecting what happened in the past to issues in our world today. Chapter 8 examines how a movie can be used to teach about controversial events in the past and their legacy to the present. In the first decade of the twenty-first century, conflict in the Middle East remains one of the gravest political issues facing the world. Militant Islamists in their opposition to Israel and Western nations frequently evoke the memory of the Crusades. Some Western opponents of militant Islamism decry a clash of cultures, seeing the Holy Land today as a battleground between the West (with its historical legacy of Christianity) and the Muslim world. This chapter examines the case of Mr. Jackson's unit on the Crusades using *Kingdom of Heaven* (2005) to explore the important historical issue of the Crusades and religious conflict over the Holy Land, particularly attitudes toward Muslim historical figures and Islam. In Mr. Jackson's view, this movie is uniquely positioned to get students thinking about the Crusades and their relevance to the world today. His unit chiefly aimed at getting students to recognize and evaluate multiple perspectives from the period and different perspectives about the legacy of the Crusades. To help his students understand the perspectives, he identified six major characters in the film and assigned each student one of them to "shadow" while watching the film, paying particular attention to their experience and taking detailed notes focused on them. Mr. Jackson's lessons revolved around understanding Saladin and the Islamic perspective featured in the film. His unit culminated in asking students to evaluate the different perspectives, the movie's historical accuracy in presenting those perspectives, and the legacy of the Crusades for the world today—with explicit connections to President George W. Bush, Osama bin Laden, and the U.S. war against terrorism.

Part V: Using Film to Visualize the Past and as Narrative

Teachers' choices about using "Hollywood" movies in the history classroom often involve a desire to motivate student interest. Students can't actually see history, only what is left behind, and some question how the study of the past holds any value for their lives today. Movies have the potential to help students visualize the past and to challenge students to examine history through films that present competing narratives about the past.

Chapter 9 looks at how a movie can be used to help students visualize elements or experiences in the past as real and immediate. This chapter examines the case of Mr.

Irwin's Civil War unit using *Glory* (1989) to "bring the past to life" for his Connecticut eighth graders. He used the film as a tool for recreating the life of Civil War soldiers, particularly African Americans. Students were given guiding questions to support their viewing of the film, drawing their attention to aspects of the soldiers' experiences such as why they enlisted, how they were trained, relationships between white and black soldiers, what battle was like for them, and how they changed over the course of the film. He wanted to help students not only to "see" the recreated past in terms of uniforms and battle scenes but to get a feel for some of the "conditions" of the past, such as race relations, that provide context for people and events. Mr. Irwin then led discussions of these elements to check for student understanding and elaborate on aspects of the film he felt were important. Following the activities with *Glory*, Mr. Irwin had students read about Connecticut's own black regiment during the Civil War and compare their experience to the soldiers in the film.

Films recreate or represent past eras or time periods. They also use particular genre and narrative tools to help the audience to follow along or to challenge viewers' common understandings of a historical event. Each film tells a story (narrative) of people and events in the past. These film narratives can sometimes parallel the way that genres of history are taught in schools. For example, the traditional Western film genre often reflects the same notions of progress, expansion, and rugged individualism that are also often included in the telling of the American West in textbooks. Sometimes, however, the structure of a film's narrative can be used to challenge students' beliefs about an event or about how they view the past.

Chapter 10 examines how teachers and students can explore a film's narrative about what happened in the past and why. This chapter looks at the case of Ms. Reed's lessons on the causes of the American Civil War using *Ride with the Devil* (1999), which depicts the bloody border wars that occurred in Kansas and Missouri before and during the conflict. She wanted students in her North Carolina high school classroom to examine causes of the Civil War outside of the traditional slavery and states-rights narratives that focus on the eastern U.S. and also to reflect on how the Kansas–Missouri conflict is still reflected today in popular memory (as seen in the University of Kansas mascot, the Jayhawk, and sports paraphernalia that use the "border war" theme). Her use of the film emphasized the messiness of the conflict and let students grapple with deciding which "side" they would be on—made intentionally difficult by the film's ambiguous narrative structure and because of the historical events themselves (including atrocities that left innocent victims on both sides of the conflict). The narrative of the film challenged students to think about both the nature of the events in Kansas and Missouri in their relation to the Civil War, challenging simplistic "good vs. bad" and "right vs. wrong" classifications.

COMMENTS ON THE MAKING OF THIS BOOK

All four authors are professors at colleges or universities in different states. We all have conducted and published previous research studies on teachers using history movies in their classrooms. A chief goal in joining together for this book was to combine our interests, knowledge, and professional insights to produce a comprehensive analysis of film-based instruction through actual classroom examples of teachers in multiple secondary schools across the United States. We intentionally looked for and chose teacher-participants who had established reputations in their schools for innovative or effective use of film in their classroom. They were identified through our previous work with them in teacher education, collegiate coursework, professional development, or field research.

All participating teachers freely volunteered to be a part of this book. In order to protect their personal anonymity, we have replaced their names and the names of their schools and districts with pseudonyms. The only exception is Ron Briley, who consented for his real name to be used because he has previously published articles about teaching with movies, which we cite in our book. Additionally, the participating teachers have generously permitted us to discuss and describe their actual classroom materials so that other teachers who read this book could visualize them and use them as a basis for making their own. All figures depicting the teacher's materials are our reproductions. As much as possible, we tried to recreate the look and content of the teacher's documents. However, some edits were necessary to remove the teacher's personal identity, to remove texts with potential copyright concerns, or to conserve the amount of page space required.

Although our book is carefully informed by our collective work with research and scholarship on history teaching and learning, there are limitations to this book as a research study. First, we cannot claim that our participating teachers are representative of any particular population. In technical terms, they are a "purposive" sample purposefully identified and selected. Second, we cannot make conclusive generalizations about the practices of classroom teachers everywhere based on our limited sample of participating teachers. Third, our book offers "cases" of actual classroom practice that illustrate our themes; they are not "case studies" in formal qualitative research terms. Finally, we cannot claim that our cases represent "models of wisdom" or "best practice" (in technical phrases from the research literature). Our cases are reflections on the actual practices of real teachers in real classrooms that illustrate ideas for thoughtful, effective film-based instruction around key themes identified in the research and scholarship of reformed history education. Not everyone may find these teachers' lessons to be perfect, but we argue that their instructional experiences are good models for considering strategies for powerful educational uses of film in secondary social studies. This book offers a rich palate of real classroom lessons with innovative uses of film that span a variety of social studies courses and topics from schools in five states and that address a number of important contemporary educational issues facing social studies teachers.

CONCLUSION

Ours is not the first book to explore the use of motion pictures in K–12 schools. Scattered across libraries and the internet are any number of books and articles on using film in classrooms, although tracking them down is a considerable chore. Furthermore, surprisingly few are targeted specifically at history educators or are informed by real classroom practice. We hope this book will help to fill the gap.

In our work with history teachers and students, we have discovered a number of accomplished educators who make inventive and appropriate use of film in history classes. These teachers know that movies offer rich opportunities for learning. Collectively, the chapters seek to provide strategies for helping teachers think about issues of historical literacy in their classrooms. Each chapter is organized around a particular pedagogical theme that is emphasized in the reflection.

However, it is important to stress that these pedagogical themes are not hard-and-fast or mutually exclusive. There are connections and overlap between them. Teachers very rarely have just one goal in a lesson, and so it is appropriate that film-based lessons connect to multiple themes. Though we have identified "historical empathy" as a central theme in the cases presented in Chapters 3 and 4, we also see empathy as a goal of the teachers in other chapters. We have focused on "visualizing the past" in Chapter 9, but we will see that almost all the teachers in this book also used movies to help students envision past events or perspectives as real, believable, or immediate to them.

Ultimately, this book has one central purpose: to offer strategies for effective, educationally meaningful film-based instruction in support of rigorous inquiry into the past and, to a lesser degree, goals of democratic values of tolerance and citizenship in the present. We feel that movies are not a trivial or inconsequential contributor to how many young people learn about the past or what they think they know about history. Through developing students' historical film literacy, they will be better equipped to be critical consumers of historical documents of all kinds long after they leave the confines of the classroom. This is certainly among the principal goals of powerful history and social studies education.

CHAPTER 2
Issues in Using Film to Teach History

Figure 2.1 Pearl Harbor (2001). Two American pilots (Ben Affleck and Josh Hartnett) compete for the love of a British nurse (Kate Beckinsale) during World War II.

We hope this book will illustrate the considerable educational promise of history movies when incorporated by teachers into carefully designed lessons in purposeful ways. Carefully designed film-based lessons reflect a thoughtful approach to using film in student learning activities, an approach that equips students with content knowledge, concepts, and analytical understandings needed to make sense of the film and to meaningfully apply it to learning about the past. Effective use of film has clear academic goals and is intentional about what a film is meant to contribute to student learning. As discussed in Chapter 1, films have tremendous potential to motivate students, to offer alternative perspectives, to help students visualize the past, to introduce controversial issues, and to be examined as primary and secondary sources of knowledge about the past.

The classroom cases presented in the following chapters illustrate what purposeful, carefully designed film-based teaching can look like in practice. Before we examine the specific cases, though, it is worthwhile to consider some of the challenges and constraints to fulfilling the educational promise of history movies. The purpose of this chapter is to discuss potential challenges teachers can face in bringing history movies into their classrooms, the challenge of film selection, and other practical concerns. We also suggest possible ways to address these concerns.

THE CHALLENGE OF FILM AS A HISTORICAL TEXT

Underlying many of the difficulties in using film is the unavoidable reality that history movies are their own kind of historical document. A history film in the classroom can serve as one "text," or piece of evidence, to support particular student learning outcomes—possibly through presenting or covering certain content knowledge, possibly by presenting specific narratives or interpretations about the past to be analyzed or critiqued, possibly by eliciting moral or ethical reactions, or stimulating historical thinking about how the past relates to the world today. Exactly how a film supports student learning outcomes depends entirely on the intentions the teacher has for its classroom use. When intentions are unclear (either to the teacher or to the students), the educational promise of a history film can suffer. Students may end up simply watching a movie for its entertainment value, unaware of how to connect it to anything else they are learning. Worse, students may watch a movie thinking it must be an accurate representation of what occurred in the past because they are watching it in school. We suggest film-based instruction is effective when there are clear goals for what the film is supposed to contribute to the lesson and clear outcomes for what students are supposed to learn from it.

As commercial products of popular culture, movies frequently contain elements meant to appeal to a paying mass audience. For this reason, historical issues can often take a backseat to supposed entertainment value. The entertainment industry as a whole has long sought to deflect criticism about how it presents history to the public. Film-makers can deny they have responsibility for historical issues such as accuracy and representation by claiming their movies are creative entertainment products. But this argument does not stop the entertainment industry from marketing these products to an educational audience. Film companies often have education-oriented materials on the websites promoting history movies, in hopes that teachers might encourage students and their parents to see the film in theaters or buy the film on home video. In recent years studios have partnered with cable television networks to produce educational documentaries as part of the mass media marketing campaign.

This "education vs. entertainment" constraint can pose practical problems in the classroom. The film industry knows that adolescents, teenagers, and young adults make up the bulk of audiences for theatrical releases and heavily markets movies to them. As a consequence, students typically are used to thinking of all movies, history or other, as vehicles for entertainment. They tend to reflexively evaluate them in terms of how fun or exciting they are. It can be a challenge for teachers to get students to view movies as more than just entertainment. Prior research suggests that, absent direct guidance from teachers, students may not naturally view films critically (Marcus, Paxton, & Meyerson, 2006; Seixas, 1994). This is not to say that students automatically believe everything they see on the screen is historical truth—students can be curious about what elements in the film are "real" and which are fictional. However, without support by the teacher, students may commonly lack the understandings needed to discern important historical issues or the personal motivation to look for answers.

History movies feature many elements with educative potential, but it is a mistake to presume that the act of simply watching a movie automatically teaches the viewer factual information. As fictionalized, dramatic stories, Hollywood movies contain a tremendous load of visual, auditory, and emotional stimulation. In order to attract an audience, and therefore make money, filmmakers take liberty with the stories they tell—even when a film is based on real historical events. To better connect with audiences, additional drama in the form of a love story or inflated action sequences may be added. Stock or compilation characters are also common in order to help the audience follow the story more easily. For example, one character may be used to represent the experiences of whole groups or of several people, as it would be difficult for an audience to follow a story with too many main characters.

In addition to the impact of the decisions made by a film's producers about how the story is presented, viewers will "read" a film differently based on their own knowledge of the past, critical literacy skills, and experience watching films or engaging with other forms of media. Different viewers are going to focus their attention on different things and have different mental and emotional responses to the content. This is especially the case when a film is not made with a particular type of viewer in mind—or with only a particular demographic in mind. Students from different racial backgrounds in a diverse classroom may look at a history movie with mostly white characters differently from majority white theatrical audiences. Teachers are often surprised by what students focus on when watching a film in the classroom. Just because the teacher showed a film that depicted a particular piece of factual historical content does not mean that all students noticed and remembered it. Whatever educational potential a movie has can be realized only by the active guidance of the teacher operating within a purposeful lesson structure that supports students in identifying, integrating, and applying elements in the film to specific learning outcomes.

There are additional intellectual and academic concerns. If "doing" history should involve more than just passively watching a story about the past, what should students do during and after a movie to tap into its educational value? If movies tell only one "side" of a complex historical episode, what should teachers do to help students recognize multiple perspectives (particularly those that might be missing)? If most movies contain interpretive or moral messages about the past, how should teachers get students to reflect on the meaning of the film? However, these concerns are problems only when they are ignored or neglected. When handled thoughtfully and skillfully, these questions can become useful means for inspiring powerful historical thinking in the classroom.

It is important to keep in mind that films by themselves are not lessons—teachers create lessons, and films are just one possible resource. Like any resource, film may not always be appropriate for every lesson. By first considering the motivation and intentions for deciding to utilize a history movie, teachers can reflect on whether the film is the right resource. This "reflective planning" can avoid the potential headache of upset students, parents, and administrators concerned about class time being taken up by a movie that doesn't convincingly relate to student learning. We suggest that misconceptions about teaching with history movies result from a lack of attention to reflective planning on the part of teachers or communication of motivation and intentions to students, administrators, and parents. Being able to articulate motivation and intentions is an essential step in making film-based instruction viable and valued by the school community.

When students are encouraged to watch a history movie critically for educational ends, they are likely to have a lot of questions about fact and fiction, about how the film constructs the past and the people in it, and about how the film encourages the viewer to think about connections between the past and present. Guiding students to ask and address these kinds of rich questions is one of the most educationally powerful outcomes of film-based lessons, but it places serious demands on the teacher. Teachers need considerable content knowledge about the historical period and elements in the film. Although it may not be important to be able to respond to every question about minor details ("Were those uniforms really that color back then?"), it is very important that teachers have enough subject-matter knowledge to help students evaluate historical accuracy and representation in a film. Acquiring this sometimes specialized knowledge requires time to research topics in books, to watch informational documentaries about the period, and to read what scholars are writing about the movie. Using a history film in the classroom requires the teacher to do homework first.

Central to maximizing the educational power of history movies is equipping students to view them as sources for historical ideas rather than just vehicles for entertainment. A teacher needs to consider how the film-based lesson will fit into the broader unit. Does the activity serve as an introduction to issues or events that will be explored further through some kind of historical inquiry? Does it serve as one interpretation or perspective on an event or issue that is used in conjunction with other sources (e.g., first-hand accounts, documents, news articles) that present complementary or even contradictory accounts? Teachers need to think strategically about how they will introduce students to the film. How will they structure the viewing? How will they help students make sense of the film and debrief or deliberate on the issues a film raises or the complex ideas it may present? All this needs to be aligned with goals for using the film as part of a curricular unit.

It is important to be explicit with students about what they should focus on during the viewing. Students need to have a task during the viewing that helps them to gather information or focus on the parts of the film that align with the teacher's goals. Some form of data collection instrument, which could take the form of a graphic organizer or even a list of ideas or questions, may help students identify and record information from the film that they will need for activities, assignments, or assessments. A teacher may also want students to view the film with a particular perspective in mind—for example, students might view the film from a vantage point of being witness to the events in the film. A teacher may also want students to be able to interpret what they are viewing through a conceptual lens based on a sociological or psychological theory, such as how group mentality develops and operates (see Chapter 4 for an example of this). Alternatively, a film may be examined like a historical text, using the same critical analysis skills that may be applied to other historical sources.

Once the viewing is done it is important to remember that, even given a task to do, students will interpret or read the film differently and will benefit from hearing how others in the class made meaning of what they saw. Some form of a structured discussion that allows students to debrief and hear the accounts of others can be most beneficial. This can be done in small groups or as a whole class, like a Socratic seminar in which the film serves as the text to be interrogated. This activity leads to better understandings of what is in the film, centered around the goal and focus set by the teacher, and also helps students experience how history and historical films are open to multiple possible interpretations.

Implementing rigorous, purposeful film-based instruction can be daunting. Teachers can find themselves constrained by the considerable knowledge needed and the time required to find it. Fortunately, there are resources available to help. Many education-oriented journals, such as the National Council for the Social Studies' *Social Education*, *The Social Studies* now by Taylor & Francis, and the Society for History Education's *The History Teacher*, publish short articles about classroom uses of history movies. Journals such as *Film & History*, a publication of The Historians Film Committee, presents in depth analysis of history-related films for teachers who want to do further research from a scholarly perspective. Articles about particular history movies often provide the kind of content knowledge a teacher needs to support the classroom use of the film and can save considerable time in the teacher's research process.

Likewise, documentary films are frequently made to coincide with the release of many mainstream history movies and are aired on cable outlets such as Discovery Channel or The History Channel. Typically with running times of no more than 45 minutes, they can be concise resources for information about the film and the history it depicts. Some DVD releases even include the supporting documentary films as bonus material—for example, the expanded DVD release of Ridley Scott's *Gladiator* (2000) contains a very useful documentary film about gladiators in ancient Roman history. It certainly can be worth a teacher's time to take advantage of special features on DVD releases, which can go beyond informational documentaries to include interviews with consulting historians or the filmmakers. Some even contain audio commentary tracks along with the film in which historical issues are discussed—for example, the DVD release of *The Alamo* (2004) features a commentary track by the two historians who were consultants for the film. Taken together, these features add educational options and help to emphasize the creative and constructed nature of historical narratives in movies.

Finally, the internet provides many resources that can help teachers find information about history movies, particularly their public receptions. Rotten Tomatoes (http://www.rottentomatoes.com) contains links to dozens of reviews for virtually every movie released in theaters. The Internet Movie Database (http://www.imdb.com) provides a tremendous amount of information about the production of a film. The database also links to a large number of reviews from the time the film was released. Reviews can be useful in helping teachers and students get a sense for how a film was received during the time it was made and whether the public responded positively or negatively to a history film. The database also links to numerous other resources and detailed information on the director and actors in the film, including links to other films the same director made and background information. This can be useful if a director was known for making films with particular political or social goals in mind.

THE CHALLENGE OF FILM SELECTION

Another important issue is the challenge of choosing which particular movies to use in the classroom. Key criteria to consider in choosing films include the factual historical validity of the film, the way the film presents the past, the "age" of the film, the teacher's goals in using a film, the perspectives of a film, and the others resources being used for the lesson.

One of the biggest considerations teachers are likely to face is whether a history movie is "good" or "bad" for the classroom. Some history movies have a reputation for being accurate, valuable, or informative—for example, initial research suggests that *Glory* (1989), about an African-American regiment in the U.S. Civil War, has been widely used in classrooms at least in part because it is considered accurate (Marcus & Stoddard, 2007). Other movies have a negative reputation for being inaccurate. For example, *Pearl Harbor* (2001) focuses mostly on the adventures and romances of its protagonists with authentic historical elements only in the background. Using *Glory* in the classroom is usually an easy sell, whereas a teacher using *Pearl Harbor* may be subject to disapproval from parents, administrators, other teachers, or even students aware of its reputation. Despite its positive reputation, *Glory* also contains fictionalized or invented historical elements—characters, events, and even entire scenes (such as when Colonel Shaw browbeats a quartermaster to get footwear for his black soldiers, an event not recorded in any of the actual sources from the time). Despite its negative reputation, *Pearl Harbor* contains some elements that are historically accurate or at least informative, such as the sinking of the U.S.S. *Arizona* or the "Doolittle raid" in early 1942 to strike back against Japan for the Pearl Harbor attack. In other words, even the "good" film has some potential historical problems and the "bad" film has some potentially informative aspects.

What matters most is not whether the movie itself is "good" or "bad" but how it is used and for what educational ends. A good movie can be used poorly and contribute to no meaningful learning outcomes. A bad movie can be used well to help students engage in critical historical thinking and apply content knowledge. This is not to say that the quality of a film isn't a consideration. As will be seen in several of the cases in the following chapters, the most important approach to being prepared to deal with historical accuracy in movies is to extensively research the film's historical content. Several of our participating teachers considered the opinions of historians reviewing a film as well as doing their own factual research in order to decide if a film was appropriate for meeting their learning objectives.

A second issue with film selection is the way a film presents the past and the "age" of the film. If a film is poorly made or overly dense for young audiences, students may grow bored or restless and try to resist even important teacher goals. It is also possible that films have a "shelf life" in terms of their appeal to students. At a certain point a movie no longer feels a part of youth culture and instead feels like an artifact from a previous generation. For this reason, some teachers may be wary about using older, especially black-and-white, movies. This is not to suggest that films more than a couple of decades old should be avoided, but teachers may need a different approach to older films from more recent movies starring contemporary celebrities. Likewise, films do not need to be recent "blockbusters" to be motivational or interesting in the classroom. Given that box-office hits often have an overly dramatized or simplistic storyline, some of the films that were well made but less successful financially (such as the aforementioned *Glory*) may be more effective in the classroom. For example, Chapter 6 features a teacher who effectively uses *The Alamo* as part of a unit on Westward Expansion. The film flopped at the box office but is generally factually accurate and can be very engaging for students.

Whether a film is engaging in the classroom depends on what the teachers asks students to do with it. Almost any film can be interesting to students if they are applying what they see to something exciting or important. For this reason, it is essential for the teacher to be explicit about why the particular film was chosen and what students are supposed to get out of the experience. The more mentally engaged students are required to be with the film, the more attentive and involved they will be with the lesson. By explaining why the particular film was selected and the purpose for the lesson, a teacher will also show that this is an important, well-designed lesson and not a diversion.

Students also need to be positioned to view the film with the teacher's goals in mind. They need a task during the viewing that will help them reach the desired outcomes. If students are expected to be passive during viewing, they will probably not be very engaged with the lesson as a whole. This is just as true for the contemporary "blockbuster" as it is for an old black-and-white film. Although students may be more initially excited about seeing a recent movie they already know, that excitement alone does not automatically translate into learning about history. Even if students are initially resistant to watching an older movie, they can become engaged if the teacher gets them intrigued in what the film has to offer.

It is tempting for teachers to think of film selection simply in terms of plot or setting. For example, a teacher may gravitate toward *Kingdom of Heaven* (2005) for a unit on the Middle Ages because the film is set during the Crusades. This consideration is reasonable and often appropriate but should not be the only characteristic for selection. There are other nuanced but just as important characteristics besides setting and events in the plot. With which characters does the film want the viewer to empathize and why (who are the "heroes" or "villains")? Does the film depict alternative perspectives on history to what students might otherwise see in their textbooks or regular lessons? What messages are conveyed by the film about gender roles? Does the film depict the historical experiences of marginalized groups that might otherwise receive little attention? What political or social values are reflected by the film and which are disparaged or ignored? Some movies may have the desired historical setting but lack other important elements that lesson is meant to emphasize. For example, *The Patriot* (2000) is set in South Carolina during the American Revolutionary War and might be a good tool for a engaging students in analyzing decisive battles in the South, but it would be a weak choice if the teacher really wanted students to focus on the institution of slavery (since very few characters are slaves or even slave owners).

As discussed earlier, all films contain particular perspectives and reflect the time and place of production. The story will always be influenced by the sources used to compose the script, the target audience, the ideological beliefs and artistic motivations of filmmakers, and market pressures that encourage the film industry to avoid offending a potential paying audience even if it means distorting or leaving out large portions of the historical record. If teachers recognize that all films will represent particular values and beliefs then they can better select a film with the perspectives that best serve their intended goals.

Finally, one further issue teachers should keep in mind for film selection is how clearly and usefully it will connect and interact with other kinds of materials used or topics covered in the lesson. If a film, no matter how well made or exciting, is too tangential to the other elements of the lesson, its educational power will be lessened. If the information or perspective in the film simply reiterates other sources that are being used, another film with a complementary or even contradictory perspective may be more valuable. Students will appreciate the use of film in class if they can understand its role and the value gained from the often considerable time spent. Students know when their time is being wasted. Hence, it may be better to select particular films that clearly and strongly connect to other materials in the lesson, such as primary documents or excerpts from books. When students see that the teacher's background instruction, their textbooks, other kinds of readings, and the film selected all relate and add up to something cumulative, they are more likely to treat film-based lessons as serious learning experiences.

OTHER COMMON CHALLENGES

Factual accuracy and choosing the right film are not the only issues at stake. There are a host of very practical concerns. Movies can be very long and require a great deal of class time. In addition, movies often contain objectionable violence, language, and sexual content.

Time is a serious constraint. Teachers are often pressed for time and must choose what to cover, what not to cover, and how much attention to devote to any particular topic or teaching technique. Movies are no different—just potentially more time-intensive. When a teacher presents direct instruction to students for 30 minutes, he or she has complete control over what content is included in that time. When a teacher spends 30 minutes on a film, content control is limited to what the film contains. If a teacher chooses to show an entire mainstream movie (with a typical running time around 120 minutes), two to three class periods are required simply to watch it, depending on whether the class runs on a traditional or block schedule. Content the teacher wants to present beyond the film adds to the instructional time required, as does time spent preparing students to critically view the film and subsequently to apply what they have learned. A film-based lesson using an entire movie often can require a full school week or more (at least five periods). Finding enough time for this kind of lesson—as well as justifying doing so—can be difficult, particularly as many schools are under the pressure of high-stakes assessment aligned with state curriculum standards. There is no easy answer to overcome the time dilemma.

Some teachers choose to show clips rather than the entire film, but this is dependent on whether clips can fully meet objectives. Judicious use of particular scenes in a movie can address the time constraint. Mainstream history movies frequently have lengthy running times, yet not all of that time may contain historical information or issues that the teacher will focus on in the lesson. It is possible to show students only selected portions of a film that will be directly engaged with in the lesson. In a sense, this approach treats the film like a series of short readings, each one used by students as evidence or interpretations to address particular questions or tasks in the lesson. However, it is important to acknowledge that there are trade-offs in using film clips over the whole film. The teacher may gain greater efficiency and control over time, but the cohesiveness of the movie narrative suffers. It can be difficult for students to follow or emotionally connect with a narrative that is chopped up or with characters who are not introduced or developed in the selected sections. Students may resent only getting to watch part of a movie and not the whole story, especially if they become engrossed in a dramatic narrative. If one of the goals is to help students develop empathy for particular perspectives or experiences in the past, clip scenes may be less effective than the total narrative of the whole movie. For this reason, it is essential for teachers to decide their goals in advance and to be clear to students about what use they are supposed to make of the film.

Clarity of instructional intentions and educational goals is also essential to justifying why large portions of class time are devoted to a history movie. With many schools under pressure to improve student performance on high-stakes achievement tests aligned with state curricular standards, questions can be raised about whether a teacher should devote class time to teaching with history movies. Underlying such questions is the assumption that class time is better spent on covering content explicitly stated in the standards in some other way. Teachers need to be prepared to justify film-based instruction in terms of academic standards. History movies are well positioned to serve the critical thinking benchmarks that are featured in most states' history academic standards. Most standards call for students to be able to analyze historical narratives or interpretations (historical thinking), to engage in critical thinking about consequences of the past for our world today (historical significance), or to recognize and explain the viewpoints of various groups in the past (historical empathy). Film-based instruction can make a unique contribution to meeting these kinds of standards.

Teachers also need to carefully watch the history movie before using it in the classroom in order to deal with objectionable content that may not be appropriate for young audiences. This means critically viewing the film with students in mind, attentive to elements that might go unnoticed in a casual viewing for personal entertainment. Many history movies are rated R by the Motion Picture Association of America (MPAA) on account of graphic violence, obscene language, sexual situations, or nudity. Many teachers are constrained by school or district policies that limit the use of R-rated films, although great differences exist in this regard depending on local context. What can make this frustrating is that certain films that contain objectionable content also can have considerable educational potential. A popular example is the opening half hour of Steven Spielberg's *Saving Private Ryan* (1998), which depicts the World War II invasion of Normandy in harrowingly violent detail and with some obscene language. Although the gore and language are problematic, that film visualizes D-Day in a uniquely powerful way. Many teachers struggle with the constraint of objectionable content interspersed in movies that also contain unobjectionable elements that are educationally useful.

The best defense for concerns over objectionable material is careful prior screening and selection. DVD technology makes it easier than ever before for teachers to control what portions of a film to show. Most mainstream movies released on DVD are divided into dozens of short "chapters" or tracks. This makes it possible for a teacher to show unobjectionable portions and quickly skip past scenes with objectionable content. If a cut scene contains important information, the teacher can pause before resuming and summarize the information bypassed. By showing only portions of a film that contain historical elements without objectionable material, teachers frequently can use film in their lessons without risking angry reactions from the school community.

However, in some movies objectionable material is so heavily interspersed that cutting scenes is impossible or insufficient because virtually every scene contains something potentially offensive. In such a case, the teacher must carefully consider the values of the local community and whether the school administration, parents, and students can be convinced that the educational value of using the film in the classroom outweighs other concerns. Communication is essential. School administrators and parents may be more accepting of a request brought to their attention in advance than willing to forgive a problematic use of film over which they felt they had no input or control. Many teachers have successfully secured parent and student support for controversial films in the classroom by sending home a letter explaining the educational goals and inviting questions or feedback. The letter can be accompanied by a permission slip requiring parents or guardians to give their child permission to watch the film in class. Some schools even have official policies requiring permission slips (particularly for movies rated PG-13 or R). Of course, teachers need to be prepared to deal with parents who decline to give permission. This typically means creating an alternative but comparable educational experience for students who do not have parental permission, such as independent research on the historical issues represented in the film.

IN CONCLUSION

While serious and important, the constraints working against film-based instruction should not dissuade teachers from using movies in the classroom when it is an appropriate educational resource for a clear and purposeful educational goal. The classroom cases in the chapters that follow will illustrate this is greater detail. Though the challenges and constraints are very real, there are possible adaptations and techniques for addressing them. There is no magic formula, however. Every school, every classroom, and every teacher and student is unique. What works in one school community may not work in another. Nonetheless, U.S. schools share enough in common that we feel comfortable offering constructive ideas that teachers may consider. Ultimately, the teacher must implement and adapt film-based instruction in ways suited to the particular school and classroom context.

PART II

Using Film to Develop Empathy

The term *historical empathy* has been used frequently in the field of social studies education over the past three decades, but there is no consensus as to what historical empathy means. What is agreed upon is the belief that a student's ability to empathize with historical agents is important, even though there are few examples of how this actually occurs within a classroom (e.g., Ashby & Lee, 2001; Barton & Levstik, 2004; Seixas, 1996; Wineburg, 2001). Most historians and educators agree that the development of empathy in high school and middle school students is extremely difficult as they tend to make sense of the past using the values and norms from present-day culture and society. So, what is empathy and how can we use films to develop students' abilities to be historically empathetic?

The development of historical empathy is a somewhat contested concept as the notion of being able to understand the actions, experiences, and decision making of people in the past is tenuous at best. Different models for developing historical empathy in students have been promoted in the history education literature framed in terms of developing attitudes of "caring" or as "perspective taking" or "perspective recognition" (Barton & Levstik, 2004; Davis, 2001). In all of these models, the main goal of empathy is the attainment of a limited understanding of the experiences of people in the past, often with a focus on understanding how and why certain decisions were made in order to develop "cognitive" empathy (perspective recognition) or in terms of developing understandings of, and tolerant and compassionate attitudes toward, others (for caring). However, some would argue that the notion of "perspective taking" is limited in its usefulness as a construct as it would be virtually impossible for a high school student to truly take on the perspective of a 16th-century Spanish conquistador, for example, even after a close reading of first-person journals and secondary accounts.

Instead, Barton and Levstik (2004) frame historical empathy in terms of "for caring" and "perspective recognition" with the former focused on the development of more affective feelings and tolerant beliefs as a result of being able to empathize with those in the past, and the latter focused on the attempt to gain a sense of the perspective of historical actors. In any conceptualization of historical empathy, the goal is not for students to excuse or forgo evaluating or judging the actions and decisions of people in the past, but instead to gain a better understanding of peoples' reasoning within the given historical social, cultural, and political context (Seixas, 1996; Yeager & Foster, 2001). One key to developing the ability to empathize and recognize past perspectives is the attainment of the metacognitive ability to recognize how our understandings in the present make it difficult to comprehend the experiences of those in the past (Barton & Levstik, 2004; Epstein, 1998; Wineburg, 2001). The ability to recognize how one's beliefs and experiences are used as a lens for viewing the world is also key to the ability to evaluate historical films and how they represent the past.

Although empathy will always entail the use of "imagination restrained by evidence," the ability of students to empathize with individuals and groups in the past and present is valued greatly within the field of history education (Davis, 2001, p. 4). In addition to a better understanding of history, it is also believed that the ability to empathize leads to students who value tolerance and humanity, and are open to the perspectives of people who are different from them (Barton & Levstik, 2004; Wineburg, 2001). In this way, empathy can be conceived of both as a process and as an outcome. It also means that film can be a useful medium for engaging students in developing empathy because of its structure and point of view: viewing historical events through the perspectives of historic characters.

For the following cases of how film can be used to develop historical empathy, we rely primarily on Barton and Levstik's (2004) typology of empathy as "for caring" and "perspective recognition."

EMPATHY FOR CARING

It is easy to imagine that viewing a film will provide an affective response in the audience to identify with, and care about, what happens to characters in the film, especially when those characters play a part in a heroic or harrowing historical event. Whereas many historians argue that affective elements of empathy should be limited, such as feeling sorry for, or gaining a sense of the hardships experienced by, individuals or groups in the past, the historian Natalie Zemon Davis (2000) argues that this may be impossible as empathy will often "include emotional dimensions." This is especially true for films that represent powerful and compelling events in history such as cases of slavery, genocide, or other forms of persecution of marginalized groups. Films in particular evoke an affective response to how historical characters are portrayed, as they are designed to tell stories from particular points of view. For example, films are often structured from the perspective of either a character that we want to cheer for as the "good" character or one that you want to feel compassion for because of their experiences. Of course these structures also often include a "bad" character that we do not care for because of the way she or he is portrayed. For example, in *Dances with Wolves* (1990), the story is told from Kevin Costner's vantage point and leads us to view the Lakota that he ends up living with as "good" and the U.S. Army and rival Pawnee as "bad."

The representations of different characters and groups in the storyline, camera work, and the music that is used to introduce them emphasizes their "goodness" or "badness" and promotes particular emotional responses on the part of the audience. Because a film is often structured to view the events from a particular character's perspective, enhanced by the camera angles used, the narration, and how the story is structured, it is easy for an audience to be drawn in and really care for or about the protagonist in a film (Smith, 1995). For example, in *Schindler's List* (1993), Oskar Schindler is portrayed in a way that humanizes his character and makes the audience feel for his mission and want him to succeed in saving more Jews from the Holocaust. The perspective from which a film is told is one of the main narrative devices used in film, along with the formulaic storylines that are often used. When these common narrative forms are broken in a film, such as *Ride with the Devil* (a film examined in Chapter 10), the narrative shift may drive the audience to question who is good and who is bad. This may in turn drive students to care for characters that have been rarely thought about in the past. Given that the teacher recognizes the above limitations, many films can be used to help students learn to care for others, and especially groups of people who are often marginalized in history, in the hopes that it will affect their decision making and relationships with people in the present and the future.

Chapter 3 examines how a teacher utilizes a number of films, both feature and documentary, and other sources (e.g., novel) to help students develop an understanding of Hmong culture and the Hmong experience in the United States. Through this unit, he wants students to both develop a better understanding of the Hmong and also foster a sense of caring about the Hmong in order for his students, who are largely white, to develop humanistic and tolerant views toward others in general, and the often misrepresented and misunderstood Hmong in particular.

EMPATHY AS PERSPECTIVE RECOGNITION

Barton and Levstik (2004) argue that understanding the experiences of people of different groups, especially those who have been traditionally marginalized, can help students to gain a better perspective of issues of justice and power in past societies. For example, the film *Smoke Signals* (1988) provides a perspective of contemporary Native American culture and could be used to help disrupt some stereotypes of different Native American groups. By asking students to recognize aspects of the perspective from the film and then guiding them to attempt to make sense of the complexity of the issues that are viewed, teachers can help make students more aware of the nature of multiple perspectives in both the past and present. Barton and Levstik (2004) would also claim that this might help students to be more empathetic in their daily lives as citizens.

Films can act as a powerful medium for recognizing perspectives as they attempt to provide characters' viewpoints, motivations, and to some degree inner thoughts (Smith, 1995). These perspectives, however, also reflect the time and place of production. For example, a film about Stalin's perspective on the United States and Britain during World War II made by a director from the United States and for U.S. audiences probably provides a limited or more Western interpretation of Stalin's beliefs. Teachers need to take care to help students make sense of how the place and time of production in the film will impact how the perspectives in the film are portrayed. In some cases, a film may serve as a better vehicle for recognizing the perspectives of the time and place it was made than for that of the historical character it portrays. Despite these limitations, films provide a medium for recognizing, discussing, and deliberating various perspectives on historical events and issues when used thoughtfully in the classroom.

The case presented in Chapter 4 utilizes a number of sources, including a made-for-television movie, a feature film, and documentaries to engage students in the difficult but persistent question of "why did the Holocaust happen?" The teacher in the case engages her students in attempting to understand the mindset and decision making of the perpetrators, bystanders, and victims of the genocide and especially the dire consequences of the type of group mentality fostered by the Nazis and other totalitarian states.

CHAPTER 3
Empathy for Caring

Figure 3.1 Gran Torino (2008). Cultures clash when retired autoworker Walt Kowalski (Clint Eastwood) encounters his new immigrant neighbors.

There may be many reasons teachers may wish their students to "understand" or "empathize" with individuals and peoples of the past and present. The case described in this chapter highlights a teacher who gained an affinity for the peoples of Southeast Asia during and after the days of the Vietnam War, and then found their stories omitted from the social studies curriculum. The teacher also has a deep appreciation of the discipline of anthropology, and knew that it takes anthropologists years of immersion to truly comprehend an unfamiliar culture. The tools of a classroom teacher are limited, at best, but surely the social studies classroom is the proper place to experience people and cultures truly foreign to our own, to seek to understand "the other." This is particularly the case when this understanding has relevance to the present day and indeed the future. Helping students to develop tools of understanding, including a compassion for peoples in the past and in the present, is an aspiration most social studies teachers rightly hold for their students.

As a rule, history's victims are poorly represented in our textbooks. Current efforts to address this perennial problem notwithstanding, the truism that history is written by the winners and the powerful is still very much part of the "hidden curriculum" of social studies education. Many important narratives are ignored or relegated to the periphery of commercially produced textbooks and state-mandated curriculums. The student observer is left to conclude that these missing stories are unimportant.

Movies can be useful pedagogical tools in this regard. As discussed in Chapter 4, most movies (be they feature or documentary films) come from distinct and evident perspectives, and this opaque sourcing can be used to assist in the construction of historical film literacy. However, comprehending a perspective may fall well short of a teacher's objectives. Understanding, compassion, and acceptance are laudable goals, in particular when it comes to the study of peoples and cultures far different from our own. As Keith Barton and Linda Levstik remind us, "empathy without care sounds like an oxymoron. Why would anyone expend energy trying to understand historical perspectives if they had not care or concern for the lives and experiences of people in the past?" (Barton & Levstik, 2004, p. 228).

The affective elements of Hollywood movies make them unique historical sources when it comes to making us care. For example, it is very difficult for Westerners to truly comprehend the enmity that exists between the tribes of Africa, but a movie such as *Hotel Rwanda* (2004) places viewers in the middle of one of history's most appalling genocides and gets us to sympathize with the powerless caught in tribal violence. Likewise, a movie such as *Ararat* (2002), which includes graphic sequences depicting the horrors of the Armenian genocide, allows the audience to see, hear, and listen to a narrative some may wish to suppress.

The unit described in this chapter asks students to comprehend the perspectives of the Hmong people, and it goes further than that. The Hmong are the epitome of a misunderstood, misused, and marginalized people and, like the Romani (Gypsies), Native Americans, or Jews, their plight provides an opportunity for the social studies teacher. There is nothing natural about modern Western students coming to understand the cultural practices of other people. However, caring about the historical event or group being investigated is often a powerful motivating force behind doing historical work. For example, many a unit on the history of the Holocaust begins with a reading of *The Diary of Anne Frank*. The notion of empathy in history has been challenged by some in the field as potentially leading to presentism or allowing emotion to cloud historical interpretation. However, empathy is not sympathy. It doesn't require that we take sides. Nor is empathy an emotional shortcut that upends historical reasoning. Empathy does not trump reason; it informs reason.

In this case, Mr. O'Brian uses a contemporary movie along with an interesting assortment of other sources to attempt to develop in his students a knowledge of the history and culture of the Hmong people, but also an empathy for who they are as fellow human beings.

MR. O'BRIAN'S CLASS: AN ETHNO-HISTORY OF THE HMONG PEOPLE IN AMERICA

Case Description

There are a few centers of Hmong culture in the United States, places where these exiled clans gathered after their torturous exodus from the mountains of Laos in Southeast Asia. None of these enclaves, however, lie within the boundaries of Mr. O'Brian's particular high school. So when he begins a unit on the history and culture of the Hmong people, he faces a considerable challenge in raising both awareness and empathy.

O'Brian teaches social studies classes at a large downtown high school in Portland, Oregon. Although a few Hmong students attend the school (three by his count), most students are unaware of their rich yet unsettled history. His two sections of Anthropology host a diverse group of mainly juniors and seniors—whites, Asians, and African Americans, among others, but no Hmong.

"I ask them what they know from their history books about the Vietnam War," O'Brian said. "First, have you ever heard about the Hmong? No. And then what do you know about the Vietnam War? And they know just a *tiny* bit, and I usually assume that they know next to nothing. They've heard of Southeast Asian refugees, but they don't even know what drove them out of Southeast Asia."

Some 150,000 Hmong people immigrated to the United States in the aftermath of the wars that raged in Laos during and after what Westerners refer to as "The Vietnam War." Yet many Americans are perplexed by their presence and, in particular, their apparently peculiar cultural practices, which include shamanism, animal sacrifice, and a general unwillingness to dive into America's "melting pot." What's more, many first-generation Hmong refugees survive on welfare payments, money they feel wholly entitled to on account of their service to, and bargain with, the U.S. government; a verbal contract they refer to as "the promise." Some Americans are less than sanguine about this arrangement, however, even if they do not fathom its origin. Among the most important goals of this curricular unit is to humanize the Hmong in the minds of students. With a Masters degree in Anthropology and more than 30 years of classroom experience, O'Brian does not shy from controversial topics, complexity, or the use of motion pictures.

> It started a long time ago because I love film and I had professors in college who used film, both in anthropology classes and in other classes as well. So I was early on introduced to the idea that what we are looking at here is a different narrative structure and it can be complementary to reading. But you have to invite your students to read film like you ideally invite your students to read text. You have to make it as attractive as possible. Of course as a teacher you know that these kids love film. They watch and watch and watch, but they watch pretty indiscriminately.

During the course of this sequence of lessons, he pushes his students to challenge their preconceptions and biases by focusing deeply not only on chronological history, but on what might appear at first to be strange ethnic customs. These practices, in point of fact common throughout the world, serve as fence posts in a year-long exploration of anthropology.

O'Brian has developed a style of teaching that is popular among the students of his school. He makes extensive use of intricate handouts, teeming with questions, amusing prompts, and artwork that pushes the limits of black-and-white photocopies. The walls of the class are thick with layers of pictures, posters, artwork, and other interesting cultural artifacts. Although his courses are infused with a quick wit and droll humor, the tone is quite intellectual for a high school classroom. When using film, O'Brian does not sit down, but instead stands at the front frequently interjecting questions and comments, and often stopping the movie mid-scene for more extended discussion. "We've got to be interactive," he said. "I know they're watching me and thinking, 'Is he watching? What's he paying attention to?' There's a whole lot of things going on, but you to a certain degree play off the film improvisationally and keep them going. I've never been able to sit in the back and watch."

Unit Overview

The unit commences with two Hollywood movies intended to convey elements of the present and past of the Hmong and other Southeast Asian peoples to students who know little or nothing about the topic. First students watch and briefly discuss *Gran Torino* (2008), the recent movie chronicling the clash between a retired Detroit autoworker and his Hmong neighbors, the latest wave of immigrants in a traditionally immigrant community (see Table 3.2 for a description). Next they view *The Killing Fields* (1984), a movie set in Cambodia and not actually about the Hmong people, but used in this case to portray the horror of war in Southeast Asia and the unambiguous motive for flight.

After framing the unit with Hollywood's take on the Hmong, the class plunges quickly into more traditional and rich anthropological sources. First, they begin to read an award-winning account of a Hmong family's experience in Merced, California, entitled *The Spirit Catches You and You Fall Down* (1997), and subtitled *A Hmong Child, Her American Doctors, and the Collision of Two Cultures*. The book chronicles the massive cultural misunderstandings that occur over a young girl with a severe case of epilepsy. Along the way it gives a concise history of the Hmong people. Reading and discussion of the almost 300-page book continues throughout the rest of the month-long unit.

Along with the readings and films comes a number of response papers—assignments that prod students to understand and even write from a Hmong point of view. This task is aided by a pair of short documentary films that explore the life of a Hmong family. The first takes place soon after their relocation to the United States in Chicago, Illinois, and the second some 14 years later after they have moved to Wisconsin. The head of the family is a shaman who struggles to keep his family intact and faithful to traditional Hmong culture and religion. Another shorter and picture-filled book entitled *Shamanism* (1995) is also used to take students deeper into the world of the shaman.

Finally, after about a month of class time spent looking at texts, films, and other cultural artifacts, such as fine Hmong stitch work and fabric art, the class returns to the movie that began the unit, *Gran Torino*. In a concluding assignment, students are asked to describe an alternative screenplay—one that tells the same story from the point of view of the Hmong characters portrayed in the movie, a narrative device previously used by *Gran Torino*'s director, Clint Eastwood, in a pair of movies about the battle of Iwo Jima during World War II, *Flags of Our Fathers* (2006) and *Letters from Iwo Jima* (2006).

Table 3.1 Unit Outline

Days	Activities	Goals
1–2	View *Gran Torino*	
3	Finish and Discuss *Gran Torino*	Focus in particular on the Hmong characters
4	Students write freewrite essay on "what they know about the Vietnam War" Discuss Vietnam War Assign Book: *The Spirit Catches You and You Fall Down* (1997)	Review Vietnam War
5–7	View *The Killing Fields*	Understanding the complexity and violence of the Southeast Asian Wars, and the reason for flight
8–9	Finish and Discuss *The Killing Fields* Discuss Chapter 1–8 of *The Spirit Catches You*	Contextualize Hmong history within SE Asia, from ancient to modern
10	Watch and Discuss: *Between Two Worlds: The Hmong Shaman in America* (1984) Fish Souping Assignment	Focus on Hmong traditions and culture, in particular the role of shamanism and the Hmong perspective on healing.
11–12	Further discuss *Between Two Worlds* Continued Discussion of *The Spirit Catches You* Foua, The Legally Abusive Parent Assignment	Continue focus on Hmong culture, bridging to the experience of flight from SE Asia and the exodus to America
13	Assign Book: *Shamanism* (1995) Shaman Picture Assignment	Continue focus on shamanism and the Hmong experience in America
14–15	View Clips from *Vietnam: The Ten Thousand Day War* (1980) Continue discussion of *The Spirit Catches You*, *Shamanism*	Focus on Vietnam War, guerilla tactics, the Secret War in Laos, U.S. agreement with Hmong (or "the promise"), flight from Laos
16–17	View: *The Split Horn* (2001) Assign: Viewers Guide to *The Split Horn*	View and discuss film
18–19	Discuss *The Split Horn*, Cumulative Discussion, Guest Speakers, Additional Cultural and Artistic examples	Sum up unit, explore student questions, flex time depending on schedule
20–21	Final Cumulative Discussion and Assignment: The next Clint Eastwood movie assignment	Move discussion from past to the present

Table 3.2 Description of Films

Gran Torino (2008) Clint Eastwood (Director) Clint Eastwood, Bill Gerber, and Robert Lorenz (Producers) Warner Bros.	A retired Ford automobile assembly line worker and Korean War veteran lives in a changing Michigan neighborhood which is dominated by immigrants—the newest arrivals being Hmong.
The Killing Fields (1984) Roland Joffé (Director) David Puttnam (Producer) Warner Bros.	Highly acclaimed, academy award winning story based on the experiences of three journalists: Dith Pran, a Cambodian, Sidney Schanberg, an American, and Jon Swain, a Brit.
Between Two Worlds: The Hmong Shaman in America (1984) Taggart Siegel (Director) Taggart Siegel and Dwight Conguergood (Producers) Collective Eye, Inc.	Documentary expose of the struggle of Hmong refugees in America. Follows three Hmong families who find themselves thousands of miles from their mountain homes in Laos. In particular focuses on Hmong Shamanistic traditions, and the lives of Shamans in the United States.
The Split Horn: Life of a Hmong Shaman in America (2001) Taggart Siegel (Director) Jim McSilver (Producer) Collective Eye, Inc.	Sequel to *Between Two Worlds*. Rejoins family of Hmong Shaman 15 years later, now living in Appleton, Wisconsin. Narrated by teenage daughter of Hmong family losing touch with their ancient traditions as they turn to TV, computer games, and Christianity.
Vietnam: The Ten Thousand Day War (1980) Michael Maclear (Executive Producer) Canadian Broadcasting Corporation	Definitive Canadian television documentary series on the Vietnam War. Series writer Peter Arnett was an Associated Press reporter in Vietnam from 1962 to 1975.

FILM ACTIVITIES

From the humid mountains of Laos to crowded refugee camps in Thailand to the bitterly cold plains of North America, the Hmong are a people who have often been misunderstood by their neighbors, at times with tragic consequences. For Americans, getting to know the Hmong among us can be difficult under the best of circumstances. These are people who hold tightly to their traditional cultural practices, which include, among many other things, a dogged resistance to social and religious assimilation. So

Table 3.3 Class Texts

The Spirit Catches You and You Fall Down: A Hmong Child, Her American Doctors, And The Collision of Two Cultures (1997) Anne Fadiman (Author) New York: Farrar, Straus and Grioux	Explores in great depth the clash between a small county hospital in California and a refugee family from Laos over the care of a child diagnosed with severe epilepsy. In the process offers gripping history and ethnography of the Hmong.
Shamanism (1995) Piers Vitebsky (Author) Norman: University of Oklahoma Press	With extensive pictures and text, the author seeks to answer the questions, "What is a Shaman?," "What does a Shaman actually do?," and "What effect is there on the people around them?"
The Latehomecomer: A Hmong Family Memoir (2008) (Chapter 2 only) Kao Kalia Yang (Author) Minneapolis: Coffee House Press	This chapter describes the horrific flight from Laos by a young family of Hmong refugees who, along with other clan members, are pursued by Laotian and Vietnamese soldiers, many being slaughtered along the way.

when Mr. O'Brian started a unit on these Southeast Asian people for his two sections of Anthropology, he began with a field trip to a local movie theater to watch the blockbuster Clint Eastwood movie *Gran Torino*. There was little preparation for viewing the film, as O'Brian wanted students to simply immerse themselves in the theater experience and encounter the characters on their own terms.

Featuring a predominantly Hmong cast, *Gran Torino* chronicles the clash of cultures between a retired Detroit autoworker (Walt Kowalski as portrayed by Eastwood) and his Hmong neighbors. One young neighbor, Thao, is forced by Hmong gangsters to try to steal Kowalski's prized Ford Gran Torino. After failing in the heist, Thao is attacked by the gang, and Kowalski then attempts to defend the family and keep the young man out of gang life.

"It's a complex film," O'Brian said. "It's both simple and complicated at the same time. It introduced a whole bunch of questions and perspectives."

After watching the movie, discussion ensued back in class. In particular, the class focused on the Hmong characters in the film and what led the Hmong to far away inner-city Detroit. Students for the most part expressed unfamiliarity with the Hmong, and indeed about the Vietnam War. O'Brian noted, but was not surprised by, the general lack of knowledge about the wars that raged in Southeast Asia from the 1950s through 1970s. As he was a high school graduate of the class of 1966, the Vietnam War affected many aspects of his life, not least the decision to become a teacher.

"Do you think the role that the Hmong played in U.S. history rises to the level of inclusion in our history books?," his classroom voice reaching a crescendo. It is difficult for students to answer the question at first, in no small measure because they have so little upon which to draw. One thing they do seem sure of is that the Hmong did not appear in their history survey textbooks.

In order for students to truly comprehend Hmong culture (a primary goal in this Anthropology course), a large swath of history also needed to be examined. So the class took a step back before it proceeded with an investigation of Hmong culture. This began with a freewrite asking students simply, "What do you know about the Vietnam War?" At this point, O'Brian also assigned the book *The Spirit Catches You and You Fall Down*, by Anne Fadiman. This is a substantial and engaging narrative, but O'Brian knows he needs to push students to keep up on the reading of what is undoubtedly a very grown-up book. "In working through this book with previous classes, it is pretty clear to me that it is a book that is of compelling interest in teaching high school classes," he said. "With a decreasing interest in reading, it's important to have a text that will capture the interest of students. And this is a very well written book, with a powerful but complicated narrative which does capture the interest of most of the students." Meanwhile, the class began viewing the haunting movie *The Killing Fields*, a film that is paradoxically not actually about the Hmong.

> The atmosphere of the emotion of *The Killing Fields* was something I wanted kids to get, because it replicates analogously the emotion of dedication and loss the Hmong went through as we read in *The Spirit Catches You and You Fall Down*. And as the Hmong describe their experience with America and the aftermath of the war in Laos—*The Killing Fields* really captures that feeling and atmosphere on film. Secondly, I wanted to begin to tune students in, without overwhelming them, to the larger context of the Indochina Wars. It's not really "The Vietnam War," it's the First and Second Indochina Wars.

Like many Americans, O'Brian's students tend to lump all Southeast Asian refugees together, rather than seeing them as different ethnic groups—Hmong, Lao, Cambodian, Vietnamese, among others—with distinct histories and cultures. This misconception is addressed during the viewing and discussion of *The Killing Fields*, as students concurrently survey both modern and ancient Hmong history while reading *The Spirit Catches You and You Fall Down*.

The first chapter of that book describes the birth of the 14th child of a Hmong couple in a Merced, California public hospital (the 13th child had been born in a refugee camp in Thailand). Immediately upon the birth of Lia Lee, literally, serious misunderstandings occur between the parents and doctors at the hospital. It is a course that continues throughout the book, as Lia is diagnosed with acute epilepsy, ultimately leading to troubling consequences for the child, the parents, and all else involved.

The next few class days are spent discussing chapters from the book. O'Brian's high school operates on a hybrid, four-day schedule in which three days feature regular, 55-minute class periods, with one day having a 1-hour 50-minute block period. This helps for viewing movies and providing time for reflection and discussion.

As the book progresses, the Lees make use of both Western medicine and traditional Hmong healing practices, in particular seeking the help of local shamans. From their perspective, taking advantage of the best features of both therapeutic traditions seems the practical thing to do. Thus is introduced the idea of shamanism, a theme examined with some intensity for the remainder of the unit. The shaman occupies a key role as a healer in many cultures, mediating between the world of the living and the world of spirits. It is an utterly foreign concept to most of O'Brian's students, so, to push this concept further, the class viewed the short documentary film *Between Two Worlds: The*

Hmong Shaman in America (1984). They were also assigned to skim through the book *Shamanism*, by Piers Vitebsky.

The film, a raw and somewhat jarring production, gives a look at a Hmong family ripped from its home in the jungles of Southeast Asia and plopped down in inner-city Chicago. It is an uncomfortable film, in many ways. The family patriarch, Paja Thao, is a respected shaman whose cultural and religious worldview seems out of place in his new home, to say the least. A particularly awkward scene features a Christian missionary who regularly visits with the stated purpose of converting the family. The missionary, who comes offering candy and gifts, appears completely obtuse to Hmong culture and has no idea that Paja is a practicing shaman. The Thao family pays little heed to the

Table 3.4 Example Reading/Film Response Essay

Fish Souping and Conquergooding the Hmong and their Encounters with the Cultures of the American West

The title of this update and opportunity sheet makes sense? We will discuss the "Conquergood approach" today and you should have a fuller comprehension.

To review, so far you have been asked to read through chapter 8 to respond to the following,

- What do you know about "The Vietnam War?"
- "Birth," for the Hmong and Lia and for you, and what does it mean when we "" a word?
- "Fish souping," explain and interpret.
- Bullet point, or otherwise display the basic narrative themes of Hmong "history."
- Did I suggest that you review "the Killing Fields"?

The above were the assigned responses as of last Friday. In addition, you also viewed *Gran Torino* and I suggested that you jot down some thoughts for future use. WE also discussed thoroughly the first 4 chapters. So, here is what you will desire to accomplish in the coming weeks.

As with past requests, the questions are intended to encourage you all to DO the reading, not just read, "read." So, after each chapter we would ideally discuss salient topics and you would have the desire to think critically and interpretively about the cultural meanings of what you have just **"read."** So, we can now dispense with the "". In order to fulfill your desire to express cultural meanings, you are asked to write responses. As you should know by now, this material lends itself to rich and diverse representations. The bottom line responses are answering the questions that the material suggests, like "birth." In addition, if you are feeling called in some other interpretive or expressive direction, go there. I will attempt to clarify some of the directions as we proceed through our reading of Hmong culture as represented in *The Spirit Catches You and You Fall Down*.

Perhaps the clearest and quickest illustration is the **3rd chapter** that carries the same title as the book, which is, interpretively, **quag dab peg**. So much is meant by the Hmong phrase? How are we to begin to understand what the Hmong themselves mean when they say Lia has/is/suffers from/is blessed by **quag dab peg**?

Table 3.4 (continued)

In addition, the good doctors at MCMC see/diagnose/treat/conceptualize "epilepsy." What does each culture intend to say and where might we find a "middle ground" of cross cultural interpretation?

And then we go to the **4th chapter** with the horror movie title, "Do Doctors Eat Brains?" And rapidly, within five pages we move into the realm of Hmong first experiences with Western medicine. The Author concisely contextualizes their responses to us by contrasting their "healers," **tsiv neebs**, with more Western expectations. What is this categorical healer, the **tsiv neeb**, and how does their healing practice differ from the stereotypical Western doctor? The larger category for the Hmong spiritual physician is **shaman**, a categorical healer whose existence is widespread documented by anthropologists in hundreds of cultures. We are also introduced to two other Western approaches to healing: Christian and "Conguergooding." Explain both. And wouldn't the idea behind the Rabies Parade make for a wonderfully dramatic scene for a play, a musical, a film? Performance Anthropology. Go after it if it calls to you.

Chapter Five is a tough one. The style is one of close-to-the-story reportage. We are there with the agonizing frustrated physicians, with the struggling and confused family. And, most tragically, with little Lia Lee as her "condition" grows worse. I guess that the essence of this chapter is to ask how fair Anne Fadiman is as an interpreter of events. Are all parties, all cultures represented with a kind of anthropological fairness? What does the title mean? This is a depressing chapter, but like many solutions to "illness" some new identification, some new diagnosis, in this case cross cultural, emerges and from the tragedy of one healing for many is possible?

"High-Velocity Transcortical Lead Therapy," **Chapter Six**, finds our anthropological journalist trying to situate herself fairly but realistically inside and in between the medical culture and Hmong culture. Does she maintain an authentically fair tone from both of the "sides" of Lia's illness? What are some of the experiences/problems faced by both the Hmong and the medical community in Merced?

Next week will you try to read through Chapter 10, "War"?

missionary, even mocking him in their own language. Nevertheless, they are outwardly polite and attentive, believing incorrectly that the missionary holds the power to cause their deportation.

O'Brian pushes the class not to accept a stereotypical impression of the missionary based on a few minutes of film. "Does the film accurately represent this Christian minister?"

"He started trying to preach to them about their sins," said one boy. "But they don't have a concept of sinning."

"Do we know that for sure?" asks O'Brian.

"I don't think they understood or maybe they didn't care what the minister was saying," the boy replied.

The narrator of *Between Two Worlds* is the anthropologist Dwight Conguergood. He also appears in the film and is mentioned prominently in *The Spirit Catches You and You Fall Down.* The class discussed Conguergood and his provocative form of "performance anthropology," such as the "Rabies Parade" he directs in a Thai Refugee camp featuring a procession of Hmong residents playing a dancing tiger, a chicken, and an evil spirit called

Table 3.5 Example Reading/Film Response Essay

Foua, the Legally Abusive, Babysitting Parent, and Lia

Thank you all for finishing the opportunities for chapter 1 thru 6, even if some of you are not quite "finished." This week we have tried to move through the next four chapters as Lia is moved to foster care and back home (ch. 7); then we come to know how Anne Fadiman found Foua and Nao Kao and thereby find Lia's parents becoming real and very human (ch. 8); Hmong healing concepts are revealed (ch. 9); and finally we come to the heart of the reason they are here (ch. 10), "War."

I suggest that you take a little quality time this weekend and consider the following, As we pass through the story of Lia's continued traumas we meet a new set of "healers." Who are these people from three different sectors of American healing culture? How does their care of and for Lia flesh out the picture of American culture's attempts to deal with Lia's problem? (Korda, Hilt, Waller) Do any of them respond to something in the Hmong that allows a more humanizing portrait to begin to emerge?

Who **are** Lia's parents? When do they become more human characters with a real voice in this narrative? Who **are** the Hmong? When and how does the story of Hmong culture and history begin to kick in? Should the author have used a different narrative strategy introducing the Hmong more completely earlier? What aspects of Hmong culture emerge early as vital to the creation and preservation of Hmong identity? Of "Hmongness?"

We watched "Between Two Worlds: A Hmong Shaman in America," a film by Taggart Siegal, narrated by Dwight Conguergood. What did the film add to your sense of the Hmong? What seemed authentic in the film? How are you understanding what shamanism is and what it does now?

Next week I will ask you to narrate as best you can the events of war and flight. Please READ! Read chapters 10, 11 and 12. Really! Read them deeply, lovingly and with imaginative empathy until you become immersed there with the Hmong traveling through their past like a shaman into the zones where life and death commingle. And, if you are successful, you can return to this world, our world, now their world, having rescued their culture's dislocated soul from oblivion and the awful death of anonymity.

---

a *dab*. It is at this point that a couple of written assignments were introduced. O'Brian employs a "wholistic" assessment method—throwing out assignments with multiple prompts, and allowing students ample time to complete them on their own terms and with a flexible time line. Tables 3.4 and 3.5 are two examples, each calling for a two-page written response. After passing out these kinds of handouts to students, O'Brian reads the assignments aloud, taking questions and initiating a discussion that helps students conceptualize their written responses.

As students mulled these take-home assignments, the discussion of Hmong history and shamanism proceeded. Students were sometimes uncomfortable with aspects of the dialogue. As embodied in the Hmong culture, shamans enter a kind of trance in an effort to push them closer to the spirit world. In addition, animal sacrifice is an important element of the Hmong religion—as a scene from *Between Two Worlds* shows all too graphically. O'Brian does not shy from these subjects: the opposite, in fact. These are topics common to the field of anthropology and will be important in the examination

Table 3.6 Shamanism Illustration Response Essay

Shamanism

To give you all a chance to let shamanism take residence in your imagination, would you please do the following:

- Page through the entire volume of shamanism by Piers Vitebsky.
- Choose six illustrations that interest you and illustrate some aspect of shamanism.
- Describe each illustration narrating why you chose it and what aspect of shamanism it makes more comprehensible.
- Connect your emerging understanding of shamanism to our study of the Hmong and to the movie *Between Two Worlds: A Hmong Shaman in America.*

An example of using an illustration could be page 8. This illustration, you might explain, comments on several components of shamanism. First, we see a reference to the use of psychotropic or hallucinogenic substances to induce visions of the other, spiritual world. Second, the imagery here represented purports to be from the point of view of the shamans themselves, which allows us to "see" the spiritual world as they see it. Third, the imagery may suggest that the Shamans are not only in contact with the spirit world, but also with each other in the alternative reality. All of these are aspects of Shamanism. Fourth, the "Spirit World" is really real.

A second example may come from pages 78–79. The several illustrations on this page evoke the role "Music" plays in a Shamanistic ritual. As we noted in past classes, music in the form of song and dance is the narrative by which trance is induced and maintained. Music also forms a basis for communicating with the "congregation" while the Shaman is journeying to find a lost soul or battling sickness-causing spirits. You get the idea?

of other cultures during the course of the year. Although some students appear leery of both shamanism and animal sacrifice, an authentic Anthropology class can hardly avoid such topics. That said, initiating a constructive conversation is not easy, but O'Brian manages to pull it off.

I do not try to establish a discussion that gives one religion or one culture preeminence in the classroom, but to try to establish a field where we can discuss one and other's belief systems, kinship systems, and languages. And so if religion is so prominent within a culture, like the Hmong culture, it's very important to find a language that allows us to see the world the way they see it. You don't have to believe the world they believe in. And I've had many Christian students say to me that they appreciated the care, but more important they appreciated the vocabulary that allowed them to look deeper into the beliefs they themselves held.

The relatively thin book *Shamanism* helps in this regard. Filled with photographs, pictures, diagrams, maps, and dense text, the book explores key aspects of shamanism throughout the world, positioning the practice as a key cultural construct shared by many, many peoples. For O'Brian's students, it serves to rest an unblinking eye on a concept that few understand and provides a fascinating opportunity to explore "the other." To this end, O'Brian gave the assignment in Table 3.6.

O'Brian pushed the discussion of shamanism and its role in Hmong culture forward on a number of fronts, including the narratives put forth in *The Spirit Catches You and You Fall Down*, *Between Two Worlds*, and *Shamanism*. Examination of Hmong history also continues, at this point with selected segments of the documentary film *Vietnam: The Ten Thousand Day War* (1980). Of this lengthy, multi-part examination of the war, O'Brian shows only carefully selected bits; specifically from part 9, entitled "Guerilla Society," which looks at guerilla warfare tactics, the leaders of the North Vietnamese army (NVA) who pioneered these techniques, and the lengths to which the Vietnamese and their allies in Laos and Cambodia went to construct the Ho Chi Minh Trail.

> I thought that that was absolutely key for at least two reasons: One is, these are the majority of the opponents that the Hmong themselves fought, that the context of that war—again the atmospherics of the jungle, the trails, the tunnels. The Hmong were supposed to interdict that trail and to fight against the NVA mainline forces. The film footage is really compelling. It's kind of raw, grainy and black and white. You're right there in the jungle. It seems to capture kids' interest and give them a sense of, "Oh, *this* is where the Hmong come from. *This* is why the war was so difficult. My God, they must have been pretty sophisticated fighters if they fought these guys."

Discussion of these film clips, along with connections and analysis of the two books, more than fills a couple of days of class. By this time students have learned a great deal about Hmong history and culture, and as they made their way toward the final chapters of *The Spirit Catches You and You Fall Down* the gravity of classroom discussion took on a denser feel. It is with this enhanced comprehension and appreciation that the unit culminated, first with the documentary film *The Split Horn: Life of a Hmong Shaman in America* (2001), and then with two separate written assignments.

The Split Horn is a longer and more polished follow-up to the previously viewed *Between Two Worlds: Hmong Shaman in America*. The film revisits the extended family of Paja Thao some 14 years later, now moved to Appleton, a mid-sized town in East Central Wisconsin that has attracted many Hmong families previously scattered across the United States. Whereas Appleton is not far from the city of Chicago (about four hours' drive), the distance traveled existentially by the Thao family in the intervening years appears great indeed. The film is narrated not by an anthropologist, but instead by Paja's youngest daughter, Chai, who speaks flawless English, dresses like an American kid, and plays on her school basketball team.

As the movie begins to roll on an aging VHS machine, O'Brian stands by the television screen and points out key aspects of the film. He is animated and quick to break in with comments and analysis: "I want the shaman, Paja, to really take center stage in your viewing of this film," O'Brian cries, as students settle into their seats.

The Split Horn begins with a hospital scene in which an esteemed uncle is dying, surrounded by an emotive group of extended family. The room is full of Hmong relatives, a fact that doesn't seem to bother hospital staff in the least. This scene provides a contrast to the actions of medical workers described in *The Spirit Catches You and You Fall Down*—a book set in California a decade earlier. O'Brian suggested that hospital workers in Wisconsin have learned much about treating Hmong patients.

As the movie progresses, it is revealed that Paja is suffering from "soul loss," what Westerners might call depression caused by Post Traumatic Stress Syndrome (PTSD), as his family makes the inevitable transition to American life. A daughter marries and moves to the East Coast. A high school-aged son dates, and later impregnates and marries a local, white Wisconsin girl. Another son converts to Christianity and wants nothing to do with the shamanistic ceremonies of his father. These and other events sink Paja deep into despair, much to the dismay of his wife and family. In a climactic scene, family members from across the country converge on Paja's home for a traditional ceremony, led by a respected female shaman, intended to find and return the patriarch's lost soul. As the healing ceremony moves forward, English-language TV blares in the background—a kind of metaphor for the entire documentary.

As the film comes to an end, O'Brian emphatically highlights the literal and figurative comparison between "soul loss" as experienced by Hmong who survived the Southeast Asian wars and PTSD as experienced by U.S. military veterans. *Between Two Worlds* and *The Split Horn* taken together are a powerful look at the conundrum facing Hmong elders who seek to hold on to their traditions, but are powerless in the face of the dominant culture. For O'Brian's students, they offer a useful tool for understanding these often misunderstood immigrants. Discussion of *The Split Horn* is greatly enriched by the arc of the Hmong unit.

"I'm curious to know how their neighbors react to these ceremonies," says one girl.

"It's hard to watch it, because I don't believe in this stuff," says another girl, who claims Christianity strongly influences her thinking. "But it really helped me to see that sickness ceremony—it helped me to understand it. I think it had a big impact to make the Hmong culture more true to me."

Table 3.7 The Split Horn Viewer's Guide

The Split Horn: A Viewer's Guide to Accompany the Reading of *The Spirit Catches You and You Fall Down*

Most of you have finished reading *The Spirit Catches You…* Even more have viewed *The Split Horn*. Write a Viewer's Guide, anthropologically speaking, to accompany the film, as well as the other texts we have used. That is, incorporate also relevant, pertinent, informative parts of Vitebsky's *Shamanism*. Your Viewer's Guide can make reference to the PBS work done a few years ago: //www.pbs.org/splithorn/story.htm. However, you will find that site anthropologically and shamanistically deficient. Your task, your calling, is to remedy that sour stealing deficiency. The unwary viewer may be seduced into something resembling an "understanding" of Hmong/Mong culture and a fatuous sense that they "understand" shamanism. You know that nothing could be further from the truth regarding understand shamanism. In fact, such unwary viewers are in terrible danger: they will have unwittingly had their souls of sensibility stolen. You will, shaman-like, travel into the zone of misunderstanding and following the threads of more accurate representation of shamanism call back the senses of understanding. You will need to travel into several scenes of the film and explicate, illuminate, interpret what sense there is to be made on behalf of Hmong/Mong authenticity of representation.

Table 3.8 Final Essay

Final Screenplay Assignment

Clint Eastwood, following his dual aesthetic with *Flags of Our Fathers and Letters from Iwo Jima,* decides to follow *Gran Torino* with an inside perspective on the Hmong Exodus. Using *The Late Homecomer* as inspiration, he enlists Ms. Yang as the screenplay writer and Ms. Fadiman as producer. This chapter is the opening scene in their film. Describe in general how the rest of the movie might proceed and in particular how it might contrast to *Gran Torino*.

"There are a lot of contrasts in the film. Like when she is performing a ceremony and the kids are watching TV in the background," says a third girl. "I thought it showed the clash of cultures and generations really well. It showed everyday life and how these cultures are really reconciling."

Many of the students are impressed with the closeness of the extended Hmong families. As Paja's children struggle to live in the only country they really know, the United States, they nevertheless show a pride of culture that is impressive. "I think it is interesting we talk about the way they resist assimilation, but the kids do not," says a boy.

"They kind of still have to figure out how to live as Hmong in America," responds a girl. "The way that they choose to do things is really different. I mean it's hard for the Hmong to fit in, because they have a really different culture."

Another student points out that, although *The Split Horn* is narrated by a young Hmong girl, ultimately she is reading off a script probably written by the film's producers. O'Brian picks up on this point, noting that, although the film does a nice job of attempting to portray a Hmong point of view, it should nevertheless be analyzed critically. Once again, he urges the class to consider carefully what is portrayed about the concept of "soul loss" and the world of the shaman in the two films. As the discussion runs its course, and the end of class approaches, O'Brian informs students that a local Hmong professor from Portland State University will soon give a presentation to class.

"You watched the two documentaries and you also watched *Gran Torino*, and you saw how modernity is affecting the Hmong," O'Brian says. "They have cars and gangs and shamans. *Gran Torino* is set in the present, more or less, but this [*The Split Horn*] was the 1990s. There's a foreshadowing of that."

A culminating discussion continued over the next few days of class, as O'Brian pressed students to complete their readings and also introduced a number of handouts showing Hmong art, stitch work, and so on. Another written assignment is given in Table 3.7: a two-page viewer's guide to *The Split Horn*. Students were also invited to create interpretive works of art accompanied by two-page written artist's statements. Many did so, bringing in various original pictures, paintings, collage, stitch work, and one colorful, highly decorated Hmong-inspired chair.

Finally, the unit turns back to where it began, specifically the Hmong people portrayed in *Gran Torino*. When students first viewed the movie, they knew little if anything about Hmong history or culture. The question now is, after about a month of study, thought and discussion: How well did director Clint Eastwood really portray the Hmong? A brief chapter from the book *The Latehomecomer: A Hmong Family Memoir*, by Kao Kalia Yang, is attached to the assignment. The chapter, entitled *Enemy Camp*, describes a young Hmong family's horrific flight from Laos, pursued with deadly intent by soldiers of the Pathet Lao and North Vietnam.

At a number of times during the unit, O'Brian challenged his class on the importance of learning about the Hmong people. Do the Hmong deserve a place in the history textbooks of the United States? O'Brian worries about the prospect. "I wonder if at other high schools now, if in other school districts, if there is anything resembling the kind of Hmong studies that goes on here, if there's something that allows the students in the schools to learn about this ethnic group?" The hope is that, after this sprawling, longitudinal look at Hmong culture, students will be possessed of more than just "some knowledge," but some deep and abiding understanding of the Hmong, their humanity, and why they belong.

REFLECTION ON THE CASE

The introduction to this chapter pointed out that, of all media, films are uniquely positioned to create an affective response. The objectives of this "ethno-history" of the Hmong are varied. However, certainly among the most important is the idea of humanizing an often marginalized and misunderstood people, and doing so by using assignments that ask students to adopt and in fact advance a Hmong perspective. In this case, the various films are utilized by Mr. O'Brian to motivate students to engage and learn more about the Hmong and their culture. In turn, this awareness helps students to develop respect, tolerance, and eventually care about and for the Hmong. At least this is the goal.

The unit described above represents a new twist for Mr. O'Brian. *Gran Torino* had only just been released and was yet to make it to DVD. This constricted O'Brian's pedagogical options to some extent. In future semesters, he will have the opportunity of playing around with scenes and images from the movie, for example stopping the movie for discussion or to emphasize important points, or revisiting key scenes at the end of the unit for reinterpretation. Nevertheless, even on first attempt, the movie served its purpose of engaging students in two very different stories—those of Walt Kowalski and of his Hmong neighbors—and showing that these narratives have great relevance in the present.

That idea of bringing both perspectives is really good. *Split Horn: Life of a Hmong Shaman* is really good, but it is still not done by the Hmong themselves. Remember that movie *Letters from Iwo Jima* is dual written and dual directed by both Eastwood and a Japanese director. So that idea of bringing both perspectives together is so rare in the classroom. It's what Homer did. It's an ancient idea, but it still works.

O'Brian seeks to immerse his students in whatever culture is under study (other units cover the Mbuti, Australian Aborigines, and Iraqi Shia). This is no simple task, given the considerable limitations of a large, public high school. Yet

O'Brian has developed a method with film that helps push students out of their comfort zone into a conscious examination of ideologies and cultural practices they don't comprehend, and indeed may not appreciate.

Teachers seeking to replicate the unit described in this chapter will face a number of challenges and also a wide field of opportunity. On the challenge side, O'Brian's content knowledge on Hmong culture has been accrued over many years, as have the materials he uses for the unit. The kind of richness that this chapter frankly only hints at would be difficult to attain during a first pass through this course of study, or even the fifth. If done carelessly or with a lack of depth, such a curricular unit might lead to naïve stereotyping. Thus teachers need to develop a deep and textured content knowledge when attempting to engage students in empathy for any marginalized group.

That said, the framework laid out in this chapter offers many opportunities. Hmong people live in many corners of the world today. Just as Mr. O'Brian has sought out local resources—guest speakers, artists, Vietnam vets, and so on—so another teacher can develop community assets to enrich this curriculum. Other film and textual resources might be tried as well. There are no lack of books and stories about the wars in Southeast Asia. However, the facts that the Hmong themselves lack a written language, and that they participated in what has aptly been named the "Secret War," mean that authentic Hmong sources are more difficult (but not impossible) to find.

This case also raises the issue of effective documentary film use, a theme that emerges in Chapter 4. It is easy to see that Mr. O'Brian previews and thinks hard about films before showing them in class. As is the case with the other teachers described in this book, he uses film as only one source of information, to be compared and contrasted with other sources. O'Brian models a sensitivity to the role of filmmakers in documentaries, helping engage students in how this agency leaves clear marks on the film text. Like history textbooks, documentaries are often viewed incorrectly by students as neutral or objective. O'Brian moves to confront this misconception, pointing out that documentaries represent distinct perspectives on the past, even when they are assembled from period film footage, images and interviews. Here Mr. O'Brian took a thoughtful approach in engaging his students in an interrogation of the films as cultural artifacts.

O'Brian's approach also helps underscore the limits to which one can fully empathize with others. Although films tend to invoke an affective response, it is important for teachers who want to engage their students in developing humane or tolerant views of others to emphasize the limits to fully understanding what others have gone through. Can outsiders truly "understand" the plight of the Hmong? Perhaps not, but that doesn't mean attempting to do so is unworthy of the effort. As the quote by O. L. Davis in the Part II introduction reminds us, developing historical empathy is always using "imagination restrained by evidence."

The truth is we all want our students to "get it." Empathy is the ability to imaginatively attempt to enter into the experience of others. If we want students to attain a passion for history or anthropology, we will need to furnish them the capacity to know what is at stake.

This is central to moral and ethical reasoning—a goal of the social studies in general.

Strategies for Using Film to Teach Empathy for Caring

The general technique outlined in this chapter might be described briefly as follows: First, introduce students as soon as possible to a compelling movie portrayal of the person or group to be studied. Then use that aesthetic to breathe life into an extended study that is textured, historical, inclusive of local resources, and to the greatest extent possible immersive in the viewpoint of those under study. Finally return to the beginning, asking students to embrace the perspective of those under study to reexamine with new insight the original portrayal, essentially teaching themselves the lessons they have learned.

It is a teaching technique O'Brian has used before. In a previous incarnation of this unit, O'Brian used the movie *Good Morning Vietnam* (1987) to the same purpose. That movie has many strengths, with the violence of war set beside the hilarious star turn of the comedian Robin Williams, playing the real-life disc jockey Adrian Cronauer.

> You pick films that they thought they knew something about, and you take them apart for them. The best example is *Good Morning Vietnam*, you play one of Robin Williams' monologues—"from the Delta to the DMZ"—"little people in orange robes burning into flames"—"follow the Ho Chi Minh Trail!"—and they don't know who any of these people are, but they're laughing. So you ask them: Why was that funny? They don't know. And so you go back: "What's the Delta? What's the DMZ? Who is Ho Chi Minh?" So teaching that, and then going back, increases the sense of not only appreciation of Robin Williams, but the history book. The other thing is that it allows Vietnamese people to be real characters. Some of them [students] don't see real people in history texts; they see abstract ideas or narratives of history, unless they get a really unusual history text. In many ways the films humanize the characters in history, in particular humanize people who come from outside the mainstream narrative.

Although the movie *Good Morning Vietnam* had certain strengths in serving to "humanize" the lives of the Hmong, it also carried clear drawbacks. Among these are its focus on South Vietnam, not Laos, and the fact that the 1980s movie and its stars are barely recognizable to today's teens. *Gran Torino* represents a significant upgrade in both these regards.

Mr. O'Brian's unit on the Hmong people was multifaceted and lengthy, for sure, but this need not always be the case. One can imagine the basic technique described above being boiled down into much smaller study blocks, especially if lessons focus on peoples about whom students already have some background knowledge. In this sense, the method is fairly replicable.

Strategies for Selecting Films to Teach Empathy for Caring

Choosing movies to build a curricular unit of this sort provides a significant challenge to the teacher. Although there are certainly other Hollywood movies that offer complex portrayals of little-known, displaced, marginalized, misunderstood, or misrepresented peoples, there are not nearly enough. Further, even movies set in far-flung places and among such peoples tend to focus the camera on mainstream Hollywood stars, with other actors playing only supporting roles, roles that can serve to extend stereotypes as much as they illuminate alternative perspectives.

Fortunately for the educator seeking to engender a fellow feeling for those who have been on the wrong end of history's stick, it is not necessary that the characters portrayed in movies be represented sympathetically or even realistically, only that there be enough "meat on the bones" for students to chew on. Even stereotypical, a-historical, and/or poorly acted accounts of the past can be used by the clever teacher as "straw men" to be knocked down by students through research and analysis. Remember that any movie shown in class—whether good, bad, or indifferent—must be open to challenge from other, more authentic sources (in this case historical or anthropological).

Gran Torino offers a complex and interesting portrayal of both Hmong and white Midwestern characters. It received high praise from most reviewers and generally succeeded in raising student interest. In short, the movie is complex, interesting, and humanizing, and these are traits that might be looked at when selecting a movie to frame corollary units on other persons or peoples. Certainly, *Gran Torino* is not the only major movie with these attributes. For example, *El Norte* (1983) has been used in many a curricular unit targeting immigration from Central America to the United States. Likewise, *Smoke Signals* (1998) fits nicely into classes studying Native American culture.

Looking beyond American mainstream commercial motion pictures is well worth the time and effort. The film industry has long since become internationalized, and it is noteworthy that a number of companies have been created in recent years with the express intention of producing movies chronicling peoples previously far from the Hollywood mainstream. For example Isuma, a Canadian company dedicated to telling the story of the Inuit, has produced fascinating movies well suited to the classroom, including *Atanarjuat: The Fast Runner* (2001) and *The Journals of Knud Rasmussen* (2006). For studying the history and culture of Australian Aborigines, Mr. O'Brian recommends a number of movies, among them *Rabbit-Proof Fence* (2002), *The Tracker* (2002), and *Ten Canoes* (2006). He has also taught about Haitian culture using *Divine Horsemen: The Living Gods of Haiti* (1985).

The intrepid teacher has a wide world of cinema to search, a task greatly aided by companies that provide easy rental, purchase, and online streaming of a huge variety of movies. This kind of access to foreign and independent cinema could only have been dreamed about a decade ago.

CHAPTER 4

Using Film to Develop Empathy as Perspective Recognition

Figure 4.1 Swing Kids (1993). Protagonists (from left to right) Thomas (Christian Bale), Peter (Robert Sean Leonard), Otto (Jayce Bartok), and Arvid (Frank Whaley).

The following case illustrates the potential for using film to engage students in the perspective recognition aspect of developing historical empathy by examining a unit on the rise of totalitarianism and the Holocaust in a U.S. History class. Unlike the goal of developing empathy specifically for caring covered in Chapter 3, which takes advantage of the affective power of film to develop students' beliefs and attitudes to one of caring for others, this chapter focuses on the aspect of empathy with the goal of helping students to develop "cognitive" empathy. Empathy as perspective recognition is developed by asking students to evaluate the thinking, decision making, and experiences of individuals and groups in the past. Although Hollywood films often elaborate on aspects of the historical record being told for dramatic purposes, they can still be a powerful medium for helping students to recognize the perspectives and experiences of people from the past.

As presented in the Part II introduction, perspective recognition is possible in part because films position their audiences to particular viewpoints through the narrative and production (e.g., camera angles, editing) of the film. These film perspectives come in several forms. For example, the viewer may be positioned as a witness to the events in the film, as if seeing history through a window. In *Tora! Tora! Tora!* (1970) the viewer can witness Japanese admirals discussing their strategy for attacking Pearl Harbor in 1941. Films may also place the audience in the position of a participant in the event. For example, certain scenes in *Saving Private Ryan* (1998), such as the D-Day invasion scene in the beginning of the film, place the audience in the position of a soldier wading ashore. Similarly, in *Enemy at the Gates* (2001), the audience watches much of the events in the film unfold through the scope of a sniper's rifle during the battle for Stalingrad. This aspect of films helps students to easily identify the perspectives being portrayed in the film, and to understand potential perspectives of historical agents or groups. The downside, however, is that the film is always being told from the director/producer's point of view and reflects the period in which it is produced, sometimes more so than the period it represents, an issue discussed in detail in Chapter 5. Therefore, it is important for teachers to be explicit about the perspectives they ask students to attempt to recognize and understand, and be explicit that there are limits to how much can be understood from a film. This may be done by identifying the perspective of the film's producers, by looking at the context of when the film was made in addition to the perspectives included in the film, and by comparing the perspectives in film to those represented in other sources (e.g., speeches, letters).

Depending on the film, students could be asked to recognize perspectives that may be a more general perspective of people from particular historical groups. For example, a teacher may use *Glory* (1989) to help students develop a sense of the perspectives of different groups of African Americans who fought for the North during the American Civil War (e.g., escaped slaves, freedmen, educated, abolitionist). A film may also provide perspectives that challenge or provide depth to previously accepted historical accounts. For example, *Swing Kids* (1993), a film used in the case presented in this chapter (see Table 4.2 for description of the films for this case), attempts to include perspectives of non-Nazi German youth. This perspective is not often included in the curriculum as the focus is more often on youth in the *Hitler Junge*, who are portrayed as true believers. Finally, the teacher could ask students to recognize the multiple perspectives of the same historical figure from different viewpoints of the film's makers (e.g., writer, director, producer) or that reflect the historical understanding of the time it was produced. For instance, students may examine how the perspective of Admiral Yamamoto, the Japanese mastermind behind the Pearl Harbor attacks during World War II, is represented across films such as *The Gallant Hours* (1960), *Tora! Tora! Tora!* (1970), *Midway* (1976), and *Pearl Harbor* (2001).

Teachers also position students through how they structure the viewing and what they ask students to pay particular attention to in the film. For example, a teacher may ask students to focus on the perspectives of socialists in *The Grapes of Wrath* (1940), the experiences of the average British sailor while watching a clip from *Master and Commander* (2003), or the perspective of an idealistic congressperson in *Mr. Smith Goes to Washington* (1939). Having multiple layers of historical interpretation and perspectives, which historical fiction film often provides, can complicate instruction, but it can also provide a rich, affective, and engaging experience for students when structured with the goal of perspective recognition in mind. Films make natural supplementary resources to use along with primary documents and literature in attaining historical empathy.

MRS. JOHNSON'S CLASS: PERSPECTIVES ON TOTALITARIANISM AND THE HOLOCAUST

Case Description

The following case takes place during a unit on totalitarianism and the Holocaust in Mrs. Johnson's period five class. Mrs. Johnson's class, a survey U.S. History course, took place at Lincoln High School, a comprehensive public high school set in a mid-sized Midwestern city and was observed in the spring of 2005. This ninth grade heterogeneous class included 25 students, including a number of students of color and several Jewish students. Mrs. Johnson believed that this particular group of students was of "average" ability but they were "really good kids" overall in that they were a nice group to work with. Mrs. Johnson uses a number of films throughout her year-long course, such as *Matewan* (1987) and *The Grapes of Wrath* (1940), as well as portions of a number of documentary films.

Mrs. Johnson's goals in this unit reflected themes that ran across this course. These goals emphasized developing tolerance and a desire for social justice in her students, especially through attempting to develop historical empathy for individuals and groups in the past. She also wanted to challenge her students' assumptions about the Holocaust and the role of the United States in it.

The importance of the above goals for Mrs. Johnson is also reflected in the extended time given to this unit even though it was part of a U.S. History course. She explains:

> The larger goal was to give the students an in-depth understanding, if possible, of the mentality of a group of people who could commit something so atrocious as the Holocaust. And, of course, the conclusion they are going to is that no one can understand it. But, I wanted them to kind of get an understanding of how people can get sucked into that whole gang mentality and do these horrendous things.[1]

For her unit on the Holocaust, Mrs. Johnson wanted to provide perspectives different from what many of her students had experienced in the past. Many of the students had participated in lessons on the Holocaust in middle school that had emphasized a lot of "bearing witness" to the horrors of the Holocaust without learning much about the context of the genocide or many of the details of what happened and why. These students had been engaged in watching film and reading first-person accounts but were not able to place the events or the root causes within the context of European history or from an American perspective.

Unit Overview

For her unit on the rise of the totalitarians and the Holocaust, Mrs. Johnson wanted her students to be able to understand the psychological, historical, and social reasons why the genocide occurred from multiple perspectives. In particular she wanted her students to understand how people such as Hitler are able to come into power and why others would assist in perpetrating or stand by as these atrocities occurred. She found film to be a useful medium for helping students understand these perspectives. Mrs. Johnson utilized *The Wave* (1981) as part of a lesson in which students induce the critical conditions that exist and strategies used to form the type of group mentality that fascists such as the Nazis used by studying the students in the "Wave." Students were then asked to apply this conceptual understanding to other totalitarian regimes that existed at the time, in part through the analysis of three films that provided insights into different perspectives on the Holocaust. These three films provided the perspectives of a Jewish survivor of the concentration camps in *The Holocaust: In Memory of Millions* (1994), of non-Nazi German youth in *Swing Kids* (1993), and of political and social perspectives of Americans and America during the Holocaust in *America and the Holocaust: Deceit and Indifference* (1994).

Unit Outline

Table 4.1 Outline of Unit on Totalitarianism and the Holocaust

Day(s)	Activity	Goal
1	Lesson introducing interwar period leading to World War II. Lesson included some textbook guided reading and map activity	Provide overall context for the unit
2	Continued work on reading guides, read and discussed "Twentieth Century Monsters," students asked to interview relatives about World War II	To introduce the rise of the totalitarian leaders and also add a personal perspective to the events in the form of family experiences
3–4	Film activity with *The Wave* and discussion	Help students identify characteristics of group mentality and strategies used by those in power
5	Students evaluated the Treaty of Versailles and conditions in Germany pre-World War II. Created chart on totalitarianism (tied to *The Wave*). Shared stories from relatives	To set the context of the social, political, and economic context for the rise of the totalitarians, and to help students develop concept of totalitarianism and identify and apply the critical attributes of that concept
6	Student read portions of a speech by Adolf Hitler that places blame for Germany's problems on other countries and peoples. Students also read a piece by Elie Wiesel in order to attempt to figure out "How did Hitler come into power?"	To recognize the perspective of Hitler and Germans who helped him come into power

Table 4.1 (continued)

Day(s)	Activity	Goal
7	Film activity for *In Memory of Millions*	To learn generally about the Holocaust and to recognize the perspectives of victims, perpetrators, bystanders, and liberators
8–9	Finish viewing *In Memory of Millions*, discuss video guides, explore the inability of efforts to stop the Holocaust, and read about the Nuremburg trials	Same as above
10	Students examine pre-World War II from the perspective of the US and conditions and events that brought the US into the war. Students are introduced to essay exam that will include all films from the unit. Film activity for *Swing Kids*	To gain an understanding of the U.S. perspective and also the perspectives of non-Nazi German youth, the disabled, and German communists and their experiences
11–12	Finish viewing and conduct discussion of *Swing Kids*. Students then discuss and compare with all films in order to prepare for Essay Exam	Begin to identify themes across films and relate to personal decision making
13–14	Examine the role of the US in the Holocaust. Film activity for *America and the Holocaust*	Recognize the perspective of many in the U.S., what the U.S. did and did not do to help stop the Holocaust

Films

As introduced above, Mrs. Johnson's unit on the rise of totalitarianism and the Holocaust included an examination of the social and political context leading into World War II, an inquiry into how totalitarians such as Hitler, Stalin, and Mussolini were able to gain power, and discussion of the Nazi-perpetuated genocide of Jews, Communists, homosexuals, Roma and Sinti, and others during the Holocaust. Mrs. Johnson used film throughout the unit to bring in different perspectives on the events and groups involved, including Jewish survivors and resistors in *In Memory of Millions*, non-Nazi youth that included collaborators, bystanders, and resistors in *Swing Kids*, the mentality of would-be perpetrators in *The Wave*, and finally an American political and social perspective in *America and the Holocaust*. Mrs. Johnson selected these films specifically for the perspectives they included and the issues they raised, and in particular the inclusion of youth perspectives in the fictional *Swing Kids* and the interviews of survivors who were young during the Holocaust. Table 4.2 includes descriptions and credit information for each of the films.

Table 4.2 Description of Films

The Wave (1981) Alexander Grasshoff (Director) ABC Broadcasting	This made for television *After School Special* portrays the experiences of a California classroom social studies teacher's attempt to help students understand why the Nazis were able to gain power and commit genocide in the 1930s and 1940s. The film portrays a classroom simulation of Nazi youth indoctrination gone awry. The events recreate those of an actual classroom in the 1960s and are based on the account of the teacher.
The Holocaust: In Memory of Millions (1994) Brian Blake (Director) Discovery Channel	This documentary was produced to coincide with the opening of the U.S. Memorial Holocaust Museum and is narrated by Walter Cronkite. The film presents a chronological visual history of the Holocaust using film footage, first-hand accounts, historical perspectives, and images. The film ends with some footage taken during the liberation of a concentration camp by a British army unit.
Swing Kids (1993) Thomas Carter (Director) Jonathan Marc Feldman (Writer) Walt Disney Pictures	This film portrays the experiences of a group of young men in Nazi Germany and their attempts to resist indoctrination into the Nazi Youth. The group is joined by their love of contraband American swing music and their dislike of Nazi authority. The young characters represent different groups in Nazi Germany who were persecuted, including the disabled, Communists, and pre-Nazi German aristocracy.
America and the Holocaust: Deceit and Indifference (1994) Martin Ostrow (Writer, Director, Producer) Fine Cut Productions	This somewhat controversial episode of PBS's *American Experience* series presents a critical examination of the role of the US in what was done and not done to prevent or end the Holocaust. The film is structured around the story of an American Jew who is trying desperately to help family members escape Nazi Germany in the 1930s, and presents an unfavorable portrayal of U.S. immigration policies toward Jews, American anti-semitism, and decisions that were made related to military strategies in World War II.

FILM ACTIVITIES

The Wave

"The teacher is getting sucked in by power. Power makes you angry," one student remarked. Another student added, "The teacher was at first trying to prove something but then it got out of control." Another continued, "It is funny that the students couldn't tell they were being manipulated."

As the above quotes suggest, students were already being pulled into the drama by the end of their first day watching *The Wave*. At the end of this period, Mrs. Johnson engaged the students in a discussion of what they had viewed up to that point and asked them to begin to analyze the events in the film and start to make connections with what happened during the rise of the Nazis in 1930s Germany. Mrs. Johnson's goal for showing the film was for students to be able to develop a conceptual-level understanding of how totalitarians use psychological and social strategies to gain power, especially through creating a form of group mentality that helps them appeal to the masses, but that also led to the atrocities of the Holocaust.

The teacher's simulation represented in *The Wave* shows how even Mr. Ross (the teacher in the film) was pulled into the power that he had accumulated with the students. It got to the point where the simulation was too out of hand, so he decided to end it by calling all of the Wave students into an assembly and showing them a clip of a Nazi rally, explaining to them that they had fallen into the same trap as many Germans did with the Nazis. In the film only Lori and eventually her boyfriend Daniel were able to resist the temptation of feeling the power of the group, because they recognized the problematic nature of the way students in the Wave were acting. By viewing and analyzing *The Wave*, Mrs. Johnson was able to ask her students to develop empathy for why people could be drawn into a negative form of group mentality without asking them to directly empathize with the Nazis. Students were also able to identify the psychological roots of totalitarianism and better understand how totalitarians were able to gain power.

Mrs. Johnson set the viewing activity up so that students were able to identify the strategies used by the teacher to gain power and the conditions or context of the environment that allowed students and even parents to turn a blind eye to what was happening. The strategies in the film represented the tactics utilized by the various totalitarian leaders the students were studying as part of the unit (e.g., Hitler, Mussolini). Prior to starting the viewing Mrs. Johnson broke the students into two groups and asked the first group to look for how the students in the film were "drawn into the group" and focus specifically on the actions of, and interactions between, three groups: students and teachers, students (Wave) and other students (non-Wave), and students and parents. The second group was instructed to identify how the teacher was able to build up the group mentality with the Wave students, especially how he was able to create a bond between them. Mrs. Johnson made comments during the viewing, such as "this looks like something for [group one]" or "an important point for [group two]" to help the two groups identify important points in the film that aligned with their task. This kind of scaffolding as a form of support helped to keep students engaged and focused during the viewing and helped them to better recognize the characteristics of behavior, which was Mrs. Johnson's goal.

It was the drama of the film, and the fact that it was of the 1980s ABC *After School Special* genre, that helped to engage the students. Their affective response to the film was strong, both in empathizing with some of the high school-aged characters and in the "cheesy" moments in the film's story and acting. Students also mimicked what was going on in the class. They gave the Wave salute to each other in class when leaving (the salute involved making a wave shape with their hand) and sat up straight in their desks when students in the film were ordered to do so. Before starting the film again on the second day of the activity, Mrs. Johnson asked students from the two groups to report the strategies and conditions they had identified so far in the film. They identified the motto used by the group "strength through discipline, strength through community, strength through action" and how, along with the Wave salute, it helped to unify the group of students. The class then viewed the remainder of the film and afterward discussed the various critical attributes they had identified of the type of group mentality used to draw the students into the group and gain power. These attributes included representative attributes from historical totalitarian regimes such as providing a sense of equality in the group, developing feelings of superiority over other groups, providing a vision of progress or hope, and identifying a common enemy to blame. The students were then asked to put these attributes into a chart (see Table 4.3) to use in the analysis of historic cases of totalitarianism during the rest of the unit (e.g., Nazi Germany, Italy, the USSR). By inducing the attributes from the film and then applying them to other examples, Mrs. Johnson hoped to instill in students this concept of group mentality and how it can be used in negative ways to gain and abuse power.

The dramatic and engaging aspect of *The Wave* was again evident in the class's discussions. Students identified easily with particular characters, including Robert, who was an outcast in the school but who found a sense of belonging by joining and participating in the Wave. One student remarked "He is usually an outcast. Now he is part of the group because the teacher used him as an example [group member]." Students also recognized why Robert in particular looked crushed when the students in the film found out how they had fallen for the Wave mentality; they thought Robert would "no longer [feel] accepted in school" after the Wave was disbanded. The class also made connections between the film and what the characters and story represented in terms of Nazi Germany. One student noted "Doesn't Robert kind of represent people who were in poverty? The ones that embraced Hitler; [Hitler] recruited the lower classes." Based on the class discussions and student remarks, the vast majority of students appeared to gain the conceptual understanding and sense of empathy Mrs. Johnson had hoped for and that also worked toward her larger goal of tolerance.

As part of this discussion, the students also attempted to empathize with the decisions student-characters made to so easily accept the norms Mr. Ross introduced, and recognized how quickly these rules translated into actions on the part of the group. As Mrs. Johnson had asked, students in the first group looked at the ways students and parents interacted. Several students in this group noted that the parents had commented that Mr. Ross "must know what he is doing" and that they were actually in favor of more discipline being applied in the classroom. This discussion also led to the idea that students in the film were not culpable for their actions as "they were following orders" from an authority figure (Mr. Ross), an argument similar to one argued by many Nazis at Nuremberg. In this way, Mrs. Johnson's viewing activity worked to help students

Table 4.3 Totalitarian Techniques

Technique	The Wave	Stalin	Hitler	Mussolini
Creating terror				
Propaganda				
Instilling nationalism (building groups)				
Educating the youth				
Authoritarian figure				
Creating common enemy				

empathize with characters but also to start making links between *The Wave* case study and the context of Nazi Germany.

Mrs. Johnson then assisted students in exploring the conceptual ideas behind how group mentality can have negative consequences with the students in the Wave group. She explained "members of the group feel as if they are not responsible for actions, because they can always blame it on others in the group." She also asked students to think about how group mentality can sometimes lead to negative consequences in their own lives, for example through social cliques or gangs. Students easily brought up a number of examples of when they felt pressured to do something they did not want to, ranging from teasing other students to being involved in gangs. Mrs. Johnson encouraged students to apply these experiences using the conceptual framework they developed. She then asked the students to apply this same framework to analyze more specifically how aspects of group mentality were used in Nazi Germany and the other totalitarian regimes they were studying (e.g., Italy, the USSR) and record their findings in the chart (see Table 4.3 above).

Using the above chart and the framework they educed from *The Wave*, the class then spent the next two days attempting to answer the question "How did Hitler come into power?" They utilized primary and secondary sources to gain an understanding of the conditions after World War I in Germany and during the Depression, the impact of the Treaty of Versailles, and the feelings of Germans toward other Europeans based on how they felt they were treated in that treaty. For example, they read and discussed an excerpt of a speech Hitler gave at a rally that blamed other European powers and Jews for the Weimar Republic's problems. These lessons laid the groundwork for examining how the hate that Hitler helped foster against the Jews as scapegoats translated into the Holocaust through viewing *The Holocaust: In Memory of Millions*, and from reading a short biographical account about Elie Wiesel, who is also featured in the film.[2]

The Holocaust: In Memory of Millions

Unlike their lighthearted reaction while viewing *The Wave*, Mrs. Johnson's class appeared somber and reflective as they watched the progression of genocide in *In*

Memory of Millions. As the film presented the escalating and systematic persecution of the Jews and other groups, and then acts of genocide, some students left the room for a few minutes or put their heads down, especially during scenes that included graphic images. The most graphic scenes are at the end of the film, which includes film taken by a British Army unit liberating a camp. At this point, the students are bearing witness to the Holocaust and are mired in attempting to understand what they are seeing. *In Memory of Millions*, a documentary produced for the U.S. Holocaust Memorial Museum, guides the viewer through the context and events leading to the Holocaust, including the systematic use of propaganda and laws to marginalize Jews, Communists, and other groups, the ghettoization of Jews, and eventually the genocide and aftermath. The film includes multiple perspectives, from personal stories of harrowing survival to those of the townspeople who claimed not to know what was going on in the camp the British liberated. This film provided evidence of the negative consequences of the group mentality they had witnessed being constructed in *The Wave.* Unlike *The Wave,* however, Mrs. Johnson treated *In Memory of Millions* more objectively because of its documentary form and without critique or acknowledgement that the film was presenting a particular perspective for specific reasons and aimed at a specific audience.

In addition to the rich content on the Holocaust provided in the film, Mrs. Johnson thought that *In Memory of Millions* provided something that was "unobtainable" using any other kind of historical source because of the powerful visual evidence of hate and violence, and to a lesser degree resistance. She believed this visual imagery could help students develop empathy for the victims and survivors of the Holocaust. She warned students before the viewing about the graphic portrayals in the film and also asked them to attempt to consider what it would have been like to be treated in the way the Jews, Communists, homosexuals, Roma and Sinti, and others were treated. She provided a guide sheet for the film that had a quote by Elie Wiesel at the top—"For the dead. And the living. We must bear witness"—and asked students to identify and take notes on the "significant events, words, ideas, which you feel will help you understand what happened during this period of history." In this way, Mrs. Johnson positioned her students to bear witness to the atrocities in a very different way from how they viewed *The Wave.* Here she did not want them to question what they were viewing or interpret how the images are used to invoke emotion; Mrs. Johnson wanted them to feel the emotions invoked by the film and attempt to develop empathy for the victims. In this case, it might have been worthwhile to also spend some time talking about the powerful imagery of the film and how it was designed to elicit particular affective responses in the audience. *In Memory of Millions* functions as a vehicle both for perspective recognition and for developing caring, similar to how Mr. O'Brian uses different films in the case in Chapter 3. It would have also been powerful for her to discuss with the students the limits of what they could understand about the experiences of genocide victims (more on this later in the chapter).

In Memory of Millions did provide Mrs. Johnson's class with a powerful representation of the effects of the hatred and mindset of the Nazis and others who stood by or participated in the genocide without showing the actual violence that is front and center in films such as *Schindler's List.* *In Memory of Millions* instead was used to help students apply their abstract understandings of totalitarian power to the very real consequences in the Holocaust and some of the perspectives on the event. The recognition of the perspectives of victims, perpetrators, resistors, and bystanders continues through the final two film activities in the unit. Although Mrs. Johnson asked students to bear witness to the atrocities in the film activity, she does not go as far as asking students to "take" the perspective of Jews and other victims. However, in using the documentary account with rich first-person stories there was a tension that Mrs. Johnson appeared to feel between wanting students to be able to empathize with people from the film and her recognition that this understanding would be limited at best for students to attain.

Swing Kids

"Don't turn it off Johnson!" several students yell. It is the end of the first day watching *Swing Kids*, and the students want to know what will happen to Peter, one of the young characters in the film who is being forced to join the Nazi Youth, and his friend Arvid, a young disabled man who is being harassed by Nazi brownshirts. *Swing Kids* tells a fictional story of several teens who live in Berlin in the 1930s and who love the American swing music that has recently been banned. Peter, Arvid, and their friend Thomas also attempt to resist the pressures to join the Hitler Youth, and the film shows how powerful the pressures on youth in Germany were to be indoctrinated into the party. The film also provides stories of resistance on the part of Germans who helped their Jewish neighbors and friends attempt to escape while risking their own lives.

Mrs. Johnson thought that her students would easily be able to identify with the teens in the film and also gain a sense of how and why young people would join the Hitler Youth, building on what they had seen in *The Wave*. She shows the film also because of the variety of perspectives the film includes: Germans who resisted the Nazis, the handicapped who were also persecuted, the German elite who were not Nazis, and Communists (represented by Peter's father, who had been killed). Finally, she used the film to help students think about themes that they might include in the essay exam that was a major assessment for the unit. This essay asked students to pull themes from across three films (*The Wave, In Memory of Millions, Swing Kids*) related to choices that were made by groups or individuals in relation to the concept of group mentality, and to also apply these themes to present-day issues or events in their own lives or larger events or issues in the world. Before the class began viewing *Swing Kids*, Mrs. Johnson went through the expectations for their essay. She explained that she wanted them to write "what you learned from the three movies and making choices, [the consequences of] doing wrong."

Mrs. Johnson then presented *Swing Kids* as a "fictionalized movie of Berlin, of kids in Nazi Germany" and asked her students to pay particular attention to aspects of the film that would help them with their essays. She wanted to position the students to look for the choices the characters in the film were making and how it related to the concept of group mentality and the sometimes negative consequences of groupthink and action. By explicitly identifying the film as fictional, Mrs. Johnson frames the viewing so that students will think of what they are seeing not as real people's stories but more as representative perspectives from different groups at the time.

The students were drawn into the film and dramatic story line, as well as the swing music and dancing. The narrative of the film follows the three young men as pressure from the Nazi Youth escalates and eventually breaks their friendship and turns them against one another. Thomas and Peter are both forced to join the Hitler Youth after getting into trouble. Also, Thomas is drawn toward the power he sees in the group as a way to get back at his parents. Peter and Thomas resolve their conflict by the end of the film, but not before Arvid takes his own life rather than submit to being taken away by the Nazis for being disabled.

At the end of the film Mrs. Johnson asks the students to report what choices they identified during the film and the consequences of the characters' choices. This discussion served as both an analysis of what they viewed as well as scaffolding to help the students think through their essay ideas. Applying the film content in this way also worked toward Mrs. Johnson's goal of having students think about how their historical understandings may influence their own personal choices. Students were able to identify a large number of examples of choices, ranging from the choice of Peter's dad to "help Jews, despite danger" to himself and his family, to Peter's choice to stand up to the Nazis, to Thomas's choice at one point in the film to be drawn in by the power of the Nazis and choose them over his friends and family.

In this discussion, Mrs. Johnson attempted to get the students to recognize the perspectives in the film and use their conceptual understanding of group mentality and how totalitarians use groupthink to gain power through an examination of the decisions they made. This potentially helps students to both recognize the representative perspectives in the film and to better remember the critical attributes of the concept of group mentality and the consequences through applying it to *Swing Kids.* This case was powerful as it challenged students' common understandings by including the perspectives of non-Nazi German youth who resisted the temptations of power offered by the Nazis.

The essay exam occurred the following day, and students yet again applied their conceptual understandings of why and how totalitarians gained power and the perspectives on the Holocaust they had engaged throughout the unit. After completing the essay, and as a way to transition back to the U.S. perspective in World War II and further a discussion started earlier in the unit, Mrs. Johnson had students view *America and the Holocaust.* This documentary presents a particular view of the role of the United States in the Holocaust that is more critical than most contemporary or historical perspectives and was used to challenge the students' perceptions yet again.

America and the Holocaust: Deceit and Indifference

Mrs. Johnson wanted students to view *America and the Holocaust* to present a different and even competing perspective on U.S. policies and societal views related to the Holocaust and Jews in general before and during World War II. *America and the Holocaust* tells the history of the United States' role in the Holocaust that challenges common historical understandings of Americans as liberators of the concentration camps. The story is told from the perspective of a German Jewish man who lived in the United States and was attempting to help relatives in Germany emigrate to the United States in the 1930s during the rise of Nazi Germany. The film presents interviews and visual and historical evidence highlighting moments when the United States could have done more to help Jews escape Germany prior to the war or ways in which the U.S. could have done more to end, or at least limit the effects of, Hitler's "final solution." In particular, the film focuses on political and social conditions in the United States during the 1930s and 1940s and how these conditions influenced U.S. foreign policy and later military action regarding the persecution of the Jews. The film, which is actually an episode of the PBS series *American Experience*, included ample visual and historical evidence but was designed to present a perspective that Mrs. Johnson believed would challenge the students' beliefs and also help them have a better understanding of the complexity of the past. During the viewing students were asked to take notes in a T chart (see Table 4.4) according to what the United States did and did not do to help prevent the Holocaust.

As students watched, they dutifully wrote down evidence in both columns. Based on the evidence presented in the film, they were more likely to have a longer "did not do" list. The evidence they collected was then used in a post-viewing discussion during which Mrs. Johnson asked the students to identify what they had written in their columns and start to make some judgments on whether the United States did enough or if there was more it that could have done. Although some of the discussion was presentist in nature, as students judged decisions of the past from their contemporary understandings, many of the students were also able to put the historical decisions made by the United States into context of the times. One student explained that the United States had "more important things going on," including the economic depression, and therefore saw the persecution of Jews as "not their problem." Another brought up the nativistic tendencies in the United States at the time and the belief that "immigrants were to blame for unemployment." Other students brought up the fact that the U.S. immigration laws were not welcoming to non-Northern European Christian populations as they "didn't let in the Jewish [refugees], but let in British kids." Another student noted the feeling of U.S. anti-Semitism by quoting a statistic in the film that said an opinion poll reported that "53% of Americans . . . [believe] Jews are different." Similar to the uneven amounts of evidence in the film, the discussion also was more heavily weighted toward what the United States did not do, but many students did seem to be able to put the events into the context of the depression, isolationist and nativist policies, and to some extent anti-semitism or anti-immigrant sentiments.

Of course, the above information was also probably new or different and therefore more prominent to the students for discussion. Students were also able to compare

Table 4.4 America and the Holocaust

What the U.S. did . . .	What the U.S. did not do . . .

decisions made during the 1930s and at the beginning of the World War II with contemporary conflict in the Middle East. One student identified the similarities between current events in that region and the hesitation of the United States to back a plan to settle Jews in Palestine (later Israel) because of national security and the need to have access to oil, because of which it was afraid to "upset the Middle East." As with *In Memory of Millions*, students viewed and discussed this film with a more serious tone and purpose, most likely because of the challenging topic and the documentary nature of the evidence. This film provided yet another perspective on the Holocaust, even if a slightly controversial one.

Overall, Mrs. Johnson used film in this unit to help students to think differently about the often-simplistic explanation for why the Holocaust happened and was allowed to happen. She challenged them to look at the events from social, political, and psychological perspectives and to recognize the representative perspectives of those involved. She also attempted to force them to think about how anti-semitism was a problem not just then or just in Germany and how U.S. policies have ramifications across the globe.

REFLECTION ON THE CASE

Given the initial framework of using film to engage students in developing historical empathy as perspective recognition outlined at the beginning of Part II of this book, there are a number of key issues illustrated in the case of Mrs. Johnson and her class that are worth discussing. Mrs. Johnson appeared to effectively engage students in attempting to recognize the perspectives of a number of individuals and groups (or often individuals representing groups): Nazi and non-Nazi German youth; victims of the Holocaust such as the disabled, Communists, and Jews; various American perspectives; and perspectives of youth who are entrapped in group mentality that serve as an abstract case study. But how well did students appear to engage in empathizing with these groups, in terms of gaining an understanding of their thinking, decision making, and experiences? It appears that she was at least relatively successful in reaching her goals based on the discussions that were observed.

Several strengths in Mrs. Johnson's practice appear to be her ability to select films that students easily identify with, and whose youthful characters are relevant to the students' own understandings, albeit from the present context. It is also important to note that the films were not necessarily "blockbuster" films but were instead selected for the particular perspectives they represent and other engaging characteristics. As the Holocaust is an emotional and difficult topic, Mrs. Johnson chose to help students develop an understanding of the concept of group mentality using *The Wave* in order to emphasize that this phenomenon can occur in other contexts and to make the discussion a little safer and less emotional by focusing on a fictionalized case. Therefore, it is also important to examine Mrs. Johnson's practice with these films in addition to her selection criteria. Mrs. Johnson made it clear that *The Wave* was based on a true story but was altered for Hollywood and that *Swing Kids* was fictional, but that there were specific reasons why she was showing them.

Mrs. Johnson structured the viewing with a purpose in mind and focused students in ways to help them reach her goals through viewing tasks or data collection worksheets. These tasks did not distract the students from the viewing as some detailed worksheets can do, but focused the viewing instead on particular attributes. Mrs. Johnson further helped students through pausing the film for brief discussions, giving reminders during the viewing, and doing thorough debriefs after each day's viewing to make sure all students were keeping up. Finally, Mrs. Johnson asked students to apply the information they gleaned from the film, by way of discussions, through journaling, or as a result of a more thorough analysis—as in the essay comparing themes or the chart using the framework induced from *The Wave* to understand the tactics of other totalitarian regimes.

Although there were many strengths in this unit, there were also some areas of concern in Mrs. Johnson's practice. Mrs. Johnson failed to engage students in analyzing how the perspectives they were interacting with were affected by the context in which they were produced. For example, how were the perspectives of Thomas and Peter influenced by the fact that the film was made by an American production company during the 1990s? It is not necessary to dwell on the fact that the perspectives are created out of context, as most historical films are, but it is important to remind students of that limitation. One other issue that emerged was Mrs. Johnson's request of the students to think about how it might have felt to be a victim of the Holocaust. This example raises the question of the limits of empathy. Can a student really understand the experiences of a Holocaust victim? Although I think most teachers would concur that it would be impossible to fully understand those experiences, what elements of these perspectives can students understand through perspective recognition that would be helpful to them as citizens and human beings? Essentially, what are the limits to really developing historical empathy? There was a tension in Mrs. Johnson's practice in this area as she shifted from asking students to think about how it would feel to be working in a labor camp to taking a step back and examining the choices of the characters in the film.

This tension was amplified in her practice with the documentary films, *In Memory of Millions* and *America and the Holocaust*. Although she explicitly presented *The Wave* and *Swing Kids* as being to some degree altered for Hollywood or fictionalized, Mrs. Johnson treated them as representative case studies with specific goals for the students to understand. In comparison, the documentaries were used to bear witness to the atrocities and to challenge students' assumptions about the role of the United States in the Holocaust in a much more objective fashion, despite the quite controversial historical perspective in *America and the Holocaust*. The documentaries were instead used to examine (in *In Memory of Millions*) first-person perspectives from the experiences of real people and (in *America and the Holocaust*) the possible complicity of the United States and how it did not act to stop or even slow down the impact of the Holocaust based on policy decisions, albeit within a given social and political context. Although Mrs. Johnson used the provocative perspectives in *America and the Holocaust* to challenge her students to examine their own understandings of the role of the United States in the Holocaust, the film was not presented that way. Instead students took notes on what the United States did or did not do similarly to how they might take notes from a lecture. As an alternative, Mrs. Johnson might have considered presenting these two films in the same fashion as the fiction films by explicitly identifying the goals of viewing the films *and* by identifying the difficulty in attempting to understand the experiences of the victims of genocide and the controversial nature of the perspective in *America and the Holocaust*. When this is juxtaposed with the use of documentary film in Chapter 3, we can see that Mr. O'Brian does a much better job of asking students to examine how a documentary film reflects a group and the perspective of the filmmakers.

The issue of the extent to which empathy can and should be understood cannot easily be answered as the result of this case. However, this case reveals how the powerfully affective medium of film can lead teachers and students to believe that they can actually understand the experiences of those in the past. Despite these limitations, this case presents an excellent model for identifying and gaining a sense of abstract concepts such as group recognition and in identifying multiple perspectives on a historical event and the impact of decision making.

Strategies for Using Film for Perspective Recognition

Using film to engage students in examining and evaluating decision making and the experiences of those is the past can make for a powerful lesson. There are a few key aspects of creating a lesson toward these goals. The first is selecting films that naturally draw students into the perspectives being portrayed (more on this below). The second key is structuring the viewing so that students pay particular attention to the decision-making process or thinking of the characters during the event or period. It is also important to put this data into context, through either learning about the background of the event, group, or time period, or also looking into the background of the film, what the director/producer was trying to do with the film, and how it reflects the views of the time when it was made.

Preparing students for the viewing, giving them a job and a structured way to collect information from the different perspectives, and then debriefing students' perceptions are all key. The step that seems to be vital, however, is asking students to then apply what they learned from the perspectives in some form conceptually. In this case, the students identified the psychological and social dimensions of what the Hitler Youth did to inculcate German youth and then applied these ideas to other totalitarian states and the impact of this mentality through the perspectives of the Holocaust. This exercise helped students to both better recognize the perspectives of victims, bystanders, and perpetrators, but also develop an understanding of the larger concepts that could be applied in the study of group mentality in the present.

Selecting Films to Teach Perspective Recognition

Films that seem to work best provide first-person accounts from a compelling and, if possible, youth character. In several of the films above, a key to success was the fact that the perspective was easily related to by students because the characters either were teens or had been teens when the events occurred (e.g., *In Memory of Millions*). In addition, the film needs to provide enough insights into the decision making or thinking of the group or individuals whose perspective students are to recognize. If the character you want them to empathize with is not fully included in the film or is viewed only through the eyes of another character, it may be difficult for students to fully identify the desired perspective. At least in the case presented here, students were not picky about having a blockbuster film or even a film at all, as *The Wave* is a made-for-television movie. The key instead is selecting films with the desired perspective presented in a way that matches the teacher's goals and that students can easily recognize given some preparation on the part of the teacher and a job to do during the viewing that focuses them on their task.

The lessons on group mentality and multiple perspectives on atrocity could also easily be applied to other instances of genocide or crimes against humanity in history. For example, a teacher could have her students explore the Rwandan genocide through *Hotel Rwanda* (2004), *Sometimes in April* (2005), and *Shake Hands with the Devil: The Journey of Roméo Dallaire* (2004). These types of lessons could also easily work with films from a variety of other topics, such as understanding the life of a "mountain man" through *Jeremiah Johnson* (1972), a perspective of what it would be like to try to live like a frontier family from the context of the present through an episode of *Frontier House* (2002), or the horrifying experiences of being sold into captivity as a slave through *Roots* (1977) or *Amistad* (1997). The wealth of films that are available today provide a wide variety of perspectives that can match a teacher's goals for his or her class, with more perspectives becoming available every year from individuals and groups that have been rarely represented in film (or textbook and other classroom resources) in the past.

PART III

Using Film to Develop Analytical or Interpretive Skills

Employing primary and secondary sources in the history classroom, as an alternative to the archetypal textbook/lecture/test cycle, has been a rallying cry among historians and history educators alike for many a decade (e.g. Barton, 2005; Dickinson, Gard, & Lee, 1978; Rouet, Mason, Perfetti, & Britt, 1996). The chapters in this section illustrate two teachers adept at juxtaposing movies, documentary films, and more conventional primary and secondary historical documents in order to teach historical content and develop the complex analytical and interpretive skills that lie at the heart of "doing" history.

Using motion pictures in the history classroom is not always an easy decision. Skeptics may argue that the use of movies in the classroom is a waste of time, or not aligned with learning "real history." However, although movies can certainly be utilized poorly in the classroom, just like textbooks and worksheets, they can also be employed powerfully and to great educative effect. Furthermore, many state and national history tests call on students to possess these intricate skills of analysis and interpretation when answering "Document-Based Questions," a key assessment of many advanced courses.

Most children grow up in a video-rich environment these days. In their own ways, and without any instruction, students are used to treating Hollywood movies as texts—viewing, reviewing, reflecting, discussing, critiquing, "dissing," "giving props," "twittering," and so on. That said, most young people do not make use of movies in the sophisticated ways that adult historians approach a wide variety of historical documents, and unfortunately traditional film use in history classrooms has not always helped in this regard. Simply watching a movie and filling out a worksheet does little to teach key investigative and discursive historical skills.

When seeking models for how to use history movies in the classroom, teachers need look no farther than another, highly analogous form of historical document: the novel. Among historians, the use of "classic" or "popular" novels as primary and secondary historical documents was once controversial, but is now common. As the intellectual historian Dominick LaCapra concludes:

In a word, the novel is pertinent to historical research to the extent that it may be converted into useful knowledge or information. For example, *The Red and the Black* informs us about social and political tensions in early nineteenth-century France as well as about the problems of an upwardly mobile young man from the provinces. *Madame Bovary* tells us about longer-term trends in provincial society and the frustrations of a woman who is not adapted to its demands. Balzac is of course a favorite novelist from a documentary perspective because he manifestly tried to provide a panoramic view of contemporary life and explicitly compared the novel to social science. (LaCapra, 1985, p. 125)

Such themes may likewise be explored through the use of movies. Further, if the novel was the dominant form of artistic communication during the 19th century, surely movies more or less occupy that role today. Young people grow up collecting a considerable mental library of movie images about their world and its past (Wineburg, 2000). The main question for practicing social studies teachers, then, is not so much whether to make use of film, but how.

There is no instruction manual for using movies as historical documents. However, history teachers seeking to treat motion pictures much like other historical text might ask their students to consider some of the following questions:

- How factually accurate is the movie? How do you know whether it is or isn't?
- Whom does the movie get you to root for, and how is this accomplished?
- What motives does the movie give to the historical characters on screen? How do these compare to the motives that in your judgment these characters actually had, based on your reading of other historical sources?
- In your opinion, why does the movie portray the historical characters the way it does?
- What is omitted—left out—that would be important for a full understanding of the historical subject matter?
- What is the role of cinematography in the depiction of historical events? Does the art of film making impact your understanding of the history portrayed?
- Who are the filmmakers, and can research point you to their motivations and goals in telling the "story" they tell?
- Can you think of individuals or groups in our society who might have an interest in people having a less than accurate view of the history under discussion? In other words, what might be the politics behind the history portrayed in the movie?

The following chapters provide two examples of teachers attempting to use movies to teach some of the analytical and interpretive skills of the historian. Specifically, they explore two important aspects of these complex ideas: (1) using Hollywood *movies as primary sources*; (2) using *movies as secondary sources*.

MOVIES AS PRIMARY SOURCES

On the surface, movies appear to be very different from written texts when it comes to the study of history. However, like other historical documents, movies are created by individuals at a certain time and place and for particular (and often compound) purposes, providing ample fodder for discussion and analysis. And, unlike many historical sources, movies hold a singular relevance in the lives of today's students. As a consequence, movies are often the most influential social and cultural documents that young people encounter. In short, movies can and *should* be "read," analyzed and interpreted much like pieces of period literature; the only question is how?

Take, for example, the movie *Forrest Gump* (1994). This movie ostensibly tells the story of a man's incredible journey through the mid- to late 20th century encountering famous historical figures, influencing popular culture, and experiencing historic events first-hand, all the while being largely unaware of their significance because of his borderline intellectual disability. *Forrest Gump* presents a fictional narrative that is both humorous and poignant. Winner of the Oscar for Best Motion Picture, the film probably says just as much about the time of its making as it does the 1950s, 1960s, or 1970s. From its release, social conservatives read *Forrest Gump* as a parable of the dangers of the liberal lifestyle. In 2009, *National Review* magazine ranked *Forrest Gump* number 4 on its list of 25 Best Conservative Movies of the Last 25 Years.

> Tom Hanks plays the title character, an amiable dunce who is far too smart to embrace the lethal values of the 1960s. The love of his life, wonderfully played by Robin Wright Penn, chooses a different path; she becomes a drug-addled hippie, with disastrous results.

Liberals have a very different interpretation of *Forrest Gump*, to say the least. The point here is not to take sides, but to note that *Forrest Gump* (like any other movie portraying the past) rewrites history, and it does so using the same historical and narrative devices as any other historical text. In the case offered in Chapter 5, a teacher uses the epic movie *Bonnie and Clyde* (1967), a movie set in the 1930s, to analyze the decade of its creation, the 1960s.

MOVIES AS SECONDARY SOURCES

Hollywood films are unique secondary sources that act as "texts" to be analyzed and evaluated much like textbooks and other secondary sources and historical documents. Films are documents created with specific purposes by directors, producers, and writers that should be subject to interpretation. Movies are viewed by millions of people and may "teach" the audience about the past through a narrative, but one without the accountability of footnotes or other scholarly mechanisms. Thus, teachers are burdened with helping students make meaning of the past presented in film through developing historical film literacy skills such as considering how a film's narrative is supported (or not) by the historical record, particularly since a film's purpose is not to teach in the way a textbook or carefully planned lesson might.

There are numerous issues regarding how films are created that generate challenges in using them as secondary sources. For example, feature films often distort time, include both recreated and real footage in the film, condense many different possible narratives into a handful of stories, provide composite characters, and add fictional love stories into an account of past events. These issues will be discussed in Chapter 6, which examines how one teacher uses *The Alamo* (2004) as a secondary source within a larger unit on Westward Expansion.

CHAPTER 5
Movies as Primary Documents

Figure 5.1 Bonnie and Clyde (1967) Bonnie Parker (Faye Dunaway) and Clyde Barrow (Warren Beatty) rob banks in Depression-era America.

In the hands of accomplished history teachers, Hollywood movies can serve as rich historical sources. It may come as a surprise to some that movies can be used as either primary or secondary historical documents. After all, "history movies" are generally thought of not as the actual "stuff" of history but rather as commercial entertainment products whose creators retain a generous entitlement to artistic license (even when this interferes with historical accuracy). Yet resourceful history teachers have come to realize that movies, like written fiction, are modern-day cultural artifacts with real educative potential in the classroom.

Ortega y Gassett maintained that every age rewrites history to suit its own purposes. So it is with historically themed movies, which often have as much or more to say about the times in which they were filmed as the periods they purport to document. For example, the classic western *High Noon* (1952) is seen by many as an allegory of Cold War tensions and anxieties of the 1950s (an analysis that lead John Wayne to call it "the most un-American thing I've ever seen in my whole life": Weidhorn, 2005). The action blockbuster *300* (2007) tells the story of the ancient battle of Thermopylae, presenting the Spartans as heroic defenders of embryonic Western liberty and rationality against the tyranny, violence, and mysticism of the Middle-Eastern Persians. Made at the height of the "War on Terror," the film seemed to be a comment on conflict between the Western world and the Middle East as much as it was about the Persian Wars of antiquity.

Additionally, some movies are primary historical documents in their own right. Consider the film adaptation of Woodward and Bernstein's Watergate investigation, *All the President's Men* (1976). It was not made as a "history" movie—Watergate was a recent current event that Americans were still trying to make sense of at the time. However, as the years passed the movie ceased to be contemporary and became historical. Today, *All the President's Men* is a primary source from and about the 1970s, depicting a particular perspective from that time on Watergate and the role journalism played in exposing criminal activities in the Nixon administration. Similarly, the John Wayne movie *The Green Berets* (1968) was made at the height of the Vietnam War. Viewed today, the movie is a period document from and about the late 1960s, depicting one perspective strongly supporting U.S. involvement in Vietnam. Neither film is a dispassionate, after-the-fact documentary about a historical past. Both are commentaries about events that were current at the time they were made and have since become historical—much in the same way a diary, journal, or blog is current when written or a television newscast is current when broadcast but becomes a historical document to later generations.

Hollywood movies in the classroom can't really stand alone. That is, they are best used in conjunction with other kinds of historical documents, such as textbooks, trade books by historians, or period accounts from newspapers, magazines, letters, diaries, or other kinds of records. In comparing film representations of the past with other varieties of historical documents, teachers are able to emphasize important themes such as the constructed nature of history, corroboration between historical sources, and modes of interpretation and contextualization of historical documents. Powerful history teaching with film helps students realize the ways in which movies function as primary sources about the past. In the case presented in this chapter, a veteran educator guides his students in examining *Bonnie and Clyde* (1968) for how it uses people and events from the 1930s to comment on U.S. society in the 1960s (see Table 5.2 for a description of the movie). Whereas *Bonnie and Clyde* could be considered a secondary source for the Depression era (though a problematic one, given its selective and less than critical treatment of its protagonists), it is foremost a primary source that reflects particular attitudes and perspectives from the 1960s.

MR. BRILEY'S CLASS: TEACHING THE 1960S WITH *BONNIE AND CLYDE*

Case Description

Ron Briley's elective course, "U.S. History through Film, 1945–Present," is offered to high school seniors who have previously completed a general survey course in U.S. history. A long-time educator who has written extensively on the teaching of history (e.g. Briley, 1990, 2007), Briley instructs a number of different "history through film" courses at a high-quality private school in Albuquerque, New Mexico. An admitted film buff, Briley uses the term "movie texts" when he discusses motion pictures because, like written texts, movies are legitimate historical documents that reflect the times and contexts in which they are made. Further, experience shows him movies are a kind of historical document that adolescents are actually excited to scrutinize, critique, analyze, and discuss.

"I'm thinking of the films to be somewhat of a primary source to try to get at what people were feeling—trying to get at the values, the ideology of the time period," Briley says. "How does the film reflect the time period? Not so much in terms of the details of the film, but the milieu, the ideology, the values, the worldview." Briley utilizes films as both primary and secondary documents, often juxtaposing these with more traditional written historical texts and other types of documents. Attending a private preparatory school, his students are almost all college-bound. With a reputation for rigor, Briley's courses tend to attract students with strong academic backgrounds and ambitions. Many are concurrently taking advanced courses in mathematics and science. Briley believes it is important for all history classes to have high standards but that this is particularly the case for film-based courses, which are often (unfairly) suspected of lacking academic rigor.

In teaching about the 1960s to students who have already attended a general survey course, Briley is less interested in "covering" history and more concerned with training his students to think and act like historians, digging deep into the important issues and trends for which that decade is known. In particular, this unit focuses on the Vietnam War, youth culture, the creation of the counterculture, and conflict between "establishment" and "anti-establishment" thought. "The idea is to really dig into the grammar and literacy of film. Then students will screen a film, and what I want to see is if they can build a bridge essentially from the history of the period to this film that reflects the period," says Briley. He notes that the connections are not always obvious to students. "Many of the films we see are not directly historical films, and I want to see if they can build that bridge, making those links."

At the beginning of the school year, Briley spends weeks of class time helping students discover how to "read" film. This involves an exploration of the technical aspects of making movies as well as how to investigate the historical context of films as texts. The class focuses on analyzing movies for how they portray consensus and conflict in American history as well as what groups have been clumsily stereotyped or simply left out of Hollywood's representation of the past. Prior to the unit described below, the class had already spent a few weeks studying the 1960s. The class examined historical issues or events such as the Cold War, the Arms Race, McCarthyism, the Civil Rights Movement, and Black Power through such movies as *Dr. Strangelove* (1964), *JFK* (1991),

Mississippi Burning (1988), *Malcolm X* (1992), and *Do the Right Thing* (1989), along with supporting textbook passages and other readings.

Unit Overview

This unit began with two fundamentally different takes on the Vietnam War: *The Green Berets* (1968) and *Platoon* (1986), along with a textbook chapter that focuses on the presidency of Lyndon Johnson. For each assigned textbook chapter, students turned in a three-page summary/reaction paper. After discussing these "texts," a take-home essay was assigned.

Next students viewed *Bonnie and Clyde* (1968)—ostensibly a movie about the Depression-era bank robbers, used here as a primary historical document illuminating one take on the spirit of the 1960s. A textbook chapter that highlighted the early years of the Vietnam War was also assigned. After a full class day of discussion, students began viewing *The Graduate* (1967), a movie that follows a young man estranged from the 1960s society in which he is coming of age.

Throughout the year students intermittently read chapters from *Film Arts: An Introduction*. During this unit, chapters on aspects of cinematography and sound in the cinema were used. After viewing and discussing *The Graduate*, students read a textbook chapter on the impact of the Vietnam War in the United States and began watching *Easy Rider* (1969), the iconic cross-country motorcycle road trip of hippie soul-searching. At the conclusion of this movie, the unit ended with a synthesis essay that asked students to reflect on the counterculture movement and assess its strengths and weaknesses. Additional movies that Briley sometimes uses to buttress this unit (depending on the time available) include *The Killing Fields* (1984) about the Khmer Rouge massacres in Cambodia and the chain-gang convict movie *Cool Hand Luke* (1967).

FILM ACTIVITIES

On a sunny day in Albuquerque, New Mexico, during the winter of 2009, Ron Briley stood in front of his U.S. history class and introduced the 1960s hit film *Bonnie and Clyde*. The film portrays the infamous Depression-era gang of bank robbers, featuring the young Hollywood stars Faye Dunaway and Warren Beatty in the title roles. "This is not meant to be a historical film about the 1930s," explained Briley, a point he returned to numerous times over the next few days. In this case, the objective of showing *Bonnie and Clyde* was not to teach students about the 1930s. Instead the notoriously violent tale of love-struck criminals was shown in the middle of an extended examination of the 1960s, the decade of the film's production, and the goal was to study that time period. The unit, centered on the Vietnam War, the rise of the counterculture and the disaffected youth who coined the term "the generation gap," had begun about two weeks earlier with the John Wayne Vietnam saga, *The Green Berets*.

In a year-long course devoted to a 65-year span of American history, the decade of the 1960s looms large. Briley's course examines many aspects of this time period, and the unit chronologically follows discussion of the 1950s and precedes coverage of the 1970s and beyond. Although the study of "movie texts" lies at the heart of the course, they are

Table 5.1 Unit Outline

Days	Activities	Goal
1	Begin watching *Green Berets*	
2–3	Continue *Green Berets*; Chapter 8, *Unfinished Journey*	
4	Discuss *Green Berets*	General discussion of Vietnam; provide dominant U.S. cultural perspective on that war. Challenge student preconceptions of a monolithic war narrative
5–6	Watch *Platoon*; Chapter 7, *Film Art* (Sound)	
7	Discuss *Platoon*; assign Vietnam essay	Provide counterculture perspective on the Vietnam War; discuss Hollywood views on Vietnam War
8–9	Begin *Bonnie and Clyde*; Chapter 9, *Unfinished Journey*	
10	Finish *Bonnie and Clyde*, discussion	
11	Discuss *Bonnie and Clyde*	Discuss the rise of the counterculture and the impact of youth culture on Hollywood cinema of the 1960s
12–13	Begin *The Graduate*, Vietnam essays due	
14	Finish *The Graduate*	
15	Discuss *The Graduate*; Chapter 9, *Film Art*	Discuss alienation of youth during the 1960s and its impact on society
16–17	Begin *Easy Rider*; Chapter 11, *Unfinished Journey*	
18	Finish *Easy Rider*	
19	Discuss *Easy Rider*, counterculture essay assigned	Discuss counterculture and its Hollywood depiction. Focus on impact on society, and successes and failings of the movement, as depicted in the movie

not the only documents students read and analyze. Two different textbooks balance out course readings, and students must write many of their own manuscripts, both short and long.

The Green Berets kicks off the part of the unit addressing the Vietnam War. It is followed by the contrasting movie *Platoon*. In this curricular sequence, Briley seeks to provide students with "Hollywood's version of the Vietnam War," and two more diverging perspectives could hardly be imagined. *The Green Berets*, a pet project of the leading actor and co-director, John Wayne, presents a traditional, cheerleading U.S. war-

Table 5.2 Description of Films

The Green Berets (1968) John Wayne, Ray Kellogg (Directors) Michael Wayne (Producer) Warner Bros.–Seven Arts	*The Green Berets* is strongly anti-communist and pro-Saigon. It was released in 1968, at the height of American involvement in the Vietnam War, the same year as the Tet offensive against the largest cities in southern Vietnam. Co-director and star John Wayne made this film to counter the anti-war atmosphere and social discontent in the United States. The film has been criticized for glorifying the Vietnam War
Platoon (1986) Oliver Stone (Director) Arnold Kopelson (Producer) Orion Pictures	Chris Taylor is a young white American who has abandoned college for combat duty in Vietnam. The year is 1967. Worn down by the exhausting work and poor living conditions, his enthusiasm for the war wanes and he develops an admiration for the more experienced soldiers, despite their reluctance to extend their friendship. The story is drawn from director Stone's experiences as a U.S. Infantryman in Vietnam and was written by him as a counter to the vision of the war portrayed in *The Green Berets*
Bonnie and Clyde (1967) Arthur Penn (Director) Warren Beatty (Producer) Warner Bros.–Seven Arts	American crime film about Bonnie Parker and Clyde Barrow, bank robbers who operated in the central United States during the Great Depression. The film was intended as a romantic and comic version of the violent gangster films of the 1930s. Considered a landmark film for its graphic violence and references to sexuality, it is regarded as one of the first movies of the New Hollywood era, breaking many taboos and popular with the youth generation. Its success motivated other filmmakers to be more forward about presenting sex and violence in their films
The Graduate (1967) Mike Nichols (Director) Joseph E. Levine and Lawrence Turman (Producers) Embassy Pictures	The film tells the story of Benjamin Braddock, a recent university graduate with no well-defined aim in life. Ben is seduced by an older woman, Mrs. Robinson, and then falls in love with her daughter Elaine. In the famous conclusion, Benjamin undertakes a desperate long-distance drive to somehow head off Elaine's wedding in Santa Barbara. After a violent struggle with Elaine's parents and wedding guests, Ben and Elaine escape on a public bus
Easy Rider (1969) Dennis Hopper (Director) Peter Fonda, William Leland, and Hayward Bert Schneider (Producers) Columbia Pictures	A road movie about two bikers, Wyatt (nicknamed Captain America) and Billy, who smuggle drugs from Mexico to Los Angeles and sell them for cash. With this money stuffed into the Stars & Stripes-adorned fuel tank of Wyatt's California-style chopper, the two hippies ride eastward in an attempt to reach New Orleans, Louisiana, in time for Mardi Gras, all the while "searching for America"

Table 5.3 Class Textbooks

The Unfinished Journey: America Since World War II William H. Chafe (Author) New York: Oxford University Press	General history of the United States since WWII. Considered a college-level textbook, Briley notes it could easily be replaced with alternative books such as Howard Zinn's *People's History of the United States*, or Houghton Mifflin's *The American Pageant*
Film Art: An Introduction David Bordwell and Kristin Thompson (Authors) New York: McGraw Hill	Film Studies textbook with chapters covering a broad spectrum of topics, including movie genres, film production, cinematography, style and critical analysis

story narrative—an anti-Communist parable that could have been set in practically any U.S. war of the 20th century. In 1968 the Chicago film critic Roger Ebert called the movie, controversial from its release, hopelessly old-fashioned, representing

> the way Hollywood always fights wars: with clichés and stock characters. There is an Irishman named Muldoon, a doubting journalist, a Negro, a little refugee kid with a pet dog, a hard-bitten veteran and the rest of the stock characters who fight every war for us. Everybody is there except the Jewish kid from the Bronx and the guy named Ole with a Swedish accent. (Ebert, 1968)

Students in the class too tend to view *The Green Berets* as stereotypical and out-of-date. "Sometimes they howl at it," said Briley. "To them it's so bad it's almost funny."

This presents a dilemma for the teacher not uncommon when films are perceived as dated or lacking in production values. Adolescent students tend to view modern films, or movies with more lavish production budgets, as being more "realistic." Further, the presentisms that inevitably appear in historical movies are more easily overlooked in these productions. Briley tries to guide students toward a more nuanced understanding of *The Green Berets*. He reminds students that the movie was a box-office hit and that it resonated with a significant percentage of the country, notably "the older generation" who remembered World War II. Even today the movie has its defenders and argument rages on websites such as the Internet Movie Database (IMDb) over its historical and artistic merits. "Sometimes you have to remind the students that people took it very seriously," said Briley, who accomplishes this task both verbally and also through class assignments. In conjunction with the viewing of *The Green Berets*, students read Chapter 8 of *The Unfinished Journey* and write a three-page reader response on the chapter. They are also aware they will soon be writing a four- to five-page "Vietnam Essay" that will call for analysis and synthesis of the film.

Platoon offers a sharply divergent view of the Vietnam War. The story of *Platoon* follows the gritty actions of Bravo Company near the Cambodian border during 1967. The film's greatest strength is its effort to present the day-to-day happenings of American infantry during the Vietnam War—a grunt's-eye view (Auster & Quart, 1988). "The kids like it because it's more modern," said Briley, and, although he agrees *Platoon* is technically superior to *The Green Berets*, he is also aware that fondness can lead to lazy historical thought. "We need to interrogate it a bit more, because its production values are so good. I really try to ask some tough questions of this movie. We look at John Wayne's case for the war. Then we look at Oliver Stone's film on the war made not during the war, but a decade after the war. We talk about things such as why Hollywood didn't deal much with the war during the time period. Then we talk about some of Oliver Stone's experience he brings to the war—his perspective. Then we talk about whether with either of these films Hollywood can really deal adequately with a topic as controversial as Vietnam. It's not so much that one film is good and one film is bad, but what's missing from both?"

After viewing the two Vietnam War movies, along with a textbook reading on the time period, students turned to the Vietnam Essay. The take-home assignment gives students a chance to synthesize the written texts, film texts, classroom discussion, as well as prior knowledge. Students can choose between two different essays, each of which requires them to "pay careful attention to how these films reflect the time periods in which they were released." In short, they are asked not only to reflect upon what they have learned about the Vietnam War but also to analyze the movies as historical documents.

As students mulled over this assignment as homework, the class pivoted from Vietnam to the rise of the counterculture in 1960s America. Briley introduced *Bonnie and Clyde* as students filed into class: "We are looking at a series of films that focus on the anti-establishment." He quickly explained that Bonnie Parker and Clyde Barrow were indeed real bank robbers of the Depression era, but that the movie was never intended as a historical film about the 1930s. Briley further noted that the older movie-going audience that made *The Green Berets* a box office hit "didn't know what to make of *Bonnie and Clyde*," a movie better received by the youth audience of the time. Whereas Briley

Table 5.4 Vietnam War Essay

Vietnam War Essays

Select one of the following questions and develop your response in a well-organized essay of approximately 4 to 5 pages, using textual evidence from the films and readings from *The Unfinished Journey*. In answering the questions pay careful attention to how these films reflect the time periods in which they were released.

1 Many historians believe that the Vietnam War was much too complex of a historical conflict to be accurately explained by the Hollywood film. Based upon your screening of *The Green Berets* (1968) and *Platoon* (1986), do you agree with this assessment?

2 Film critic Steven Scheuer described John Wayne's *The Green Berets* as "more than two hours of relentlessly simple-minded, chauvinistic claptrap about a complex and profoundly important question—the American role and presence in the Vietnam War." On the other hand, Oliver Stone's *Platoon* is often praised by critics as a realistic portrayal of the American experience in Indochina. Based upon your screening of the films and readings on American involvement in Vietnam, do you agree with these critical assessments or find them to be simplistic?

introduced the movie on this particular day, on other occasions when time permits he assigns students this task after doing research on the movie at home on internet sites such as the Internet Movie Database or Wikipedia.

"This movie had a tremendous influence on how sexuality and violence will be used in films," Briley said as the opening credits rolled over a backdrop of old-fashioned black-and-white pictures. For their part, the students seemed to have little knowledge of the movie. If not for this class, they may never have seen *Bonnie and Clyde*. Students giggled as the opening scene reveals a young, beautiful Bonnie pacing naked in her bedroom, a mild semi-nude scene by today's standards, but far more risqué and innovative in 1968, Briley explained. As the movie progressed over the next two days of class time, students sat quietly and paid close attention. Briley often chimed in with comments and questions—foreshadowing themes the class would explore in future discussion (such as violence, sexuality, the role of women, youth culture, counterculture) and interjecting information about the movie (its actors, director, Oscar nominations, cinematography) as well as issues of historical film literacy (historical accuracies and inaccuracies, composite characters, scenes and images that appear to hold metaphorical references). Briley rarely sat during the viewing, either standing to the side of the classroom or pacing around the back of the room. In total, viewing *Bonnie and Clyde* took just over two class periods. About 50 minutes of class time was then devoted to discussion, with students' own ideas serving as a starting point.

"What did you think of the film," Briley asked broadly as he passed out a fact sheet (Table 5.5).

Students, in general, seemed to enjoy the film. "It's pretty action packed," said one young man, who noted the physical appeal of Faye Dunaway. "I think there was a lot of action but also good dialogue," noted a young woman. "I thought it was cool the way they developed their relationship. I mean, it seemed far-fetched at first, but they made it work."

Table 5.5 Example Film Credit Handout

Bonnie and Clyde credits

Date of Release—1967

Studio: Warner Brothers

Director: Arthur Penn

Screenplay: David Newman and Robert Benton

Producer: Warren Beatty

Cast:
> Bonnie Parker (Faye Dunaway)
> Clyde Barrow (Warren Beatty)
> Buck Barrow (Gene Hackman)
> Blanche Barrow (Estelle Parsons)
> C. W. Moss (Michael J. Pollard)
> Ranger Frank Hammer (Denver Pyle)

Cinematographer: Burnett Guffey

After an overview of students' general reactions, Briley bored in on a series of questions relating to some of the overarching themes introduced during viewing. In particular, the class explored parallels between the 1930s and 1960s, and the relationship of violence and sex as presented in the movie. "They both were not periods of consensus," said one student. "I mean, people thought the system wasn't working." As Briley invited the student to give a more specific explanation, several others responded with the idea that the country was divided over the Vietnam War, Civil Rights, and woman's rights during the 1960s, and that social consensus was likewise blown apart in the 1930s by the Great Depression. In both decades, respect for the government was challenged by segments of the population and, in particular, youth were fearful about their future prospects.

Briley asked the class to reflect on why many reviewers see *Bonnie and Clyde* as an anti-establishment film. He observed the impetus for violence in the movie for the most part comes not from the young bank robbers but from older establishment figures (police, sheriffs, a store owner, a double-crossing father, etc.). Indeed, the film renders a Robin Hood mythology, a popular legend that Briley maintained has little historical warrant. "I think at the time, a lot of them were in to rebelling against the system, and that's really what the movie is all about," said one girl. "These rebellious kids see themselves as adventurous rebels," noted a boy. "Yes, but the main point that they make is that we're folks just like you," responded the girl. A classmate added, "They're only rebelling against like the sheriffs and police and the powerful people."

At this point the discussion began to roll, with Briley stepping into the background but still sporadically cutting in to amplify student ideas, clear up questions of fact vs. fiction, or to provide terminology or cultural definitions ("the establishment," "the generation gap," "anti-establishment," "youth culture"). Students, for their part, seemed to know the routine. This unit took place about half way through the school year, and most students appeared willing to express their thoughts and opinions.

As this discussion wound down, silence eventually came over the class. It served as a handy dramatic pause for Briley's next question: "What do you think the film is saying about sex and violence?" *Bonnie and Clyde* managed what has become today's typical Hollywood screenwriting double play: injecting sex and violence within the first few scenes. Throughout the movie, sex and violence are placed side by side in a manner that could hardly elude any viewer, least of all high school seniors. The question met with a few giggles, but only a very few. The students knew from discussion of previous movies that this was a question to be taken seriously. Again the conversation began at a fairly superficial level, but additional prompts and moments of uncomfortable silence pushed the dialogue deeper. "It was like the violence was good and the sex not so much," said one girl. "I kind of just thought they were juxtaposed," said another.

Briley mentions *Bonnie and Clyde* was groundbreaking for its use of violence in a film intended for a broad commercial audience (indeed many thought this "gangster movie" would prove too violent for mass appeal). He also raised questions about the general acceptance of violence in 1960s America, as the nightly news brought viewers frontline images of the Tet Offensive in Vietnam and other Cold War proxy battles in places such as Czechoslovakia, college campus riots, the assassination of political and social leaders, and the increasingly radicalized Black Power movement. This lay in stark contrast to the emerging youth culture: 1967 was the "Summer of Love." "Some of the older generation feels threatened by the sexual revolution," said one boy. "Maybe like the sheriff sort of represents that." "Because Clyde doesn't want anything to do with sex," a girl pointed out. "Because violence has made him impotent," the boy shot back. An interesting Freudian analysis of the film followed. Individual scenes were analyzed for their sexual implication, including an early incident when Bonnie suggestively fingers the barrel of Clyde's pistol, another in which Bonnie unsuccessfully attempts to seduce the frigid Clyde on a bed that is partially covered with the gang's weapons, and a third in which Bonnie forcefully kisses a Texas Ranger caught trying to ambush the gang. The Ranger responds by spitting in her face.

In its midst of these potent images, Briley injected a number of probing questions: Does *Bonnie and Clyde* suggest that the violent culture of the United States makes us incapable of love? Or that suppression of sexuality leads to violence? Are authority figures in the film afraid of the sexual revolution? Is the film ultimately a challenge to puritanical America? Why are Bonnie and Clyde murdered soon after they make love for the first time? A number of times during the discussion, Briley implored students not to take the movie literally as history but rather to focus on what *Bonnie and Clyde* implies about 1960s America. In this role as a primary historical document—an artistic product of its time and place—the movie provides fertile terrain for the history teacher.

As the class bell approached, Briley steered the discussion to its conclusion. He asked students what the movie *Bonnie and Clyde* is actually about. Students, sensing the end of another school day, shifted in their seats and became more jocular in their responses. "Make love not war," one blurted out to general snickers. "You get persecuted for making love," spouted another. Briley smilingly accepted these interpretations and then emphasized once again the concurrent themes of youth alienation and generation gap—ideas that would be central in upcoming classes. On Monday the class would begin viewing *The Graduate*, and as students filed out on this Friday afternoon, a few were asked to do some internet surfing over the weekend to be prepared to give a brief introduction to that film.

Briley's unit finished with *The Graduate* and *Easy Rider*, both movies that present iconic images of the 1960s. *The Graduate* is a comedy/drama that explores the life of 21-year-old Benjamin Braddock shortly after earning his degree from an unnamed college in the Northeast United States. Braddock is lured into an affair with an older family friend, Mrs. Robinson, but later becomes infatuated with her daughter Elaine. Meanwhile, Benjamin is hounded by his father to select a graduate school, a suggestion he deliberately resists by spending his days sleeping in late and lounging around the family pool. "With *The Graduate*, we try to get at this idea of alienation, how many youths in the 60s were alienated," said Briley. "But these youths weren't going to be out becoming hippies, throwing bombs, joining the Weather Underground. I try to use *The Graduate* to look at this broader theme of why so many young people were alienated."

The Graduate introduces the idea of innocent youth seduced and exploited by a corrupt and decadent older generation and mirrors what some consider the anarchic mood of American youth of the 1960s (or at least a particular subculture of American youth). It also ultimately suggests the aimlessness and naïveté of the younger generation, as they move toward lives of sterile corporate work. Briley feels that the students in his class easily pick up on the themes of generation gap and alienation of youth (even upper-class youth), but student reaction to the movie is far from monolithic. "Most tend to like it," Briley said. "Sometimes students will connect it to their own lives, and sometimes students will look at it as if Benjamin Braddock needs to grow up; he's a whiner. Certainly, we try to look at the generation gap, and then also look at what happened to the affluent society of the 1960s. And one of the fun things to talk about is the conclusion. Is it optimistic or not?"

In the film's closing scene, a fantastic chain of events ends with Benjamin disrupting Elaine's California wedding to a blond fraternity boy, jamming a cross into the church door to prevent pursuit as he and Elaine escape on a city bus. As the camera pans away, Benjamin and Elaine do not stare passionately into each other's eyes but instead gaze blankly out the bus windows. "The director, Mike Nichols, said this was to show that their lives would be much like their parents. They really don't know each other very well, and off they go into the future," said Briley.

Gaining insight into the complexity of historical times is an important goal in Briley's class. The 1960s, like any era, has been hashed and rehashed in the media. The images that reside in the popular consciousness of many of today's students is more caricature than reality. "Rather than thinking of the 60s as just being *Easy Rider*, there's also *The Green Berets*," he said. "That film, which they really don't like, *was* popular. There was a generational conflict there. This idea that everyone was a hippie is simplistic. I want them to see that there was not a monolithic 1960s. And so I hope the films break some of the stereotypes as well. I hope that through reading, screening, discussing that we are able to do justice to the complexity of the 1960s."

Easy Rider, a drug-addled hippie road trip complete with a stopover at a free-living commune and a wild spree at Mardi Gras in New Orleans, may be stereotyped by some as a low-budget celebration of the counterculture, but not by Briley. "The film to me is a very complex film that seems to suggest the failures of the counterculture. To me it's a rich text that talks about a lot of things."

When viewing *Easy Rider* in class, students are initially drawn in by the two protagonists: Wyatt dressed in Stars and Stripes motorcycle leathers and helmet, Billy with his handle-bar moustache and Australian bush hat. However, as the movie progresses, it becomes clear that peace and love are hardly the only motivations of these 1960s vagabonds. In a pinnacle scene of the film, before Wyatt and Billy are gunned down by a pair of gun-toting rednecks, the two sit reflective and glassy-eyed around a campfire. Wyatt (a.k.a. Captain America) utters the revealing line, "We blew it, man."

"I think the film can be used very metaphorically," said Briley. "What did he mean by, 'We blew it?' Did he mean the two of them blew it? Did he mean the counterculture blew it? Did he mean America had blown it? And if you think about that whole trip across the country: Here they are supposedly hippies that are protesting against and dropping out of traditional society, yet they're capitalists! They're selling drugs; they're entrepreneurs." Here again Briley is analyzing a popular movie as a legitimate historical document. To what extent do other primary and secondary historical sources support (or contradict) the movie's overall narrative? Does this movie confirm or conflict with students' prior understandings of the 1960s? As Briley explained:

> I hope that they gain increased understanding of the times by looking at the film, one of the important cultural artifacts of our times. And I hope they would also get a handle for the complexity of the period. A stereotype of the 60s is often Hippies, and not much else. I always hope that what they come out of any time you're looking at, is that they come out

with some appreciation of paradox, ambivalence, historical causation and motivation. So, the complexity is what I hope they get out of it. Much like the present, there's conflict.

In order to gauge what students learned from the unit, the concluding essay assignment asked them to use the movies and written texts to come up with a synthesis of their thoughts about the counterculture movement (Table 5.6).

Of course, this curricular unit does not exist in a void. As the class goes on to study the 1970s, 1980s, and beyond, Briley does not allow the decade of the 1960s to disappear in the rearview. Movies such as *All the President's Men* (1976), *Chinatown* (1974), and *Forrest Gump* (1994) provide ample opportunities for the class to reflect upon the undoubted influence of the 1960s, and to turn the historical interrogation to Hollywood's first attempts—but hardly its last—to rewrite that decade.

Table 5.6 Concluding Essay

Anti-Establishment Cinema of the 1960s Essay

In a well-organized essay of approximately five pages, using specific examples from the film texts as well as course readings, analyze how the anti-establishment films of the late 1960s, such as *The Graduate, Bonnie and Clyde*, and *Easy Rider*, reflect the countercultural values of the time period. In conclusion, assess, using both films and readings, the strengths and weaknesses of the counterculture movement.

"For those of us who attended college in the 1960s it is indeed a sobering experience to encounter high school students who view both the Vietnam War and Peloponnesian War as ancient history," Ron Briley wrote in *The History Teacher* in 1990 (Briley, 1990). His article further notes a student habit of confusing World War II with Vietnam. Judging from the teenagers observed in Briley's 2009 class, times haven't changed much in this regard. However, his case suggests that intellectually rigorous uses of history movies in the classroom can challenge students' problematic attitudes and beliefs about the past and the culture they have inherited.

Throughout the year-long course in modern U.S. history, Hollywood movies are used as both primary and secondary historical documents. In the above unit *Bonnie and Clyde* serves as an example of a film selected for use first and foremost as a primary document. Although there (inevitably) is some discussion of the 1930s content, the primary focus is on what the movie says about the times of its production. *Bonnie and Clyde* is a movie with considerable appeal to today's adolescent student. It has aged fairly well. The fact that its striking star, Warren Beatty, is also the movie's producer offers a

REFLECTION ON THE CASE

nice segue into discussing those who created the film and their motives—a start at analyzing the film as a historical document.

Teachers and students are used to thinking of letters, diaries, and newspaper editorials as primary sources, but any product of popular culture—music, magazines, television shows, commercials, websites—is potentially a primary source for the historical and social moment in which it was created. Each is a historical artifact of that particular context, influenced by and influencing the broader public consciousness and popular culture at the time. It is no mistake that *Bonnie and Clyde* could have been made in 1967 but not 1947—the film emerges from the confluence of conflicting attitudes about sexuality, violence, and civic authority in 1960s America that were not part of the public consciousness in the 1940s. Hence, *Bonnie and Clyde* is a primary source reflecting a particular perspective on the cultural conflicts and social changes in the society and time in which it was created.

Recognizing that *Bonnie and Clyde* is a specific, if partial, perspective is essential to its educative value. It is not a neutral, detached commentary about American society. The film sympathizes with its gangster protagonists against the establishment figures who hunt them down. They are rebels against an exploitative American social order, in which banks and conservative elements hold all the power. Perhaps only through violence can humble people hope to claim any power or control. Early in the film, Bonnie and Clyde come across an impoverished Dust Bowl farmer whose home is being repossessed by the bank that owns his mortgage. They lend him one of their guns to shoot up the house, as it is no longer his home and is instead now bank property. When the Barrow gang is finally caught at the end of the film, the death of Bonnie and Clyde is not depicted as the triumph of justice or law over criminal recklessness: It is an ambush led by a resentful authority figure, a brutal assassination of two young renegades who resisted the establishment forces of their society. From this point of view, *Bonnie and Clyde* is a kind of historical fantasy using events and characters of the 1930s to comment on the 1960s. Much like most letters or diaries, the film expresses just one perspective on its time, the perspective embraced by the film creators. Hence, the film includes only personal details about the protagonists that advance their role as rebels against authority but not historical details (such as the sense of terror their killing spree elicited in much of the public in Oklahoma and Texas) that would interfere with expressing the filmmakers' social critique.

Briley's carefully guided instructional use of film positions his students to recognize historical themes reflected by a film such as *Bonnie and Clyde*. He took care to mentally equip his students to watch the film in a particular way, observing its distinct perspective and not blindly accepting it as an accurate or authoritative account of the Barrow gang. This was possible only through Briley's thoughtful planning, reinforcement through multiple sources (different texts), and scaffolding of student activities (frequent discussion, short response essays, end-of-unit summative essay).

Additionally, Briley's instructional use of *Bonnie and Clyde* was part of a broader unit. He had clear academic and intellectual goals—discussing establishment/anti-establishment conflicts in the 1960s—that built on the other unit elements, such as the social divisiveness of the Vietnam War (as reflected in his use of *The Green Berets* and *Platoon*), youth alienation among the "baby boom" generation (as reflected in *The Graduate*), and assessing the 1960s counterculture (as reflected in *Easy Rider*). Each film was used purposefully as part of a broader analysis of what the 1960s American experience was like and what it means. *Bonnie and Clyde*, *The Green Berets*, *The Graduate*, and *Easy Rider* all were used by Briley as primary sources—cultural artifacts made in the 1960s that reflected social debates and perspectives on that era.

Strategies for Using Film as a Primary Document

The introduction of this section lists a number of questions one might pose of movies when treating them as historical documents. Ron Briley doesn't read from any script, but he does take seriously the notion of "interrogating" movies set in the past, and in fact using this arc of questioning as a model that students can apply to many kinds of historical documents.

A number of useful strategies emerge in observing Briley's class. First is the idea that students are asked to do research on a movie before viewing and present their findings to class. This helps in getting students "hooked in" prior to seeing the first reel. Another point is the viewing of the film, what might be called a communal reading of the historical text. As noted above, Briley does not lounge at his desk while the movie is rolling. Rather he stalks the classroom, monitoring student engagement while intermittently throwing out comments, questions and facts. Occasionally he pauses mid-movie for discussion and questions. A balance must be struck here, because the point is not to distract and overwhelm students with the teacher's brainy repartee, but to model the habits of critical viewing. Briley's years of experience in the classroom show during this viewing process, as he continually gauges the mood of his students.

Once viewing is over, the time comes for discussion. Students in this course not only view films, but are concurrently reading from the history textbook as well as other supplemental texts such as movie reviews from the internet and the popular and academic press. These documents are subject to more or less the same kind of questioning and analysis to which course movie texts are exposed. Dialogue and written papers provide opportunities for comparing and con-trasting various historical documents, corroborating or disconfirming assorted themes and ideas. There are differences, of course, between movies and written texts, so this is not to suggest that the kinds of questions history students might pose would be *exactly* the same. Examining the kinds of questions that might be posed of different kinds of historical documents becomes another important lesson for high school students.

One can imagine all sorts of possibilities for the resourceful teacher seeking to recreate this unit or to improvise upon the theme, such as bringing magazine or newspaper accounts from the time, or the use of more non-traditional historical artifacts such as memorable posters or other works of 1960s pop art, or even classic 1960s music, whose well-known lyrics could take on a new light in the minds of students when placed alongside the movie texts. The internet today gives easy access to professional movie reviews, both from the time of release and more modern. Websites such as Wikipedia and IMDb provide easy, free access to a wealth of information. New DVD versions of movies offer bonus footage, including interviews, cut scenes, and retrospective analysis by reviewers as well as moviemakers. In short, teachers who unlock the potential of film as a historical source in the classroom have a prodigious pedagogical toolbox at their disposal.

Selecting Films as Primary Documents

All films are primary sources to the extent that they can be analyzed and interpreted as artifacts of the time period in which they were created, a fact that hardly helps in the task of film selection. Teachers using films as primary documents are likely to be covering topics situated in the 20th or 21st centuries—the age of movies. For most of this time period—say the 1930s to the present—there are likely to be countless potential films at the teacher's disposal. So how to choose?

The first consideration in film selection must surely involve course and unit objectives. What are the main objectives of this curricular sequence? If, like Briley's, the focus falls upon broad themes, the cultural milieu, the varying moods and values of the times, then a teacher must begin by reflecting upon the transparency of these subjects in given films. For example, it would not take much research and thought to identify the fact that *Bonnie and Clyde* was a groundbreaking movie in terms of its representation of sex and violence in the United States. A search of movie reviews and articles (all easily available on the internet) would reveal a great depth of scholarship identifying many historical themes in this movie, or in many, many others for that matter.

In teaching about the 1960s, Briley often tinkers with the format, sometimes using supplemental or replacement movies such as *The Killing Fields* (1984) or *Cool Hand Luke* (1967). Over the years, he has experimented with many other films, and his 1990 *History Teacher* article reflects upon on the pedagogical strengths and weaknesses of such movies as *Apocalypse Now* (1979), *The Deer Hunter* (1978), *Hearts and Minds* (1974), *Full Metal Jacket* (1987), *Coming Home* (1978), and the musical *Hair* (1978), just to name a few that address the 1960s in some way.

Notice all of the movies mentioned above were either critical or box-office successes; indeed it would not be going too far to say that they are classic movies. Not all films used in the classroom need to be masterpieces. However, after unit objectives, another consideration is a movie's ability to engage young students. It is difficult to precisely define what makes a movie popular with today's youth, a far from monolithic group. Big movie stars, complex plots, action sequences, love stories, Oscar-winning performances, lush cinematography: Filmmakers have spent no small effort trying to discover a magic formula. That said, it is relatively easy to identify if a movie has been popular with a particular audience (either upon its release, or afterward). If the movie has never been well liked by any discernible audience, what are the chances that your students will enjoy and be engaged by it?

Broad historical themes are more clearly intelligible in some movies than they are in others. These themes often lurk below the surface of films, whether they are feature movies or documentaries. In asking students to analyze movies as primary documents, we are often asking them to "read between the lines" of a movie, much like historians attempt to read the subtext of historical documents. In this aspect of movie selection, tailoring to specific classroom situations is important. The example of Ron Briley illustrates a teacher adept at the kind of communal viewings and discussions that highlight important course objectives and help his students "read" complex movie texts. To this extent it is hardly an exaggeration to say that the most important consideration is not so much which movie is used in the classroom, but *how* it is used.

CHAPTER 6

Using Film as a Secondary Source

Figure 6.1 The Alamo (2004) Green Jameson (Tom Davidson), Davy Crockett (Billy Bob Thornton), William Travis (Patrick Wilson), and Micajah Autry (Kevin Page) (from left to right) defend the Alamo.

Feature films represent the events, people, and time period depicted in their narratives in much the same way as a textbook or other secondary source treats the past. However, Hollywood films contain unique features that both add to and detract from their validity as secondary sources. The following case illustrates the potential for using film as a secondary source through examining the practices of a teacher using *The Alamo* (2004) to teach about Westward Expansion (see Table 6.2 for a description of the film).

Hollywood films deserve special consideration as secondary sources. Unlike other secondary sources such as textbooks or documentary films, which are viewed by many teachers as inherently "accurate" because of their perceived neutral, authorless tone, Hollywood films are often recognized by teachers as a challenge in terms of historical accuracy. Any secondary source, written or visual, can distort the past, limit the number of perspectives discussed, or present biased accounts, but Hollywood films are even more problematic in how unevenly films' creators research historical events and strive for historical accuracy. In addition, movies intentionally include fictional elements when representing past events. It can be quite difficult for educators to judge the historical integrity of a film and sort out which elements are invented. Showing a Hollywood film as a secondary source may be daunting for many teachers given the time and resources required first to learn about the content in the film and then scrutinize its accuracy. However, these films offer a wealth of important teaching opportunities that can enrich students' understanding of the past.

Hollywood films are unique secondary sources. Not quite historical-fiction novels and not quite documentary films, movies still serve as "texts" that can be analyzed, questioned, and discussed just like any other kind of historical document. Although the medium of film is visual and aural rather than print-based, they are still documents created by people with purposes and within a particular context and are open to interpretation and interrogation. There are other unique aspects to Hollywood films as secondary sources. First, a mainstream movie is seen by millions of people in the United States and frequently around the world. Movies are a principal source of knowledge about the past for many. Second, whereas films may function to develop empathy in viewers and raise controversial issues, at their most basic level they are commercial entertainment products that "teach" the audience about the past through telling a story. Finally, unlike books written by historians or similar secondary sources, films have no footnotes and often no way to trace how the past was recreated or hold the filmmakers accountable for how they chose to represent the past.

Therefore, an enormous burden is placed on teachers to develop historical film literacy skills in students that prepare them for a lifetime of viewing films more critically. For example, using Hollywood films as secondary sources provides a resource that can both reinforce and contradict other secondary sources in powerful ways. What happens when a film presents narratives of the past that are not present in the textbook? Which is more accurate and how do we know? Teachers and students can collaborate to evaluate a Hollywood film, facilitating how students both learn the specific content being covered as well as develop skills to decipher how past events are represented in various ways. However, teachers need to carefully scaffold the process of how to effectively analyze film. One of the most crucial elements is helping students recognize what they should "learn" from a particular film. Unlike a textbook, which may be more straightforward for students, films are not made explicitly for the purpose of educating students in history classrooms. Therefore, teachers and students can approach film as they would any source, considering issues of context and sourcing, such as analyzing the purpose and background of the author or "source" of the document, while also comparing film to other secondary and primary sources, activities crucial to using film as a primary source as well. In addition, they can focus on issues specific to film—such as how representations of the past are influenced by the way movies distort/collapse/draw out time, add fictional elements such as characters who are invented or composites (multiple historical figures represented by just one person in the story), and present narratives of "good vs. evil" in often simplistic ways.

For example, *Malcolm X* (1992), an excellent film to use as a secondary source, condenses a lifetime into 202 minutes, requiring director Spike Lee to make crucial decisions about time distortion. *Good Night, and Good Luck* (2005) is shown by some teachers during a unit on the Cold War and specifically to explore McCarthyism. Among many issues to consider with the film is that the director, George Clooney, includes both recreated and real footage in the film thus confusing recreations of past events containing fictional element with reality. Another film often used by teachers is *Glory* (1989), the story of the Massachusetts 54th regiment in the Civil War (and used by the teacher in Chapter 9 to "visualize" the past). African-American characters are composites that represent different groups, such as freed slaves, runaway slaves, and educated free blacks. These characters condense many different possible narratives into a handful of stories that make a film's narrative more manageable. One of the most common problems with Hollywood films is that they often add fictional love stories into an account of past events. Whether it is the romantic interest in *Pearl Harbor* (2001), *Titanic* (1997), or *Iron Jawed Angels* (2004), imaginary love stories distort the past by creating fictional elements and distracting viewers from the historical record and thus influence how students make sense of the film.

This chapter presents one teacher's use of *The Alamo* as a secondary source. As with many of the cases presented in this book, this teacher's lesson was not limited exclusively to the focus of this chapter and the teacher also used *The Alamo* to develop students' historical empathy and to bring the past alive. However, his primary purpose was to teach students about the struggle for control of Texas with the movie as a secondary source. In this case, Mr. Hector successfully demonstrates film as a secondary source by choosing an appropriate film that is relatively true to the historical record, by carefully preparing his lessons with research on the time period and the film, and by developing activities with *The Alamo* that thoroughly support student learning about the fight for Texas and focus students on how to use film as a secondary source more broadly.

WESTWARD EXPANSION AND *THE ALAMO*: A VISIT WITH MR. HECTOR'S CLASS

Case Description

This case describes the classroom practices of Mr. Hector in one of his U.S. History classes at Cutler High School in Hill Valley, Connecticut, during January and February 2009. Hill Valley is a relatively poor, working-class community located in northeast Connecticut. Once a booming mill town, the city has never fully recovered from the decline of its mills.

Mr. Hector's class was a "fundamental level" class, the lowest track in the school. All but a few students were members of minority groups with the vast majority speaking Spanish as a first language. Of the 20 students in the class, 14 had identified exceptionalities requiring special education or 504 services including supporting learning, behavior, and emotional disabilities. Most of the students were juniors, though three were seniors who had not passed the class the previous year. However, every student in the class during the fall term passed (three students were new to the class for the spring term).

Although the students were usually on task during class, Mr. Hector believed that most "would fail the class if I required routine homework," though the class did work on several long-term projects outside of class time. The class was generally well-behaved despite many in-class distractions that interfered with student learning. For example, in one 55-minute class there were 11 interruptions from school-wide announcements, the classroom phone ringing, and visitors at the door including a guidance counselor who interrupted class to hand out information about courses for next year, multiple students, and a security officer trying to solve the case of a teacher's jacket stolen—with car keys and wallet—from the same room the period before. Though not every day had this many interruptions, it is representative of the challenging learning environment.

Mr. Hector is a veteran teacher with 12 years of experience teaching high school in urban settings, including time as a special education teacher before teaching social studies. Prior to teaching high school Mr. Hector taught in a variety of college and clinical settings. Along with his BA, Mr. Hector earned four Masters degrees.

In addition to *The Alamo*, throughout the school year Mr. Hector also shows *The Crossing* (2000), *Mr. Smith Goes to Washington* (1939), *Glory* (1989), *The Searchers* (1956), *Dances with Wolves* (1990), *Iron Jawed Angels* (2004), and clips from dozens of documentary films. Mr. Hector has both short- and long-term goals in using these films. His more immediate goals focus on learning content, making history more concrete, and providing opportunities for students to use other senses and skills beyond traditional textbook reading. He is concerned that his students' reading abilities are very deficient and that films offer another medium through which to learn about the past—both increasing students' content knowledge as well as bolstering their self-confidence. He says his students "tend to remember the content better" from a film than from other sources and that it even improves their long-term memory of what is covered in class.

Furthermore, Mr. Hector believes that films complement and scaffold understanding from primary sources, making often abstract concepts and ideas more understandable. Thus, the films reinforce learning from other sources in class, including both primary and secondary texts. Finally, he uses film because it "helps me to get [students] involved" because they have a "better experience with history" and are more motivated—which he feels is a tremendous challenge with the students in this class. Films also support Mr. Hector's overall goals for his U.S. History course—to connect the past to students' interests, to emphasize the everyday life of people in the past, and to support the school's goal of improving students' literacy. Beyond classroom goals, Mr. Hector believes it is important for students to be able to understand and interpret film as part of their functioning as adults in a media-saturated society.

Unit Overview

Mr. Hector used *The Alamo* in lessons on the U.S.–Mexican War (1846–1848), one of eight segments of a larger multi-week unit on Westward Expansion. Other segments included the Louisiana Purchase, Oregon Trail, and California Gold Rush.

Mr. Hector's lessons on the Mexican War revolved around the use of *The Alamo*. In keeping with his overall philosophy about using film to teach history, he showed the film for a variety of purposes. First, he expected the film to help students understand "what happened at the Alamo" including the basic sequence of events, the people involved, and, to the extent possible, the "reality" of the Alamo. He expected students would leave class with an appreciation for "what the war was all about, what happened at the Alamo, [and] . . . the importance of the Alamo." This core goal of helping students understand the events, people, and reality of what happened at the Alamo demonstrate *The Alamo* as a secondary source. He believed that the film could help to take something that was abstract to his students and make it more concrete so that it was easier for them to understand and remember. Mr. Hector accomplished this goal by focusing students on the information they could learn from the film and reinforcing that information with readings and discussion. Building upon this base of knowledge, he then asked students to interpret a primary source using what they had learned from the film. This application of students' knowledge served to assess their learning and ability to analyze other kinds of sources. In addition, Mr. Hector hoped to use the film to generate historical empathy in his students, focused on the defenders of the Alamo and their American values.

Mr. Hector chose to show *The Alamo* because the film could potentially accomplish his three main goals while also motivating the students with minimal "Hollywood" distractions such as numerous inaccuracies and significant fictional elements. In past years he had shown a documentary film on the Alamo. However, he was replacing some of his documentary films with feature films because of a concern that documentary films contained too much information. He believes his students can become overwhelmed by a documentary film's bombardment of fact after fact.

Unit Outline

Table 6.1 describes *The Alamo* lessons, which occurred over six class sessions of 55 minutes each. They took place during the sixth of eight segments on Westward Expansion. After some initial preparation for viewing *The Alamo*, students watched the film over four class periods, interspersed with discussions and other activities. The sixth day included post-film analysis.

Table 6.1 Outline of Lessons Using *The Alamo*

Day	Activity	Daily Guiding Questions and Goals
1	Introduction to the unit focused on key issues of Texas independence and on geography.	Questions: How and why did Texas gain its independence? What are the Texians and Mexicans fighting for? Goals: Place the events at The Alamo in historical context. Provide background for viewing of film. Learn basic information about events at The Alamo and the fight for Texas independence.

Table 6.1 (continued)

Day	Activity	Daily Guiding Questions and Goals
2	Review of territorial expansion and preview of the battle for The Alamo. Preparation for watching the film. Begin watching *The Alamo*. Film stopped at various points to briefly discuss key characters and issues.	Questions: How and why did Texas gain its independence? ** What are the Texians and Mexicans fighting for? How do you feel about the main characters in the movie? Goals: Place the events at The Alamo in historical context. Provide background for viewing of film. To learn basic information about events at The Alamo and the fight for Texas independence.
3	Reviewing content from previous viewing of film and preview of journal writing assignment. Watch *The Alamo*. Film stopped at various points for brief discussion. Students record answers to questions in journal and share with class.	Questions: How and why did Texas gain its independence? How do the leaders of the regular army and volunteers treat each other? What are the feelings the soldiers of Texas and Mexico may be experiencing? Is the Alamo worth fighting for? For the Texians? For the Mexicans? Goals: Provide background for viewing of film. To learn basic information about events at The Alamo and the fight for Texas independence. To develop empathy for soldiers on both sides of the battle. To evaluate and improve students' writing skills.
4	Review key terms/vocabulary from the film. Watch *The Alamo*. Film stopped at various points for brief discussion.	Questions: How and why did Texas gain its independence? What happened at the Alamo? Is the Alamo worth fighting for? For the Texians? For the Mexicans? Goals: To learn basic information about events at The Alamo and the fight for Texas independence. To visualize how the battle for the Alamo looked. To evaluate and improve students' writing skills.

Table 6.1 (continued)

Day	Activity	Daily Guiding Questions and Goals
5	Watch *The Alamo*. Film stopped at various points for brief discussion. Primary source activity.	Questions: How and why did Texas gain its independence? What happened at the Alamo? Was it all worth it for the Texians? Goals: To learn basic information about events at The Alamo and the fight for Texas independence. To effectively analyze primary source documents. To visualize how the battle for the Alamo looked. To evaluate and improve students' writing skills.
6	Review key terms/vocabulary from the film. Read and discuss textbook section on manifest destiny, Texas, and The Alamo. Journal activity and discussion.	Questions: How and why did Texas gain its independence? Was it all worth it for the Texians? Goals: To learn basic information about events at The Alamo and the fight for Texas independence. To evaluate and improve students writing skills. Place the events at The Alamo in historical context.
		** Many of the questions are used over multiple days because several activities took more than one class period and as a means of reinforcing student learning.

Films

The Alamo is briefly described in Table 6.2. It was the only film used for this case study.

Table 6.2 Description of *The Alamo*

The Alamo (2004) John Lee Hancock (Director) Touchstone Pictures	*The Alamo* recreates the events before, during, and after the Mexican Army's siege and storming of the Alamo in 1836 as part of the war for the territory of Texas. The film focuses on the American perspective, particularly those of William Travis, Jim Bowie, Davy Crockett, and Sam Houston. Mexican General Santa Anna also plays a significant role in the film.

FILM ACTIVITIES

Day 1

The first day centered on providing students with background information on the settlement of Texas by Anglo settlers and their slaves, and the geography of key events in Texas history. Students spent the first half of class reading about Texas settlement in five segments: (1) Spanish settlement and initial American settlement led by Stephen Austin; (2) Mexican independence from Spain and the role of American colonists; (3) the fall of San Antonio and the Alamo; (4) the defeat of Santa Anna and Texas independence; (5) Texas statehood and war with Mexico. Each of these segments was one paragraph and asked students to use an attached map to mark the locations of key places/events (e.g., San Antonio, border with Mexico). Mr. Hector then reviewed the map with the students. These activities provided important historical context for the film emphasizing geography, an ongoing goal for all social studies courses in the school.

Day 2

Students walked into class on the second day of *The Alamo* lessons and saw key terms written on the board (see Table 6.3).

One student asked, "Who is Davy Crockett?" and then jokingly asked, "Is that like Betty Crocker?" In fact, almost none of the students in the class remembered the name Davy Crockett—though it was mentioned once in prior readings. Mr. Hector assured the students they would be intimately familiar with Mr. Crockett by the end of the film.

Mr. Hector began class by asking the students, "What happened at the Alamo?" as a way to check for prior knowledge from the reading and to arouse curiosity. A few students correctly identified the Alamo as being located in Texas and involved in a battle with Mexico. However, they improperly believed Mexico lost the battle. Mr. Hector went on to ask several questions as a way to review background and context for the Alamo battle and the film. For example, he asked students about President Jefferson's Louisiana Purchase as a means for reviewing Westward Expansion. He also asked students to define "legend" in their notes and identify a sports legend as a way to conceptualize the definition. Students mentioned Babe Ruth as a sports legend. Mr. Hector then connected the idea of legend to the film and the list of names on the board, suggesting that Travis,

Table 6.3 Key Terms for Film

Slavery
U.S. Citizens
Mexicans
Santa Anna
Legend
James Bowie
William Travis
Davy Crockett
Sam Houston

Bowie, Crockett, and Houston were all historical legends, some in their own lives and others after the Alamo. His purpose was primarily to preview the main characters in the film, but at the same time he wanted to invite students to evaluate what makes a legend, whether these men were legends, and the potential gaps between legend and reality.

To emphasize how Crockett was a legend, Mr. Hector called on a student teacher observing his class to join him in the front of the room, and the two of them sang "The Ballad of Davy Crockett" (1955). After the first line the students detected the lack of harmony and one student cried out: "Oh my God, no!" Each stanza provided some actual background on Davy Crockett while also reinforcing images of him as a legend. For example one couplet is "He went off to Congress and served a spell, Fixin' up the Government and the laws as well," highlighting his time as a member of the U.S. Congress; others read "And he patched up the crack in the Liberty Bell" and "Fought single-handed through many a war," reinforcing his legendary status. At the end of the song—a nice grabber and illustration of the term *legend*—another student remarked, "After this, it better be a good movie."

Next, Mr. Hector handed out journals that the students would use for the film and instructed students to write down three facts they learn from watching the film but did not previously know. This writing prompt focused students on using the film as a secondary source by drawing their attention to factual content knowledge in the film.

Mr. Hector began showing the film in the latter part of the class. He periodically stopped the film to review a key idea and check for understanding. For example, he paused to reiterate that the Alamo was originally a Catholic mission, to emphasize that there was a conflict between leaders of the Texan soldiers (led by Travis) and the unofficial volunteers (led by Bowie), to point out that white men controlled decision making at the Alamo, and to clarify the difference between "Texians" (American Anglos in Texas) and *tejanos* (Texans of Mexican descent). Although students protested the interruptions at first, they eventually were compliant (or at least ceased openly expressing displeasure) and Mr. Hector continued this type of instructional support throughout the viewing of the film. As demonstrated through subsequent class discussion and students' journal writing, his viewing pauses promoted a deeper understanding of the film by students, particularly in using the film as a secondary source.

A few minutes before the class ended Mr. Hector stopped the film and asked the students to record at least three things they had learned into their journals. He then briefly reviewed the main points of the film viewed so far.

Day 3

Students began by copying the daily questions written on the board into their film journals. This served to remind students of the overall purpose of watching the film: to understand what happened at the Alamo within the context of Texas independence. The questions also focused the students on several pivotal issues raised by the film, including conflicts between Texian soldiers and volunteers, the mindset of the defenders, and the purposes of fighting for the Alamo. Mr. Hector, over the protests of students anxious to continue the film, reviewed key events and people from prior viewing (Travis, Bowie, Crockett, Houston, Santa Anna, the Alamo as a mission) and previewed what they were about to watch. This review and preview provided excellent scaffolding for the students,

Table 6.4 Vocabulary Listed on the Board

militia, mission, palisade, pyre, republic, revolution, siege

reinforcing the focus on the film as a secondary source while also highlighting issues of empathy required for answering the journal questions.

Most of class was spent viewing the film. Mr. Hector stopped the film briefly at several points to check for student understanding and to clarify important points. For example, he paused to emphasize how Travis and Bowie disagreed as a representation of soldier vs. volunteer dispute, and he also stopped the film to repeat the line by Colonel Neill, "as goes the Alamo, so goes Texas," in order to stress the value of the Alamo as a symbol. Once again the students grumbled about Mr. Hector's interruptions, but these clarifications and highlights appeared to focus students on his learning goals without significantly distracting from students' enjoyment of the film.

For the last segment of class, Mr. Hector reviewed what the students had just seen and then students wrote answers to the questions in their journals. Mr. Hector asked a few students to share their responses as a way to assess understanding, keep students on task, and provide a model for any students who were struggling with the assignment.

Day 4

Students arrived on day 4 eager to begin the film. Tension and suspense in the film had been building and the students were "ready for [the Alamo] battle." Consistent with his prior practice, Mr. Hector began by reviewing a list of vocabulary from the film and asking students to define the words they knew. Students copied the words (see Table 6.4) into their journals along with the definitions. Mr. Hector reviewed vocabulary for this segment of the film because of the number of terms used that the students would not recognize or be able to define. Given the students' literacy skills and that many spoke English as a second language, the vocabulary review helped to reinforce Mr. Hector's literacy goals while also allowing students to focus on the content of the film.

After the vocabulary review Mr. Hector highlighted key moments in the film from the previous class and previewed what the students were about to watch.

Similarly to day 3, the majority of class time was devoted to viewing the film with periodic pauses for Mr. Hector to emphasize and clarify various events in the film, including cooperation between Travis and Bowie (as a turning point in the film) and Crockett's reaction to the death of a young Mexican soldier, and to ask, "What does Sam Houston believe those in the Alamo are fighting for?" Class concluded with time for students to write in their journals, answering the daily questions about how and why Texas gained independence, what happened at the Alamo, and whether the Alamo was worth fighting for. As before, Mr. Hector engaged students in pre-film and in-film activities that helped students to make meaning of the film, to reinforce the film as a secondary source, and to build their literacy skills.

Table 6.5 Travis Letter of Appeal for Reinforcements

Directions: Travis' appeal. "read the following letter written by William Barret Travis on the second day of the Siege of the Alamo. Journal exercise: Travis' son was six years old during the battle of the Alamo. Discuss how Travis' son possibly reacted to this letter when he became old enough to understand what the battle was about."

Commandancy of the Alamo– Bejar, Fby 24th 1836–

To the People of Texas & all Americans in the world–

Fellow citizens & compatriots—I am besieged, by a thousand or more of the Mexicans under Santa Anna—I have sustained a continual Bombardment & cannonade for 24 hours & have not lost a man—The enemy has demanded a surrender at discretion, otherwise, the garrison are to be put to the sword, if the fort is taken—I have answered the demand with a cannon shot, & our flag still waves proudly from the walls – I shall never surrender or retreat. Then, I call on you in the name of Liberty, of patriotism & everything dear to the American character, to come to our aid, with all dispatch—The enemy is receiving reinforcements daily & will no doubt increase to three or four thousand in four or five days. If this call is neglected, I am determined to sustain myself as long as possible & die like a soldier who never forgets what is due to his own honor & that of his country—Victory or Death

William Barret Travis
Lt. Col. comdt

P.S. The Lord is on our side – When the enemy appeared in sight we had not three bushels of corn – We have since found in deserted houses 80 or 90 bushels & got into the walls 20 or 30 head of Beeves

—Travis.

Day 5

After students wrote the daily questions in their journal, Mr. Hector provided a very brief preview of the upcoming film segment. Students then watched the end of the film, culminating in the storming of the Alamo and the subsequent battle at San Jacinto. The students seemed most riveted during this segment of the film, perhaps because of the battle in conjunction with connections they had developed with the characters.

Following the conclusion of the film, Mr. Hector asked students to apply what they had learned to the analysis of a primary source document. As a whole class Mr. Hector and the students took turns reading the letter sent by Travis during the siege at the Alamo appealing for reinforcements (Table 6.5). Parts of the letter were read in the film—one of several places in which the screenplay actually employed primary sources to frame events or tell the story. By reading the letter out loud, Mr. Hector was able to clarify issues of language and content.

Students were asked to write in their journals a reaction to the prompt: "Travis's son was six years old during the battle of the Alamo. Discuss how Travis's son possibly reacted to this letter when he became old enough to understand what the battle was about." This exercise was designed to assess students' understanding of what happened at the Alamo and its significance as well as to develop historical empathy and analyze a primary source.

Day 6

Mr. Hector came full circle by placing the Alamo back within the broader context of Texas settlement and Westward Expansion. Although he had done this to some degree prior to the film, he felt it was important to revisit the broader context now that the students had a better understanding of the battle and historical figures at the Alamo.

Mr. Hector began by reviewing the vocabulary from day 3 to check for understanding. He then asked students to complete a reading from the textbook and answer questions. The three-page reading included the major topics: manifest destiny, Americans in Texas, the Alamo, and war with Mexico. Students were asked to answer several questions: "How did people travel west in the first half of the 1800s? Who fought the battle of the Alamo? As a settler living under Mexican rule in the Southwest, why might you have wanted your own independent state?" Mr. Hector and the students then discussed the answers to the questions, both drawing from and adding to information from the film.

Finally, Mr. Hector asked students to complete a summative journal entry answering the question: "Was [the battle of the Alamo] all worth it to the Texians?" The students relied on details from the film as well as their previous journal entries to answer the question.

REFLECTION ON THE CASE

Mr. Hector described the lessons with *The Alamo* as "an improvement in my teaching . . . an improvement in [students'] learning." The film provided a tool that made the content more understandable for students and provided a "better learning experience" in their history class. Students were engaged with, and enthusiastic about, *The Alamo* and willingly completed assignments related to the film. They demonstrated an understanding of the larger historical context within which the conflict at the Alamo was situated as well as knowledge of the key events and people associated with the conflict. In this respect the film and related activities met the teacher's instructional goals. Based on the students' previous performance and motivation during the year, Mr. Hector believed the film both motivated students and supported their learning. This success was rooted in part by Mr. Hector's choice of film as well as the supporting activities.

Mr. Hector researched *The Alamo's* background as part of the process of deciding to use the film and in determining how to use the film. He compared the film with other sources of information about the Alamo and assessed how accessible the film would be to his students. He determined that the film was very appropriate given the film's content, his own objectives, and the abilities and interests of his students. In terms of historical accuracy, *The Alamo* does a good job at recreating the period, covering the main events, and putting the conflict at the Alamo in a broader strategic and political context (Metzger, 2007a)—precisely Mr. Hector's objectives for the film. Mr. Hector was less concerned with the factual accuracy of small details, such as whether Davy Crockett uttered the specific words in the film, and more focused on the basic premise of what happened and the connections to the larger context. Thus, the film was well suited for the lessons. His background research on the film was a critical component of his successful lessons.

Mr. Hector's lessons were arranged to guide his students through their learning experience. He supported his objectives through a variety of activities before, during, and after the film viewing that were essential to student learning. Prior to the film he provided students with important background information through reading, map work, and discussion. Students were then prepared to understand what they would view. During the film Mr. Hector required journal responses to various questions and prompts, reviewed key vocabulary used in the film, and periodically stopped the film to check for understanding and to clarify or accentuate key elements. This approach guided students to pay attention to particular events and people in order to learn the material. Through this focus, students were less likely to be confused or miseducated by fictional elements in the film. In addition, students were learning literacy skills to enable them to use secondary sources to understand the past. Whereas this might be taken for granted in some classes, this group of students required these most basic skill boosters. Although there was some student grumbling about the film being stopped from time to time, they still were drawn into the narrative and the pedagogical advantages outweighed the classroom management inconveniences. After viewing the film Mr. Hector asked students to apply and extend their knowledge through analysis of a primary source and a journal prompt. He also asked students to complete a reading that reconnected what they had learned in the film to the larger context of Westward Expansion, Texas Settlement, and the U.S.–Mexican War. The primary source activity not only checked for student understanding but illustrated how secondary sources are created based on primary sources. Mr. Hector specifically chose a primary source that was directly used in the film to reinforce this point. He also pointed out to the students other examples of primary sources cited in the film, such as journal entries by characters.

Finally, his activities before, during, and after the film appeared to meet his content and skill objectives. Mr. Hector skillfully supported learning from the film based on his students' abilities, carefully adjusting for student needs. Given his students' ability levels and prior experiences, this assistance was critical to student learning. It was hoped that students came away from the lesson with an understanding of what happened at the Alamo and the conflict's historical context.

Despite the overall success of the lessons there are a few potential concerns that emerge. If Mr. Hector were to extend the lessons he could consider addressing the fictional elements of the film, adding documents that both support and contradict the film, and do more to evaluate the film as a source of knowledge about the past.

First, there was a lack of attention to elements of the film that were fictional. Whereas Mr. Hector focused on many of the key events and people and the "big picture" issues, he did little to specifically point out to students the fictional elements such as Davy Crockett shooting at Santa Anna, which was representative of his excellent marksmanship, but did not specifically occur. Although we have specific historical evidence to support many scenes in the film, there are also significant gaps in the historical record such as much of the specific dialogue spoken during the film. Unlike a textbook, which is supposed to be a synthesis of up-to-date, accurate scholarly knowledge, using film as a secondary source requires adequate analysis of both the more factual representations and the fictional or more blurry representations of the past. Mr. Hector expressed concern about this issue going into the film. He was aware of the potential pitfalls and conducted background research on the film; however, this did not translate into an effective strategy to compensate for the film's deficiencies. Students in Mr. Hector's class may have a good understanding of what happened at the Alamo, but they would be hard pressed to point out any misrepresentations present in the film.

A second, and related issue, is the lack of other documents used during the lessons, particularly documents that might contradict events or perspectives presented in the film. Whereas Mr. Hector did provide readings prior to and after showing the film, these readings acted as a reinforcing mechanism. In some respects this had a positive impact by fortifying students' understanding of events at the Alamo and the broader context, at least as presented in the film. Students were able to learn the information from more than one source. However, a more sophisticated use of secondary sources, and one that promotes historical film literacy, would include multiple sources of information about events at the Alamo and the broader context, some of which provided contradictory information and/or alternative points of view; for example, documents from the Mexican perspective including that of Santa Ana and newspaper accounts of the events at the Alamo, some of which discuss the broader issue of Texas settlement and slavery. Given the context of the students' reading abilities and prior practice analyzing Hollywood films this may be an unrealistic observation; nonetheless, it is an important consideration for the larger discussion of films as secondary sources. Students with more advanced skills, or these students with additional practice and scaffolding, could be asked to do more analysis and evaluation of the film and to use the film as one of numerous sources much like the work of historians. In fact, for the next part of the unit in Mr. Hector's class he asked students to be more critical consumers of film by thinking about how Native Americans are represented in film during different time periods (specifically *The Searchers* and *Dances with Wolves*), in other words evaluating films as primary sources—as products of the time in which they were produced and viewed. However, in this instance he focused more on the actual events and historical context so traded one type of learning and understanding for another.

Third, although the students learned to glean information from the film—in other words, using it as a secondary source similarly to how they might use their textbook—Mr. Hector was less successful at asking students to critically analyze the film as a source, such as considering the film's context or purpose, for instance a pro-multicultural perspective that is inaccurate for the time represented in the film but that might resonate with viewers. This critical analysis would have required more time and additional scaffolding in order to tackle these more sophisticated types of historical film literacy given all of his other goals.

As we know, all teaching is contextual. Despite these limitations of Mr. Hector's lessons, this is a very good model for using *The Alamo* as a secondary source. Given the contextual constraints, teachers need to consider the needs of their own students and the requirements of their own objectives to effectively use the film.

Strategies for using film as a secondary source

Mr. Hector's use of *The Alamo* illustrates several important issues in considering the use of film as a secondary source. These include researching the film for accuracy, providing proper background for the events/people in the film, focusing students on what is important for their understanding including stopping the film for clarifications and enhancements, using other primary and secondary documents, and evaluating the film as a source of knowledge about the past including analyzing non-fictional elements of the film.

Teachers rely on the authority of textbooks and certain other sources such as some documentary films and trust they are "accurate." However, even feature films such as *The Alamo* that use professional historians to bolster their accuracy contain significant fictional elements and do not have the footnotes or other scholarly mechanisms to guide learning from them. Therefore it is the responsibility of the teacher to do the homework on the films' historical accuracy. The background research supports all other aspects of using the film as a secondary sources including creating guiding questions that focus students, helping students analyze the film, and choosing other documents to use in conjunction with the film. Mr. Hector conducted extensive research on the film in deciding to use it and to then help him determine appropriate activities.

A second component of good practice with film as a secondary source is to provide adequate background on the film and on the content of the film. As with any source, students will get more out of the source if they have contextual information that helps them understand the source. This is especially important when using film since there are fictional elements woven into the historical narrative. Mr. Hector provided the historical context for the battle at the Alamo as well as background on the key historical figures. This background enhanced what students took away from the film.

It is also critical to focus students based on learning objectives. Just as reading guides help students to distinguish between what is important and what is trivial in a textbook or other reading, students require scaffolding to decipher what is "important" in a film, what is of lesser importance, and which elements are entirely fictional. There is a danger in asking students to learn too much information from a film. In this case Mr. Hector provided guiding questions to focus students' viewing and paused the film at various points to keep the students focused on key events, people, and ideas.

Another feature of good practice with films as secondary sources is to use multiple other sources—primary and secondary—that both support and challenge the film portrayal of the past. A crucial element of any historian's practice is to examine multiple documents in order to make sense of the past. Films may come across to students as authoritative documents (Marcus, Paxton, & Meyerson, 2006) and it is a delicate balance for teachers to challenge that authority with conflicting accounts while not completely undercutting a film's version of the past, otherwise the value of the film as a secondary source would be lost. In this case Mr. Hector used sources that supported the film's version of events at the Alamo, but did not provide any contradictory sources that might help the students evaluate the film as a source.

Finally, it is important to evaluate films as sources of knowledge about the past. Unlike a textbook, which may be more straightforward for students, films are not made explicitly for the purpose of educating students in history classrooms. Therefore, teachers and students can approach film as they would any source, considering issues of context and sourcing, such as analyzing the purpose and background of the author or "source" of the document, while also comparing film with other secondary and primary sources, activities crucial to using film as a primary source as well. In addition, they can focus on issues specific to film—such as how representations of the past are influenced by the way movies distort/collapse/draw out time, add fictional elements such as characters who are invented or composites (multiple historical figures represented by just one person in the story), and present narratives of "good vs. evil" in often simplistic ways.

Strategies for choosing films as a secondary source

Perhaps the most important aspect of using film as a secondary source is the choice of film. Some films are better suited for classroom viewing. Some adhere to higher standards of reporting the historical record.

Accuracy is a crucial issue in choosing a film as a secondary source. Without some adherence to the historical record a film loses all value as a secondary source whereby students can learn about "what happened" at an event or learn about people in the past. Obviously, films that have readily available research are easier to use, though compiling background about the content covered in a film will greatly support using it well.

Textbooks are also secondary sources. What distinguishes films from textbooks is not just added fictional elements, but a powerful audio-visual medium. Therefore, when choosing films to use as secondary sources it is important to consider how engaging the film will be to students. How well will it motivate them?

A third consideration when choosing films to use as secondary sources is the availability of other primary and secondary sources that meet the goals of the lesson and work well in concert with the film. Without these complementary sources the film will not be as effective as a secondary source.

Finally, it is important to reflect on other goals for using a film. In most of the cases in this book a film served multiple purposes. A film used as a secondary source may also be chosen because it can help students visualize the past, and/or develop students' historical empathy, and/or present alternate perspectives. Multiple films may work as secondary sources, but a smaller number may be able to also work in achieving other goals at the same time.

Among the many films that are well qualified to be used as secondary sources, one particular gem is *Iron Jawed Angels* (2004). *Iron Jawed Angels*, an HBO film, centers on the work of Alice Paul and Lucy Burns to pass the women's suffrage amendment to the United States Constitution. The film has its share of fictional elements, but the majority of the film's narrative follows the historical record, such as a 1913 suffrage march in Washington, DC, a split within the women's movement, picketing in front of the White House, and the jailing and force-feeding of Alice Paul. The film also relies heavily on primary sources and cites many of them in the film, such as newspaper articles and excerpts from speeches. In addition, the film's modern film-making style and contemporary music are particularly engaging for students. The combination of an engaging film, accuracy of major events in the film, and obvious reliance on primary sources makes *Iron Jawed Angels* an excellent secondary source. It is also a fabulous resource for historical empathy through its depiction of multiple perspectives.

Another film that also works well as a secondary source is *Fat Man and Little Boy* (1989). The film tells the story of the Manhattan Project to build the atomic bomb during World War II. The narrative focuses on the lead scientist, Robert Oppenheimer, and the lead army officer, General Groves. The film closely adheres to the historical record including how the bomb was built and the controversy about building and using the bomb that occurred both within and outside of the community of scientists building the bomb. Although the outcome is known—the bomb was successfully built and used—the film provides an engaging and provocative narrative that draws in the viewer. As with *Iron Jawed Angles*, there are dozens and dozens of documents that can be used with the film, particularly from the U.S. government. Asking "should the United States have dropped the bomb in World War II?" is commonly explored in U.S. history classrooms and *Fat Man and Little Boy* is an excellent resource to use to learn about the background to the question.

Using film as a secondary source can be very challenging owing to the background research required and decisions about how closely to analyze a film. It is also potentially more time consuming than using other secondary sources. Despite these drawbacks, the benefits of using film as a secondary source—increased student motivation, making content knowledge more accessible for students, and the potential for developing historical film literacy skills—make a good case for periodically using film as one of several sources of knowledge about the past.

PART IV

Using Film to Teach about Controversial Issues

History and the social studies have long been rife with academic controversy and heated debates over what topics and perspectives should be included or emphasized (Cornbleth & Waugh, 1995; Evans, 2004; Nash, Crabtree, & Dunn, 1997). Social issues, group identities, and historical experiences that people often feel most passionate about are fundamental to the social studies curriculum. Social studies teachers need, at least to some degree, to recognize and teach about conflicts, exploitation, and other contentious events that happened in the past and that continue to have implications for the present world. Historical issues such as racism, genocide, and religious strife and contemporary issues such as gun control, the death penalty, and gay rights are important to include in classroom activities in order to understand the past and participate as a citizen in the present.

Because social and political power and identity are at stake, there is tremendous educational power for teaching about participation in a democracy to students through exchanging diverse views and openly discussing controversial issues in the classroom (Epstein & Shiller, 2005; Hess, 2009; Parker, 2003). The ability to discuss controversies, consider multiple perspectives and value sets, and come to reasonable decisions about them is essential to democratic citizenship. There are likely to be differences and heated disagreements over controversial issues in the past and present, and easy answers or consensus often will prove elusive or impossible. Indeed, even deciding whether an issue is controversial and open for debate can be divisive when different groups in a community argue over whether an issue is closed and should not be debated within the school curriculum (Camicia, 2008).

These kinds of issues can be controversial because how they are interpreted and the meaning attached to them in the present day depends heavily on teachers', students', historians', and general public values, beliefs, and identities. The status, power, and position of individuals and social groups are on the line when controversial issues are open to debate. Raising controversial issues in the classroom can be messy, demanding, and risky for teachers. The legacy of societal and cultural conflict as well as newly emerging issues can be difficult, awkward, or even painful for teachers to confront with students. It can be challenging to find ways to show to students multiple perspectives on a controversial issue or to find strongly presented dissenting or minority points of view. Here films about and from history can serve as a powerful instructional resource. As narrative stories, movies by their very nature present a particular point of view (usually from a main protagonist, though sometimes films can follow the perspectives of multiple representative characters). A film's narrative, in a sense, provides a particular "frame" on a controversial issue in the past or present and conveys certain messages, interpretations, or conclusions to the viewer. In-depth discussion of the film may help students tease out the issues, ideas, and values behind the filmmakers' perspective on the controversy. The film also could be used as one source in a deliberative or debate-style activity, as long as other sources are also provided to make sure that multiple sides are presented and treated with comparable evidence.

History movies can be useful for raising controversial issues in the classroom by serving as a vehicle for envisioning the background context, dramatizing particular perspectives or interpretations of the issue, or conveying particular messages about what the issue means. These aspects have rich possibilities for student learning when rigorously studied with appropriate content knowledge and analyzed in critical but civil debates. Of course, just because history films have this potential does not mean they inherently will achieve these outcomes on their own. Everything depends on the willingness or ability of the teacher to select appropriate films for raising the controversial issue, devote sufficient class time to supporting instruction and activities, and take the risk of confronting unpleasant topics with their students. It is possible even for committed educators with good intentions to use history movies to avoid or skirt around discussing controversial issues, presuming that just the movie on its own is sufficient for students to understand the complexities of a controversial issue (Metzger & Suh, 2008). However, films by themselves do not teach students careful consideration of controversial issues—this learning outcome requires active teacher guidance, involvement, and structured support for students. It is important to keep in mind that posing an open question on an issue and then using a film as the principal source of evidence can be problematic, as films often present just one preferred stance on issues with which students and even teachers may not unanimously agree (Stoddard, 2009).

In the following cases on using film to teach about controversial issues, we explore two different dimensions: (1) teaching *contemporary controversial issues* through historical and recent films; (2) teaching *controversial issues in history* through films about the past. Although they are similar and closely related, there are important distinctions worth noting.

CONTEMPORARY CONTROVERSIAL ISSUES

Movies from and about the past can raise or comment on controversies in our world today. Films used this way can allow a teacher to teach about the present through connections to the past. The present-day controversy is the focus, and the film provides historical context or demonstrates how perspectives can change (or remain stable) over time. Sometimes films are set in the past but comment on conflicts or social issues in the present. Consider how *300* (2007), made during the U.S. wars in Iraq and Afghanistan, presents the ancient battle between Greeks and Persians as a clash between the liberty and rationality of Western civilization and the fanaticism and tyranny of Middle-Eastern cultures. Teachers also may use films from the past to teach about a present-day controversy. In the case in this book, a teacher used *The Jazz Singer* (1927) to teach students about the controversy over "blackface" and to introduce controversies over depictions of race in entertainment and racism in society more broadly. The film was then compared with modern portrayals of race in film and racial controversies in society today.

CONTROVERSIAL ISSUES IN HISTORY

Movies set in the past can comment on historical controversies that have shaped our world today or that have been persistent over time. Films used for this purpose can allow a teacher to teach about the past by making connections to the present. When movies dramatize controversial historical events, they often are meant to have meaning for contemporary viewers. They convey messages about how past events relate to, cause, or continue to be concerns or heated debates today. Consider how *The Last Samurai* (2003), set during the modernization of Japan in the 1870s, presents the samurai as an indigenous tribe that, like Native Americans, were crushed by Western industrialization and capitalism. Is "Westernization" an imperialistic force that crushes local cultures around the globe? Of course, what controversies will resonate with contemporary viewers often change and depend on the social context at the time. In the first decade of the 21st century, one of the most pressing controversies is religious warfare and terrorism, and schools have struggled with how to teach about the September 11 attacks and the subsequent U.S. wars in Muslim countries. In the case in this book, a teacher used *Kingdom of Heaven* (2005) to teach students about the Crusades as a controversial historical event. The film was used to help students visualize multiple perspectives on the conflict, both Christian and Muslim, and to consider implications for the U.S. fight against terrorism today.

CHAPTER 7

Using Film to Teach about Contemporary Controversial Issues

Figure 7.1 The Jazz Singer (1927). Jakie Rabinowitz (Al Jolson), in blackface before a show, struggles as his family and professional life pull him in different directions.

It is natural to include lessons on controversial social and political issues in history and other social studies classes. Films can be excellent tools with which to introduce and examine these issues as they explicitly and implicitly deal with contemporary controversial issues and issues that connect the present to the past. The case in this chapter is an example of using film to teach about contemporary controversial issues and reveals how one teacher promotes open and powerful discussions of race and racial conflict in his diverse classroom.

Promoting the discussion of contemporary controversial issues in social studies classes is itself controversial for some, but in our view, exceedingly important. Discussions of contemporary controversial issues that are well scaffolded and purposeful can promote the broad goal of preparing students to participate in and contribute to our democracy. These discussions strengthen students' understanding of real world issues, enhance students' communication skills, develop students' critical thinking abilities, and bolster students' ability to thoughtfully analyze sources, all important attributes of an involved democratic citizen. Hess (2009) provides two additional arguments for including controversial issues in the social studies curriculum. First, led by a trained teacher, classrooms are a unique space for the open discussion of controversial issues because they can support a diversity of ideas that might not be duplicated in students' lives outside of school. Second, not discussing controversial issues sends the message to students that these discussions are taboo, that the political realm is not important, and that there is natural agreement on what the public good is and how to achieve it.

Of course, contemporary controversial issues are difficult to teach, and teachers have legitimate reasons to be cautious. The content of a particular controversial issue may still be evolving, so teachers must be vigilant for the latest events and ideas and constantly update their resources and teaching materials. In addition, teachers may not have the support of administrators, parents, or the larger community, particularly around heated social issues such as gay rights or abortion, which can leave teachers, particularly new or untenured teachers, feeling vulnerable. Hess (2009) argues that another barrier to teaching controversial issues is that developing students' abilities to participate in a democracy is not supported by the job marketplace, in comparison with their abilities in subjects such as science and math.

There are also key pedagogical challenges to discussing contemporary controversial issues, including the need to present a balanced perspective beyond the teacher's personal views or the views of a majority of students and the time it may take away from official prescribed curriculum or textbook coverage. In addition, teachers need to consider the difficulty of sustaining an open, supportive, and tolerant learning environment, and the official positions of power that teachers, schools, and curriculum represent that can intimidate, unduly influence, or turn off students.

Films, when used in conjunction with other sources, offer the opportunity to scaffold the teaching of contemporary controversial issues. For a rigorous and balanced treatment, they cannot be the only source used. As seen in the cases in this book, films are one of many sources that support effective lessons on contemporary and historic controversial issues.

Films are often created by filmmakers with distinct messages, and for that reason they can serve as a good introduction to a controversial issue in the classroom. Although not a neutral source, using films to introduce contemporary controversial issues takes the burden off the teacher to be the one presenting a perspective, while at the same time adding the burden of providing other viewpoints. These distinct messages are especially effective at providing alternative perspectives that might not be present in official school sources such as textbooks or in the mainstream news media outlets. As discussed in Chapters 3 and 4, the powerful audio-visual nature of film uniquely promotes the development of empathy, particularly the ability to learn about and understand multiple perspectives. A key attribute of effective teaching about contemporary controversial issues is presenting and helping students understand multiple viewpoints or alternative frames.

An additional reason that using film to support teaching about contemporary controversial issues is important is because they can help students develop essential analytical and evaluative skills. Developing these skills is crucial because movies have the potential to be a powerful influence on young people, considering how many they watch as part of youth popular culture. Therefore, training students to critique the messages in films and think for themselves is vitally important and part of what we label historical film literacy. Finally, certain films are valuable for providing background information on contemporary controversial issues in powerful, engaging, and sometimes time-efficient ways.

This chapter explores how history classes are a natural place to include lessons on controversial social and political issues and how films can be powerful tools with which to introduce and examine these issues. Specifically, this case study examines Mr. Clark and his use of *The Jazz Singer* (1927) as well as clips from several other films to explore controversial issues of race and identity from the 1920s to today. All films are described in Table 7.2.

Mr. Clark uses film in this case as an effective means of developing students' ability to understand race and engage in public discussion of touchy social issues. The contemporary controversial issue for this unit was the intersection of race and identity in modern society and how it can generate conflict. The activities supported the enhancement of students' critical thinking and communication skills, and their ability to confront real-world issues and to analyze the meaning and messages of a variety of sources. Mr. Clark's case illustrates the features of effective practice with film to explore contemporary controversial issues. For example, he created and maintained a safe and supportive classroom environment, presented historical context for the contemporary controversial issues, chose activities that enhanced student understanding of the issues, and connected the topic and films to students' lives. And, although Mr. Clark believed race in society was a difficult topic to cover in class, he was willing to focus an entire unit on the topic because of his local context where issues of race and conflict are prominent in the school and community. For example, there was a heated curriculum controversy about the use of *The Adventures of Huckleberry Finn* in school and the students were in this heterogeneous class together after years in a mostly racially segregated leveling system. Mr. Clark believed this unit's focus on race created an excellent prospect for student growth and learning.

RACE THEN AND NOW: THE 1920S, *THE JAZZ SINGER*, AND TODAY

Case Description

Mr. Clark teaches a social studies elective class that studies U.S. history through film and music at Shermer High School in Central Connecticut. Shermer High School is one of the largest high schools in Connecticut with almost 2,000 students. The heterogeneous student population mirrors the state's diversity in terms of student backgrounds, socio-economic status, and second language learners. Approximately 20% of the student population is African American and 14% is Latino/a; 39% of the students receive free or reduced lunch.

The class, "History through Film and Music," is one of only three non-tracked social studies classes in the school and therefore is composed of students with a wide range of abilities and previous academic success. The class has 29 students, who are also diverse in terms of race/ethnicity, mirroring the school's population. The course is offered as a half-year senior elective in the spring and is very popular (there are two sections of the course, the other taught by a different teacher). Despite being an elective, the course is quite demanding of students with a heavy workload both in terms of the number of assignments and readings and in terms of the higher-order thinking required of students. Mr. Clark works hard to balance treating the students as young adults while pushing students to avoid "senior slump."

Mr. Clark views the class primarily as a history class that uses film and music as key media, as opposed to a film and music class that uses history as a context. The class focuses on 20th-century social history of the United States. The curriculum is chronological, working from the 1920s through the 1990s, as well as thematic. The major theme of the course is studying identity conflict as expressed in film, music, and society. In addition to a unit on the 1920s and race, other units range from the 1930s and the Great Depression using *O Brother, Where Art Thou?* (2000), to the 1950s and the birth of rock and roll using *La Bamba* (1987), to the 1980s (what he calls the "Cosby Era") using *Footloose* (1984). Each unit allows students to analyze a film with a focus on issues of social identity and music. In addition to these content goals, Mr. Clark's major objective is to make students critical consumers of film and music—not only to enjoy film as entertainment but to broaden their understanding by contemplating the place of film in society. Specifically, he wants students to analyze film for messages. He asks students to evaluate what filmmakers are trying to convey and how in different time periods music and film can stimulate larger social discussions.

Mr. Clark has been teaching for 10 years, all at Shermer High School, is actively involved in the school district and local community, and has become well known for his infusion of film and music into his history courses. He continually seeks out new challenges and learning opportunities and is currently working on a doctorate.

Unit Overview

The contemporary controversial issue for this unit was the intersection of race and identity in modern society and how it can generate conflict. The specific focus was on "blackface," an entertainment form dating back to the 19th-century U.S. South in which white performers would use makeup and costumes to appear as African Americans, and whether or not blackface is acceptable in today's society.

Mr. Clark's unit on the 1920s begins with activities that explore theories of blackface, including viewing *The Jazz Singer*. During and after viewing the film Mr. Clark asks his students to consider the ways in which identity conflict—racial, religious, generational, cultural—is shown in the film. The students are also required to consider how the film connects to historical trends such as the migration of African Americans from the South to Northern cities, the Harlem Renaissance, and the entertainment industry. Finally, the students examine the ways in which the film celebrates or demeans African-American culture. Next, Mr. Clark assigns readings about modern examples of blackface or race identity—1990s rapper MC Hammer, a blackface college party, and a protest against the film *Norbit*. He further illustrates the issue by showing clips depicting blackface from

Norbit, 1990s pop-rapper MC Hammer, the popular animated series *Sponge Bob Square Pants*, and the movie *Soul Man* (1986). Students are asked to discuss the similarities and differences between the historic and modern examples. The modern examples are then used as a mechanism for exploring racial attitudes and issues today and support a rich dialogue among the students. As Mr. Clark taught the unit, national and local contexts were discussed, ranging from protests over the depiction of African-American women in *Norbit* to Shermer High School's Board of Education considering a request from African-American parents to ban the teaching of Mark Twain's *The Adventures of Huckleberry Finn*. Throughout the unit students were continually asked to reflect on issues of identity (particularly racial) for both the films/video clips and personally for themselves on how the issue in the present connects to painful conflicts in the past.

Unit Outline

Mr. Clark's unit occurred over 10 class periods. Table 7.1 provides an overview of each day's activities. The class met every other day on a block schedule for almost 90 minutes, though several days were shorter on account of state-mandated testing. *The Jazz Singer* was viewed on days 3 and 4 of the unit.

Table 7.1 Outline of Lessons, Race: Then and Now

Day	Activity	Daily Guiding Questions and Goals
1	Define and discuss race and culture. Listen to and analyze music from U.S. history. View documentary film clip on music in U.S. history. Overview of the unit.	Questions: What is race? What is culture? Goals: Provide introduction to the unit. Analyze the historical context for the use of blackface in entertainment in terms of identity, race, and music.
2	Review historical context for the 1920s and *The Jazz Singer*. View documentary film clips on the roaring 20s, jazz, and black music in Harlem. Film stopped at various points for brief discussion. Listen to, analyze, and discuss Bessie Smith song "Pigs Feet." Homework: each student completes one of four readings on the history of blackface.	Questions: What is the historical context of the 1920s? Why was the African-American experience so central to American film and music in the 1920s despite the relatively small percentage of African Americans in the United States at the time (~11%)? Why did people do blackface in entertainment? Goals: Review/provide historical context for the 1920s and *The Jazz Singer*. Evaluate the role and contribution of the African-American experience to film and music of the 1920s.

Table 7.1 (continued)

Day	Activity	Daily Guiding Questions and Goals
3	Introduction to *The Jazz Singer.* View clip from documentary on the follies and jazz. View *The Jazz Singer.* Film stopped at various points for brief discussion.	Questions: What are the connections between *The Jazz Singer* and historical trends (e.g. great migration and Harlem Renaissance)? In what ways do you see African-American culture celebrated or demeaned in *The Jazz Singer*? What are the ways in which identity conflict is seen in *The Jazz Singer* (musical, racial, religious, generation)? Goals: Explore the role of race and identity in history as expressed through film. Analyze the connections between identity, race, *The Jazz Singer*, and historical trends.
4	View *The Jazz Singer.* Film stopped at various points for brief discussion.	Questions: What are the connections between *The Jazz Singer* and historical trends (e.g. great migration and Harlem Renaissance)? In what ways do you see African-American culture celebrated or demeaned in *The Jazz Singer*? What are the ways in which identity conflict is seen in *The Jazz Singer* (musical, racial, religious, generation)? Goals: Explore the role of race and identity in history as expressed through film. Analyze the connections between identity, race, *The Jazz Singer*, and historical trends.
5	Discussion and analysis of *The Jazz Singer* and readings on history of blackface. Homework: Read articles and answer questions about modern-day examples of blackface.	Questions: What are the ways in which identity conflict is seen in *The Jazz Singer* (musical, racial, religious, generation)? Is *The Jazz Singer* a good representation of racial issues in America during the 1920s? Goals: Explore the role of race and identity in history as expressed through film. Analyze the connections between identity, race, *The Jazz Singer*, and historical trends.

Table 7.1 (continued)

Day	Activity	Daily Guiding Questions and Goals
6	Discussion of examples of modern blackface in America.	Questions: What is the role of blackface today? What is the intent? What is the impact? Goals: Explore connections between historical uses of blackface and the use of blackface today. Evaluate the intent and impact of blackface today. Analyze and critique modern issues of identity and race.
7	View documentary clips of modern-day issues of identity and race. View popular culture clips of blackface and/or racial identity. For each clip, whole-class discussion of the similarities and differences to *The Jazz Singer*, connections to issues of identity and connections to American history.	Questions: How are issues of identity and race important today? Is blackface today okay to do? Under what circumstances? Goals: Analyze blackface in modern popular culture. Evaluate the intent and impact of blackface today. Analyze and critique modern issues of identity and race.
8	Continue viewing video clips and discussion of modern-day issues of identity, race, and blackface.	Questions: How are issues of identity and race important today? Is blackface today okay to do? Under what circumstances? Goals: Analyze blackface in modern popular culture. Evaluate the intent and impact of blackface today. Analyze and critique modern issues of identity and race.
9	Students work on film analysis paper. View documentary about blacks in Hollywood. Discussion of the historical context and current status of blacks in Hollywood.	Questions: What is the status of blacks in Hollywood today and what historical trends and influences remain? Goals: Explore the role of race and identity in Hollywood and the potential impact on films.

Table 7.1 (continued)

Day	Activity	Daily Guiding Questions and Goals
10	Discussion of controversy at Shermer H.S. over the use of *Huck Finn* in the curriculum and larger issues of race in the local community.	Questions: What issues of race and identity exist today in our own community? What is the line between lampooning racism and being racist? Goals: To connect issues of race and identity to the students' current community and personal lives.

Films

Mr. Clark showed all of *The Jazz Singer* as well as short clips from several other films and television shows. Each of the films/videos used is described in Table 7.2.

Table 7.2 Description of Films/Video Clips

Check and Double Check (1930) Melville W. Brown (Director) RKO Radio Pictures	*Check and Double Check* brought the "Amos 'n' Andy" radio characters to film. Amos and Andy were African-American characters who were grossly stereotyped. The film starred Freeman Gosden and Charles Correll, who were the radio voices. Since they were white, they appeared in the film in blackface. The storyline of the film has Amos and Andy running an open-air taxi business. In the specific scene shown they are in their taxi office fielding phone calls and trying to attract business.
The Jazz Singer (1927) Alan Crosland (Director) Warner Brothers	*The Jazz Singer* was one of the first films to have sound and stars Al Jolson as Jakie Rabinowitz, a cantor's son in New York. However, instead of going into the family business of being a cantor, Jakie prefers to sing jazz and ragtime. Becoming Jack Robin, Jakie leaves home and is disowned by his father. He builds a successful career as a jazz singer and eventually comes home to New York to sing on Broadway. Throughout the film Jakie is conflicted between his professional ambitions and his Jewish heritage. In the end he is able to reunite with his family and keep his career. As part of his show, Jakie performs in blackface.

Table 7.2 (continued)

MC Hammer MTV Hip Hop Video Awards (1990)	MC Hammer performs "U Can't Touch This" at the 1990 MTV Hip Hop Video Awards. His song-and-dance draws from 1920s follies.
Norbit (2007) Brian Robbins (Director) Dreamworks through Paramont Pictures	Eddie Murphy stars as Norbit, who is raised in an orphanage. Murphy also plays the head of the orphanage (who adopts him) as well as Rasputia, an overweight and overbearing woman whom he marries. In the end he dumps the evil Rasputia for his childhood love, Kate. The film contains many racial stereotypes and was widely panned by critics.
Soul Man (1986) Steve Minor (Director) New World Pictures	Mark, played by C. Thomas Howell, is a white man who pretends to be black in order to receive a scholarship to attend Harvard University by taking "bronzing pills" and "acting" black. He finds that being black in American society is harder than he realized and also falls in love with the student whose scholarship he took (because he took her scholarship she has to work a job while going to school and raising a son). He comes to regret his poor choice and decides to repay the money.
Sponge Bob Square Pants "Squirrel Jokes" (TV show, 1999–present) Stephen Hillenburg (Creator) Nickelodeon	Sponge Bob is a cartoon sea sponge (who looks more like a kitchen sponge) who lives in the Pacific Ocean town of Bikini Bottom. In the episode "Squirrel Jokes," Sponge Bob is doing stand-up comedy. When he does poorly, he reverts to telling squirrel jokes (one of the audience members is a squirrel) and dresses up in "squirrel face" (like blackface but using squirrels). The audience loves his show, but the squirrel, his friend Sandy, is offended.
Various documentaries (in the order in which they are shown in the unit)	Day 1 *American Experience: Stephen Foster* (2000) Randall MacLowry (Director) PBS Day 2 *American Experience, New York: A Documentary Film* (1999) Ric Burns (Director) PBS

Table 7.2 (continued)

> Day 3
> *The Age of Ballyhoo* (1986)
> David Shepard (Director)
> Egami Media
>
> Day 7
> *People Like Us: Social Class in America*, Part 3:
> Salt of the Earth (2001)
> Louis Alvarez and Andrew Kolker (Directors)
> PBS
>
> Day 9
> *America Beyond the Color Line: Black in
> Hollywood* (2002)
> Henry Louis Gates, Jr. (Writer)
> PBS

FILM ACTIVITIES

Day 1

Mr. Clark began the unit by facilitating a whole-class discussion about defining race and culture and the differences between these two terms. Students who volunteered responses described race as something "natural" that included issues of place of origin and skin color, whereas culture was described as "learned" and encompassing issues of lifestyle, expression, and family. Mr. Clark emphasized the socially constructed nature of race and used this discussion to set the context for the intersection of race, culture, and identity in media depictions.

Next, Mr. Clark played three songs that communicate messages of culture and identity. He chose to use songs from a historical context to demonstrate the historical continuity of the issue: the Dutch song about the first Thanksgiving, "We Gather Together"; an early Irish settler song, "Whiskey in the Jar"; and a slave song from Africa. Mr. Clark provided a listening guide with questions that focused on the larger issues of music and culture: "How is American music like a melting pot? Like a salad? Like gumbo? What issues do you believe may exist/have existed in U.S. history due to American music being a mix of cultural/racial influences when for much of this history society has been segregated along cultural/racial lines?" Students were also asked to list what they saw as influences on music.

After a brief discussion of the songs and answers to the questions. Mr. Clark showed a very short video clip from the PBS program *American Experience: Stephen Foster* (2000) that discussed music in U.S. history ranging from Westward Expansion and "O, Susannah" to the invention of the phonograph. Finally, Mr. Clark previewed the remainder of the unit and explained the unit's summative assessment to his students.

Day 2

Mr. Clark provided the historical context for the 1920s and *The Jazz Singer*. He asked students to discuss as a whole class what they already knew about five topics: the "Great Migration" (of African Americans from the South to Northern urban areas), the Harlem Renaissance, Prohibition, new media (radio and movies), and the media industry (radio business, movie industry). For each topic students provided basic information and Mr. Clark added depth.

Mr. Clark then showed a short documentary video clip from the PBS program *American Experience: New York, A Documentary Film* (1999) that presented these five topics through visual representations. He periodically stopped the film to connect images and ideas in the film to the five topics. Afterward, Mr. Clark handed out lyrics to the Bessie Smith song "Gimme a Pig Foot and a Bottle of Beer" and played the song. The class briefly analyzed the song, looking at how it addressed the five topics, and he asked them to connect the message of the song to today. For homework students were required to complete their analysis of the song utilizing a guide provided by Mr. Clark that also asked students to provide historical context for the music, to provide music industry context for the music, to connect the music to the course theme of identity, to discuss the aesthetic qualities of the music, and to pull all of these pieces together for a final conclusion. Using this song served to deepen the students' understanding of the context, to provide a primary source example of music from the era, and to scaffold activities with *The Jazz Singer* in which students would also be required to connect a 1920s entertainment product to today.

Day 3

Mr. Clark began by introducing *The Jazz Singer*. He "warned" the students that it was an older film with only partial sound. He also explained its basic premise and discussed some of the film's issues of identity. Next, he provided students with copies of a film viewing guide (Table 7.3).

Mr. Clark explained that all of the big issues for the unit are covered in the film except for the connections to today. He also checked for student understanding of the difference between celebrating and demeaning and reminded them that by the end of the unit they would have to decide whether the film did more to celebrate or demean African-American culture.

In order for students to understand what the follies were Mr. Clark showed a clip from the documentary *The Age of Ballyhoo* (1986) that focused on Aunt Jemima follies. Mr. Clark and the students discussed the message of follies in comparison with jazz (one perhaps more demeaning, the other more celebrating), where they each occurred (on Broadway, in nightclubs), and caricatures and stereotyping. Students brought up the issue of team mascots such as the Cleveland Indians (baseball) and Washington Redskins (football), and Mr. Clark reminded them of the Shermer H.S. mascot (also a term

Table 7.3 The Jazz Singer Film Viewing Guide

For your final film review you will need to cover several topics so please cite specific evidence in each of the following categories:			
Connections between film and historical trends like great migration, Harlem Renaissance, prohibition, new forms of media, and the media industry:			
Ways in which you see AA culture celebrated or demeaned			
Celebrated		Demeaned	
Ways in which identity conflict is seen in the film:			
musical identity	racial identity	religious identity	generation identity
Production quality of the film including all the major areas we discussed in class and that I again photocopied for you on the back of this here paper.			

related to Native Americans)—a connection that made the discussion very personal and real to the students. Toward the end, the class began watching *The Jazz Singer*. Mr. Clark periodically stopped the film or spoke over silent portions of the film to scaffold student viewing by pointing out key issues, elaborating on something in the film, and probing student understanding through questions. For example, Mr. Clark stopped the film to ask students how, in the 1920s, it is possible to have a major film with Jewish characters and to explain how the record with music that went along with the film was a big deal and the first real movie soundtrack. He also asked students to indicate issues of identity they were seeing in the film.

Day 4

Mr. Clark began class by handing out homework readings on the history of blackface. Each student was assigned one of five readings to be read for a discussion on day 5 of the unit. The five readings included:

- *Bert Williams, Black-on-Black Minstrelsy and the African American Diaspora*, Introduction, by Louis Chude-Sokei (2006);
- *Raising Cain: Blackface Performance from Jim Crow to Hip Hop*, Chapter 3—"Blame It on Cain," by W. T. Lhamon, Jr. (2000);
- *Black Like You: Blackface, Whiteface, Insult & Imitation in American Popular Culture*, Chapter 3, "Black Like You, Blackface Minstrelsy, the Rock & Roll Years," by John Strausbaugh (2006);

- *Black Like You*: *Blackface, Whiteface, Insult & Imitation in American Popular Culture*, Chapter 6, "Black & White Film, Reel One, Uncle Tom's Cinema," by John Strausbaugh (2006);
- *Black Like You*: *Blackface, Whiteface, Insult & Imitation in American Popular Culture*, Chapter 1, "A Pestilence of Ignunce, Blackface in the Twenty-first Century," by John Strausbaugh (2006).

To support understanding of the readings the students were provided guiding questions: (1) Why was blackface performance present in America before the 1920s? (2) What was the intent of blackface performance, and why did people perform in this way? (3) What was the impact of blackface performance on all Americans?

For the remainder of class Mr. Clark and the students watched *The Jazz Singer*. The students continued to take notes on their worksheet and once again Mr. Clark periodically stopped the film (or spoke over the silent portions of the film). For example Mr. Clark pointed out instances of generation identity conflict, explained the significance of Yom Kippur to Jews, and asked students to think about how they thought jazz was being received by people in the 1920s. Mr. Clark also kept playing up the conflicts in the film to "keep students on the edge of their seats." At one point he stopped the film and asked student to predict what would happen—what would the main character, Jackie, decide to do? Would he choose his father and religion or his work and passion for performing?

Day 5

Mr. Clark set up the discussion by asking students to think about the intent of entertainment, particularly blackface, against the actual impact blackface might have on people's attitudes, beliefs, and identities. He also asked students to think about the context of the readings, highlighting the fact that they were written by white males who are all historians and asking students to think about what that means about the articles' bias. Then, using the "intent vs. impact" framework, students formed jigsaw groups so that each had one person who had read each of the homework articles on the history of blackface and spent 11 minutes discussing the issue. Following the small-group work, Mr. Clark asked students if they had something they did not understand that the class should discuss so "everyone was informed." Several students asked questions or made statements: "What is the deal with the white circle around their eyes and mouth [when doing blackface]?" and "The article made me mad—how they were treating blacks—but now that I know it was a white guy [who wrote it] I'm confused."

Mr. Clark proceeded to ask groups to report out what they learned from their articles about the intent and impact of blackface. One of the prominent issues of intent that arose was whether some blacks did blackface as a way to counter whites who performed in blackface. One of the key issues of impact was whether blackface was a self-fulfilling prophecy whereby blacks began to believe that reality matched what they saw in blackface. Mr. Clark then refocused the intent/impact discussion on *The Jazz Singer*: Was Scott Joplin (Jackie) doing blackface in a bad way? And why couldn't he sing jazz on Broadway as a white man? Student responses indicated they were clearly engaged with the film and the issue of blackface and identity. Most defended Jackie and thought his intent was not harmful. However, they also believed the impact of the film may have been more detrimental. Mr. Clark also asked about connections between the readings and *The Jazz Singer*.

Next, Mr. Clark asked about the rapper Eminem and his dress and behavior and how that spoke to issues of race and identity. Again the students defended the entertainer and believed his intent was not bad. Students also brought up the issue of their own identity with one student commenting identity should be "about how you view yourself and not how others view you." Some students agreed but other students remarked that you could not escape how others judge you. This series of discussions served to connect *The Jazz Singer* to a broader historical context and begin the process of relating issues raised in the film to today.

For the last segment of class Mr. Clark provided a handout that listed seven "main theories of blackface performance in America": (1) the "Cain" and freedom phenomenon; (2) a dominant culture demeaning an oppressed culture through imitation; (3) a satire of racist views; (4) justification of racism; (5) an agent of cultural diffusion in a culturally segregated society; (6) a caricature that African Americans were forced to portray to please the dominant culture in a time when there were no other opportunities for African Americans in entertainment; (7) a caricature that African Americans developed to poke fun at the dominant culture's view of their identity. At the end he reviewed each one, many of which were discussed in the articles read for today. These theories would be used for the homework as well as activities on day 6. For the last segment of class Mr. Clark assigned the homework: readings and questions about modern-day examples of blackface. The readings included:

- an article from MSNBC, " 'Black-Face' College Party Causes Controversy," about a college party at Clemson University;
- a short excerpt describing a protest by black activities in Los Angeles against the film *Norbit*'s portrayal of black women;
- a short excerpt from *Raising Cain: Blackface Performance from Jim Crow to Hip Hop*, "Finding Jim Crow," by W. T. Lhamon, Jr., that discusses the entertainer MC Hammer;
- an excerpt from *Black Like You: Blackface, Whiteface, Insult & Imitation in American Popular Culture*, Chapter 1, that discussed "Shirley Q. Liquor," a white man who does blackface as a black woman; and
- a newspaper letter to the editor from *The Hartford Courant* (2/7/07, p. A10).

To guide the readings students were asked to answer the following questions: (1) Why is blackface still used in America today? (2) What is the intent of blackface today? (3) What is the impact of blackface on America today? (4) What theory of blackface can be applied to the modern examples of blackface you read about? The articles varied in their length and difficulty so Mr. Clark assigned the longer and more difficult readings to higher-performing students.

Day 6

Class began in small jigsaw groups with one person in each group having read each article. After small-group discussions, Mr. Clark asked each group to report out to the whole class. One of the key issues that arose was whether blackface in 2009 is acceptable. The students were divided (not along racial lines) about the appropriateness or offensiveness of blackface and other types of racial stereotyping. For the remainder of class Mr. Clark facilitated (and at time moderated) a passionate discussion of race and identity that touched on popular culture, broader societal issues, and the students' personal lives. Although the readings generated the initial issues, Mr. Clark let the students determine the direction and scope of the discussion. For example, several students discussed what they saw as generational differences. They discussed events their parents may have lived through, such as the Civil Rights movement, that give their parents a different perspective on issues of race and, in several students' view, made their parents more passionate about the topic.

Other students did not think there was a generation conflict in their family, but agreed that each individual reacts to racial issues such as blackface based on their own experiences and personal biases. All of the students agreed that racism still exists and is an important issue in society and to them personally.

At this point the conversation turned to the difference between *Norbit*, in which Eddie Murphy, as an African-American male, is making fun of African-American women, and Shirley Q. Liquor, a white male making fun of African-American women. The students who spoke believed there is a difference even if their intent may be the same. Murphy, as an African American, is "allowed" to do this or it is at least seen as relatively acceptable, but Shirley Q. Liquor is less acceptable and more likely to be seen as racist. Students then related this to two similar issues in their own lives. An Asian student said he and his Asian friends will "rag on each other" and specifically make remarks that are Asian stereotypes, but that this is okay because they are all Asian. However, if a non-Asian made these remarks they would be very upset. An African-American student echoed these sentiments and commented about how "everyone knows" that blacks can call each other "nigger" but that whites cannot use the word without being offensive Mr. Clark's lesson facilitated a rich discussion because he had created a safe and open classroom environment. It also illustrated how film can help spark discussion about contemporary controversial issues—students used blackface as an important reference point and couched many of their comments in terms of intent and impact and issues of identity. However, the students were also emotionally on edge and several were clearly agitated. Toward the end of class an African-American female said (quietly to herself) "I can't listen, I can't handle it."

Day 7, 8

Mr. Clark began by asking students to reflect on the previous discussion and "write one thing you wanted to say or ask last class but did not OR something you were thinking. Have it be like a bathing suit—long enough to cover the topic, but short enough to be interesting." He was concerned that students with minority opinions or who were shy may not have expressed their views and wanted to assess their learning and obtain a clearer picture of how the students were thinking about the issues of identity and race. Students turned these in under their own names but with the assurance that Mr. Clark would be the only person to see them. (He later commented that quite a few students wrote things that were not discussed in class and that this writing exercise was very helpful in assessing his students' learning.)

Next students folded a paper into four quadrants and labeled them: (1) similar to *The Jazz Singer*; (2) connections to identity and music themes; (3) connections to American history; (4) different from *The Jazz Singer*. The students viewed a series of documentary film clips from *People like Us: Social Class in America* (2001) and filled in the four-quadrant sheet. The documentary clips provided examples of Americans dealing with issues of identity, class, and race. For example, in one scene college students are followed out on a weekend night for what they called "dive bar weekends." The students went to "corner" bars rather than "trendy" bars because they thought they could interact with more "genuine" people. Many of these "genuine" people see the college students as "yuppie" outsiders. The point of the clips was to segue to the contemporary issues in popular culture.

At the end of the period and continuing into the next day, Mr. Clark showed students more clips from popular media: one older (Amos 'n' Andy) and four more recent, (*Sponge Bob*, *Soul Man*, MC Hammer's performance, and *Norbit*). Students were provided a film guide that asked them to list what theory of blackface best fit each media clip, to list any other modern examples of blackface they could think of, to describe connections between the historical examples of blackface discussed during the unit (e.g., Bert Williams) and the modern examples, to complete a Venn diagram comparing historical and modern examples of blackface, and to answer a final question: "Ultimately, when push comes to shove how do you think that the blackface phenomenon in American history should be studied or do you think we should try to collectively forget about this phenomenon and leave it out of historic and academic studies? Why?"

Throughout, Mr. Clark highlighted important points related to race and identity and answered students' questions. He emphasized that blackface is not the only issue—that the students should contemplate broader issues of cross-cultural imitation and insult. The day concluded with a short discussion of some of the issues in the film. Interestingly, the clips were all essentially comedies that the students seemed to find entertaining, yet they also were effective in raising important issues of identity.

Day 9

Students spent half the period working on their summative assessment for the unit. For this assignment students had to write a review of a modern movie that deals with issues of blackface, cross-cultural imitation, and/or racial identity. Five films were suggested: *White Chicks* (2004), *The Nutty Professor* (1996), *The Nutty Professor II: The Klumps* (2000), *Norbit* (2007), and *Soul Man* (1986). Students could ask for approval of a different film. Their review had to include a main thesis describing their overall analysis of the film followed by connections to the course theme of identity, inclusion of historical contexts related to American cultural history, and incorporation of modern perspectives on the use of blackface and depictions of African Americans in film today. Students were expected to use their class notes as well as the class readings as part of their film analysis. In the second half of class, students watched excerpts from Henry Louis Gates, Jr.'s documentary *America beyond the Color Line: Black in Hollywood* (2002). The clips focused on Gates's interviews with black Hollywood stars on race in Hollywood. Following the clips Mr. Clark led a discussion about whether the students believed conditions in Hollywood for black actors and filmmakers had changed.

Day 10

The final day of the unit focused on a class discussion on issues of identity and race at Shermer H.S. and in the local community. The centerpiece of the discussion was a controversy over the use of Mark Twain's *The Adventures of Huckleberry Finn* in the school curriculum. Some African-American parents had complained that the book was racist and should be removed from the curriculum. The Board of Education agreed. After a backlash from other parents and teachers, the board reversed its decision and reinstated the book into the curriculum. The class discussed how Mark Twain was a white man who created a black character (the slave Jim) and debated the fine line between lampooning racism and being a racist.

Mr. Clark's unit on race and identity is a powerful example of using film to discuss contemporary controversial issues. Students explored the controversy of racial identity in its historic context and in society today, with blackface as a focal point. The lessons helped students to develop critical thinking skills (impact vs. intent of popular culture), to confront real-world issues (race and identity in society and popular culture), to enhance communication skills (discussing issues, writing ideas), and to analyze the meaning and messages of a variety of sources (text readings, feature films, documentary films, newspaper articles, and fellow students' personal lives). The unit also took advantage of the diversity of opinions among students.

Several aspects of Mr. Clark's practice are exemplary. He created and maintained a safe and supportive classroom environment, provided significant historical context for the contemporary controversial issues, connected the topic and films to students' interests and experiences, and chose activities that assisted student learning and thinking about the issues. These are good practices in dealing with contemporary controversial issues with or without the use of film. However, his use of film clearly enhanced these practices.

The use of film contributed to the positive learning environment by providing a medium familiar to students and through the use of comedy. It also took the burden off of Mr. Clark to introduce the topics and allowed him to be more of a facilitator and moderator than a "source" of ultimate knowledge, perhaps promoting more freedom of discussion. *The Jazz Singer* served as an accessible means of learning historical context and, through the focus on blackface and comparison to recent media clips, provided a conduit from the past to the present. Finally, the films also helped to connect the issues of race and identity to students in ways more effective than non-visual sources. The students' written and oral responses to *The Jazz Singer* and the modern film clips demonstrated that the films acted as powerful audio-visual stimuli that helped students directly visualize many of the messages and narratives.

REFLECTION ON THE CASE

Perhaps the most impressive aspect of Mr. Clark's unit was the careful thought he gave to anticipating how the unit might play out and to potential complications both for the issue of race in general and for the issue of blackface specifically. First, he considered whether the topic and film fit within his course curriculum. He realized that he could have used *The Jazz Singer* and focused on the issue of generational gaps and still fit within the course's curriculum. However, although he recognized that race is considered "a fairly dangerous topic," he felt strongly that it was important to discuss. His rationale was that the local community has a 50/50 white/minority population and the issue of race has played out at the intersection of the community and school through controversy over a school redistricting plan and the debate over *The Adventures of Huckleberry Finn*. In addition, he believed his students "are kids who have been culturally and racially segregated through the school's leveling system for three years and are now together in this class." Mr. Clark considered these factors and saw this unit as a great opportunity to discuss issues that were prevalent in the school community and students' everyday lives and to place them in a historical context.

A second area of reflection for Mr. Clark was predicting possible reactions to the unit from his administrators, parents, and the broader community. He felt comfortable with the unit given the congruity between his goals and activities and the course's goals as approved by the district. Therefore, he did not feel he needed to clear the unit with anyone. He also recognized that race is "a most touchy issue in the district right now and on most people's minds" and felt at times that there "was almost a McCarthy [attitude] related to issues of school and race." At the same time he believed it "is okay to talk about it, kids want to know [about issues of race]," and "it is also difficult not to talk about it." In addition, he was concerned about showing blackface in film even in a historical context. Many see blackface as particularly offensive, so his choice of these particular films required careful calculation. Mr. Clark is also an experienced and tenured teacher. He acknowledged that "there are people who would stay a million miles away and I understand."

Third, Mr. Clark anticipated students' potential responses to the topic and specifically to *The Jazz Singer* and other film clips. Not only does the topic lend itself to potentially powerful reactions, films can also be particularly effective at evoking emotional responses thanks to their unique audio-visual communication. Mr. Clark was concerned about the potential reaction from one student, whom he knew well from a previous class, and who he worried might get upset. Anticipating this, he contacted one of her parents ahead of time to explain the unit and discuss ways to offer support at school and at home.

There are two specific problems visible in Mr. Clark's approach. First, the unit used a rich array of resources and asked the students to complete numerous higher-order thinking tasks. However, at times the breadth and depth of resources and activities seemed overwhelming and perhaps distracting. This was exacerbated by the length of time it took to complete the unit (a month and a half for the ten class periods) due to the school's block schedule, snow days, testing days, and winter vacation. Fewer, more select resources and activities might allow for a less frantic pace within class and more cohesion around the central themes. Specifically, whereas the preparation of students to view *The Jazz Singer* and clips from other feature films was outstanding, many of the documentary clips could be better supported by teacher instruction and integrated into the unit, with some cut altogether. In his own reflections on the unit, Mr. Clark agreed and commented that next year he would need to do more to condense some of his materials, particularly around the historical context.

The second problem revolves around classroom discussion. There were many rich and powerful discussions throughout the unit. However, despite what was mostly a supportive and friendly classroom environment, at times a handful of students seemed to withdraw from the conversation or not have time to express their views. Although *The Jazz Singer* and other feature film clips seemed to grease the wheels and stimulate dialogue, students could benefit from more time to process and alternative ways of expressing their views. The pace of discussion was often so fast that students who need to process before speaking may have been left behind. Other students may be willing to write their views or express them in small group, but not to the whole class. Mr. Clark proposed that next year he would provide more opportunities for students to express views in other ways than whole-class discussions including small groups and personal reflection writing.

Strategies for Using Film to Teach about Contemporary Controversial Issues

Mr. Clark's specific practices point to broader recommendations when using film to teach contemporary controversial issues. Although these practices are generally good teaching and not necessarily exclusive to using film, they are particularly effective for incorporating film. First, it is important to consider how a film and topic fits within a course's and school's curricular objectives. Being able to directly connect a film and topic to these objectives can inoculate a teacher from disgruntled parents and administrators. When controversial issues arise in textbooks or more traditional curricular materials they are easier to defend, but with film there is often an extra burden to justify its inclusion.

Second, it is critical to reflect on possible reactions from administrators and those in the broader community to determine whether a quick check-in with a department head or principal might be appropriate. However, we must not avoid teaching these issues because it is precisely these controversial issues that can resonate with students and help them understand the world around them—both in real life and in film. Understandably, new teachers and those without tenure may be reluctant to tackle such issues. However, if it is done wisely—situated within the curriculum, presenting balanced views, honoring students' views and diversity of opinions—even untenured teachers should be on solid ground.

Third, as much as possible, it helps to anticipate potential student responses to particularly controversial issues and specific films, especially given the power of films to enhance emotional responses more than most other sources. These can be addressed with the student and if necessary others to support the student to participate in the lessons in a constructive way, such as when Mr. Clark contacted the parent of the student he expected might get upset. The critical issue is to meet both a student's intellectual needs and academic requirements of the unit as well as their emotional needs.

Strategies for Choosing Films to Teach about Contemporary Controversial Issues

Mr. Clark chose *The Jazz Singer* because it is a landmark American film and because it "hits the nail on the head for jazz culture and identity for a new generation." He believed it did an excellent job at exploring issues of identity while also providing historical context for racial issues. He also chose the film because it focused on music and entertainment (one of the themes in the course curriculum) and provided a musical connection to the time period being studied. However, Mr. Clark was concerned that the movie was long, much of it silent, and nearly a century old and therefore students could be bored; however, he felt that the connections to today and to the unit's objectives were worth the risks.

More broadly, there are several criteria to consider when choosing films as part of a unit on contemporary controversial issues. Mr. Clark suggests that the most important criterion is to choose films that strongly connect to the overall theme of the course as well as specific unit objectives. This criterion applies for all uses of film, not just teaching about controversial issues. Mr. Clark also believes that films need to be engaging. Some students may be tempted to shy away from participating in conversations about contemporary controversial issues, so having films that engage them may be able to draw them into the conversation. However, a potential hindrance with overly engaging films is that they may become the basis for too much of their beliefs and ideas and become what Mr. Clark says is the "norm"—a reference point for all discussions of the contemporary controversial issue. Instead of the powerful medium of film supporting the discussion, it could blind students to seeing other perspectives or contexts.

Additionally, Mr. Clark says film should offer different perspectives that students might not be exposed to. A critical component of effectively discussing controversial issues is to provide multiple perspectives, and employing a variety of films that can do this. In this respect films can be used to provide a counter-perspective from what is being offered by other sources. On the other hand, powerful films that represent the dominant social discourse today may themselves need to be counterbalanced by the inclusion of other sources.

Another consideration in choosing films to discuss contemporary controversial issues is that many of these controversial issues, and the portrayal of them in films, can be distressing for students. Contemporary controversial issues often involve human suffering and in some cases may be relevant to students' own lives. Taking into account the specific issue, the portrayal of the issue in film, and the personal experiences of students is crucially important. In this case, an African-American student became upset because she personally connected so strongly to the issues discussed in class. Other students did not became publicly upset, but did express in writing being highly emotional during several of the class conversations.

A final issue to consider when choosing film relates to the appropriateness of clips in terms of genre. In this unit the modern film clips were primarily comedies. The use of comedies can be a great way to defuse the tension that might exist around a controversial issue. For example, we have seen many teachers use clips from *Seinfeld* or films as a way to introduce the issue of gay rights. However, although comedies can ease anxieties and engage students, they risk the potential of undercutting the seriousness of the issue and should be used carefully and appropriately.

There are numerous films to consider using to teach about contemporary controversial issues. A few examples include *Hotel Rwanda* (2004), *Good Night, and Good Luck* (2005), and *Redacted* (2007). These three films can be effectively used to introduce students to a controversial issue (or continue a dialogue about an issue), to powerfully bring the controversial issue to life, and to offer alternative perspectives. In addition these films are the appropriate genre for the given topics and fit within most schools' history curriculum.

Hotel Rwanda is one account of the genocide in Rwanda during the 1990s where in a 100-day period almost a million people were killed. The story, about the conflict between the Hutus and the Tutsis, is told through the eyes of Paul Rusesabagina, a Rwandan who saved many of his fellow countrymen. The film is an emotionally captivating way to capture students' interest and motivate them to learn more. It exposes students to an event many of them do not hear about in the mainstream media and can be part of broader discussions about human rights issues and the role of Western nations and the United Nations in protecting human rights.

Good Night, and Good Luck is a Cold War narrative and tells the true story of Edward R. Murrow's battles with Senator McCarthy and his attempts to expose McCarthy's Red scare tactics through his television show. The film is overtly about the Cold War, but also contains messages about modern-day America and the role of the government and the media in society. The film can be shown to discuss issues of the role of government in society and what limits should be placed on government power, the role of the media as a government watchdog, and the use of scare tactics to influence public opinion. The film can present a perspective critical of the government not present in textbooks, without the teacher being critical.

Redacted is a fictional story based on real events from the war in Iraq. It focuses on a group of American soldiers at a check-point in Iraq and provides the perspectives of the soldiers, the media, and local Iraqi people. It can be used to discuss the controversy around the war in Iraq as well as the role of the media in society today. It offers powerful images of the consequences of war, provides multiple perspectives, and provides teachers with a way to approach discussing the Iraq war without having to be the "source" themselves.

Teaching contemporary controversial issues is an important part of preparing our students to effectively participate in a democracy. Film is an important resource to consider using as part of activities that discuss these controversial issues.

CHAPTER 8

Using Film to Teach Controversial Issues in History

Figure 8.1 Kingdom of Heaven (2005). Balian of Ibelin (Orlando Bloom) fights for Jerusalem during the Crusades.

Although all historical events have consequences, certain events or issues in the past are particularly profound in their effects or historical reach. These events or issues remain controversial because they are divisive, painful, or ambiguous in the moral responses they elicit in people today. Depending on the social identities, ideological perspectives, or values of the individual, the event or issue can be interpreted and given meaning in very different ways. For this reason, controversies in history naturally point to connections between the past and the world today. History movies can serve as dramatic tools in the classroom to focus student attention on controversies in the past and think about their legacy for the present and future. The following case explores how film can be used to teach about controversial issues in history, focusing on a unit that used *Kingdom of Heaven* (2005) to teach about the medieval Crusades and religious conflict in the Middle East (see Table 8.2 for a description of the film).

The defining features of a historical controversy are that it casts a long shadow down to the present, that it remains of special interest to people today, and that there is still disagreement or debate over how to evaluate its meaning and legacy. Some issues are controversial only in historical context—for example, slavery no longer exists in the United States and its existence is not a debate in our society today, yet the nature and effects of slavery are still heated issues in American history. Other issues may not have been controversial in the past but are considered controversial in light of present-day values or have become controversial because they have implications for political debates today—such as historical discrimination or past legal restrictions against particular social groups now seeking greater representation, rights, or resources. Some historical controversies revolve around a specific event that can be meaningfully looked at on its own, such as the attack by U.S. forces on Native Americans at Wounded Knee in 1890. Others consist of a longer series of interconnected or consecutive events, such as Indian removal in the eastern United States in the 1830s and the Trail of Tears. Historical controversies also can be persistent social or political issues across time, involving similar or interconnected events that take place over decades or even centuries—such as religious conflict between Christians, Jews, and Muslims. As shown by these examples involving race, racism, and ethnic conflict, what happened in the past directly relates to social and political conditions and national or ethnic identities in the present.

Historical controversies are important to history education because by their nature they involve multiple perspectives and alternative interpretations over what they mean for our world today. Unlike basic memorization of historical events, controversies in the past engage students in critical thinking, evaluating arguments, and interpretation of meaning. Fundamental to this learning outcome is helping students to recognize that there is no one simple answer or innately correct way to look at the issue—it can be interpreted in alternate ways depending on the values and identities brought to how it is framed. This can even extend to how the event or issue is labeled or named. Is what happened at Wounded Knee a "battle" or "massacre"? Were the Crusades a European invasion of the Muslim lands in the Middle East or a defensive war to protect Christians in the Byzantine Empire and the Holy Land?

Such ambiguities, alternative interpretations, and multiple perspectives can make it difficult to teach controversies in the history classroom. Many students come with established notions that the history is only "what happened" in the past and that there is just one right answer. Considering multiple interpretations or alternate viewpoints in history can be a strange new demand—part of why educational researcher Sam Wineburg has called historical thinking an "unnatural act" for young learners (Wineburg, 2001). "Presentism" is a natural instinct for many students: evaluating the past exclusively in terms of present-day attitudes, values, and knowledge. Even when modern viewpoints are diverse or have room for disagreement, they are still modern-day constructs that are anachronistic to people in the past. When students settle for presentism, they simplify a complex past by looking for one easy conclusion that comfortably fits with what they already know and think about the world. Getting students to recognize and challenge presentism requires the intervention of a teacher prepared to provide appropriate content knowledge. Teaching controversies in history can be daunting because it often involves difficult or dense content topics and can require considerable scope of subject matter knowledge, for both the teacher and the students.

History feature films have much to offer teachers when it comes to raising historical controversies in the classroom. First, movies can help students visualize an otherwise abstract past. Seeing what happened as a kind of realistic experience can make the controversy more approachable for students. Second, the dramatic storytelling essential to most movies can engage students emotionally in the issues and values at stake. Being emotionally engaged in the controversy can make it seem more immediate and important rather than distant and unfathomable. Third, most history movies emphasize a dramatic or controversial event in the past and offer a particular viewpoint on it. Sometimes movies intentionally try to incorporate the perspectives of multiple sides or alternative viewpoints—though the viewpoints are not necessarily treated equally. Other movies strongly emphasize just one perspective and clearly want the viewer to empathize with it. Either kind of film has educational potential. A film with multiple perspectives can be used to get students to recognize and consider each; a film based in just one perspective can be used to get students to examine its strengths and limitations and consider what other possible viewpoints are missing from the film.

Most importantly, history movies convey messages about what the filmmakers believe a controversial past means for contemporary audiences. Often this plays out in movies as portraying one side or perspective as the heroes and another side or perspective as the villains. Of course, real history does not divide so clearly or cleanly and always involves shades of gray. History movies can be used by teachers to draw student attention to a historical controversy, to examine the side or perspectives taken by the filmmakers, and to critique the messages that the film narrative aims to convey about what the issue means for our world today. Ridley Scott's *Kingdom of Heaven* is an example of a film that attempts to portray multiple perspectives on the medieval Crusades: Christian settlers who are willing to coexist with Muslims (represented by Tiberias and Balian); reasonable Muslim rulers willing to make truces and negotiate trade with the Christians (represented by Saladin and Nasir); and militant Europeans and Muslims who push both sides into war. The film clearly wants the viewer to empathize with the characters it presents as religious moderates over the factions it presents as fanatical. The main character becomes a passionate multicultural defender who rejects religious extremism in the Holy Land. This message is a powerfully presented interpretation of the Crusades and their legacy of religious conflict that students can analyze using the content knowledge and instructional support provided by the teacher (Metzger, 2005).

The rest of this chapter explores how history movies can be a powerful tool for engaging students in examining a controversial issue in history and its connections and implications for the world today. This case specifically examines the instructional use of *Kingdom of Heaven* to teach about the medieval Crusades (1095–1291) and their legacy of conflict with the Muslim world. Mr. Jackson's case illustrates important features of effective practice in using a movie to teach about a controversial issue in history. Most notably, his unit emphasized multiple perspectives. The film served as a tool for visualizing and dramatizing perspectives. He wanted students to consider that the Crusades meant different things to different groups in the past and were subject to a variety of motivations. Mr. Jackson wanted to move student thinking beyond presentism to look at how crusaders and Muslims at the time felt about the conflict. Furthermore, a chief goal was for students to reflect on the legacy of the controversial historical event for our world today from alternative viewpoints.

THE CRUSADES AND *KINGDOM OF HEAVEN* IN MR. JACKSON'S CLASS

Case Description

This case describes the classroom practices of Mr. Jackson in one of his Early Western Civilization classes at Winchester High School in Connecticut. Located several miles outside one of the state's major cities, it is in a thriving suburban and largely white and middle-class community. The school itself is large, contemporary, and well funded. There are approximately 1,500 students; 85% of them are white. In terms of quality and academic performance, Winchester is considered one of the more successful school districts in the state.

Mr. Jackson's Early Western Civilization class is a one-semester course that he teaches twice every year to mostly ninth graders (with some tenth graders). It surveys the eras in Western history from ancient Greece and Rome through the Renaissance. He focuses on significant historical contributions and events and how they connect to the world today. His Crusades unit builds on the course's broader unit on the Middle Ages. He teaches regular mixed-ability and mainstreamed special education sections of the course. The class observed for this case was a mainstreamed section team-taught with a special education instructor. About half of the 25 students in the class received special education services. At the time of observation, Mr. Jackson had been teaching for six years. He did his undergraduate teacher certification at a Connecticut college and was currently working on a Masters degree.

Mr. Jackson is a frequent and avid user of film-based instruction because "anytime you can use anything visual, I think the students can connect with it a lot more." He added, "It makes history come alive. These kids grow up in a really visual world, and they're used to seeing things." Mr. Jackson uses film to some extent in many of his courses, on average once a week. Most are short clips from movies or portions of documentary videos. *Kingdom of Heaven* is the only feature-length movie that he uses in its entirety in Early Western Civilization. He carefully chose this film because he believes it is a strong fit for his instructional goals, holds value as a historical account, and is effective at visually engaging students. In the past he has used or considered using other movies. He used to show Stanley Kubrick's *Spartacus* (1960) but felt that its topic was not significant enough in his curriculum to warrant the time required and that it was largely lost on the current generation of students because of its age. He has considered using parts of Mel Gibson's *Braveheart* (1995) but decided not to because of its historical inaccuracies. Mr. Jackson did have concerns about *Kingdom of Heaven* due to its total running time (around 140 minutes), the complexities of its story, and its R rating. Ultimately, he felt the movie's value in helping students visualize the different perspectives, locations, and events in the Crusades outweighed the concerns and justified the time required. In his view, the film pays enough attention to historical accuracy to be valuable and is powerfully contemporary. Despite the R rating, the film's violence is not extreme enough to cause parents to object—he requires a permission slip for students to watch the film, and only one parent so far has ever refused.

The Crusades are a controversial issue in history because of their legacy of religious violence in the Middle East—a legacy that resonates in debates today over political, economic, and military involvement of the United States and European nations in Islamic countries or in support of Israel. In Mr. Jackson's view, it is necessary for students to understand the complexities and long-term consequences of the Crusades from both Western and Muslim viewpoints. He believes the unit is important and effective because "the focus is on understanding the Crusades from multiple perspectives." Historical understanding emerges from considering alternative frames: He believes we can "find the reality somewhere in the middle, in the common ground." *Kingdom of Heaven* is his chosen resource for getting students to identify, analyze, and compare the different viewpoints of European crusaders and Muslims.

Unit Overview

Mr. Jackson designed and implemented his Crusades unit at a time when the United States was engaged in military action in Iraq, Afghanistan, and parts of Pakistan. The issues of terrorism, religiously inspired violence, and military intervention in Muslim countries give the Crusades a particularly potent and controversial resonance today. Are the Crusades an inspirational precedent for a global war against terrorism? Are they an example of pointless religious fanaticism? Are the Crusades the beginning of European intervention in Muslim lands in the Middle East? Are they the beginning of Islamic violence against Christians and Jews? The Crusades are controversial because how someone thinks about these historical questions has implications for beliefs, values, and political policies in the contemporary world.

For Mr. Jackson, dealing with the Crusades as a controversial issue in history means grounding his unit in multiple viewpoints and getting students to consider the experiences of the different sides in the conflict. He believes that *Kingdom of Heaven* is the right resource to use. "When you talk about multiple perspectives [on the Crusades], this [film] really brings it alive for the students because [the filmmakers] do a lot with looking at the Muslim side." This is important to him because students otherwise might reach comfortable, simplistic conclusions that do not recognize the complexities behind the conflict or the importance of the consequences. As Mr. Jackson points out about *Kingdom of Heaven*, "There's not a clear good guy and bad guy. I think inherently [students] want the crusader to be the good guy and Saladin to be the bad guy, and I think what they find when they watch this [film] is that's not really the case . . . It shows them the different perspectives, and it shows them the complexities." Throughout the unit Mr. Jackson involved students in activities and asked them questions that required them to focus on the multiple perspectives in the film. By first providing background content knowledge about the medieval crusading period and societies involved and by positioning the film within a supporting activity that required students to focus on a particular

Table 8.1 Mr. Jackson's Outline for His Unit Using *Kingdom of Heaven*

Unit: The Crusades

Unit Focus: To understand the importance of examining the Crusades from multiple perspectives.

Essential Questions:
What were the causes of the Crusades?
Why was Salah al-Din an important leader?
What were the Crusades like for those who embarked on them?
What is the legacy of the Crusades?

Day 1	**Introduction to the Crusades** What led to the Crusades? What role did Pope Urban II play in motivating knights to go on Crusade?
Day 2	**Motivations for Crusaders** What were the four main reasons Christian knights took up the Crusade? How are these factors reflected in selected primary sources?
Day 3	**Life in Muslim Lands** What was life like in the Holy Land for both Christians and Muslims? How were their experiences similar? How were they different?
Day 4	**Military Encounters** How did Christian knights and Muslim mujahids view each other?
Day 5	**Comparing and Contrasting Leadership** How did contemporary accounts view the leadership of King Richard the Lionheart and Salah al-Din?
Day 6	**Salah al-Din as a Leader** How did contemporary sources view Salah al-Din? How is Salah al-Din portrayed in the film Kingdom of Heaven?
Day 7	**Introduction to *Kingdom of Heaven*** Why are we watching *Kingdom of Heaven* in class? What is the outline of the film? What is empathy?
Days 8, 9, and 10	***Kingdom of Heaven***
Day 11	**History vs. Hollywood** How historically accurate is the film? What can we learn from the film?
Day 12	**The Legacy of the Crusades/ Review day** How has the legacy of the crusades manifested itself in modern politics?

character's historical perspective, Mr. Jackson prepared his students to study and analyze the historical value and messages in *Kingdom of Heaven*.

Unit Outline

Table 8.1 is a reproduction of Mr. Jackson's actual outline for his unit on the Crusades, which occurred over 12 class sessions of 45 minutes each. After several sessions that provided students with background knowledge about what the Crusades were, their causes, experiences of those who fought them, and famous leaders, students watched and analyzed specific clips from *Kingdom of Heaven* the next period and then spent three days watching the whole film in class. Additional class sessions were devoted to post-film analysis and review.

The Film

Kingdom of Heaven is briefly described in Table 8.2. It was the only feature film used in this unit.

Table 8.2 Description of *Kingdom of Heaven*

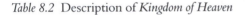

Kingdom of Heaven (2005) Ridley Scott (Director), 20th Century Fox	*Kingdom of Heaven* dramatizes historical events in the late 1180s at the height of medieval Europe's Crusades to the Middle East. Balian (Orlando Bloom) is an illegitimate blacksmith from France encouraged by his father (Liam Neeson) to go to the Holy Land and take his place as a lord in the Christian Kingdom of Jerusalem. There Balian finds that fanatical elements are pushing for a new war between Christians and Muslims. After defeating the crusader army, Muslim ruler Salah al-Din (Saladin) lays siege to Jerusalem. Only Balian remains to lead the defense of the city and protect its diverse population of Christians, Jews, and Muslims.

FILM ACTIVITIES

Days 1–5

The first five periods of the unit were devoted to providing students with background knowledge about the Crusades. Mr. Jackson's lectures and use of maps, primary document readings, and illustrations (of knights, Jerusalem, and medieval depictions of battles) were organized in a computerized projected slideshow presentation, each day revolving around a series of slides devoted to the class content and student activities. His initial lesson taught students that the crusades were a series of wars between Christian knights and Seljuk Turks and other Muslim armies from the Middle East over control of the Holy Land. His presentation opened with a quote from President George W. Bush on September 18, 2001, describing the war on terrorism as a "crusade" that will take a long while. He then had students read and analyze an excerpt from Pope Urban II's Clermont speech in 1095 calling a war for the Holy Land. The purpose was for students to identify the papacy's motivations of unifying European Christianity and channeling military violence from Europe to conquering the Holy Land.

In subsequent periods Mr. Jackson used his slideshow presentation to overview the results of first four crusades, explain reasons why medieval Europeans went on crusades, look at what life was like in advanced cities of the Holy Land, and examine perspectives on King Richard I of England and Salah al-Din (Saladin), the most renowned Christian and Muslim leaders. He focused on Richard and Saladin as well as the religious-military orders (Templars, Hospitallers) because they appear in *Kingdom of Heaven*. Each day Mr. Jackson also provided students with various documents to analyze, mostly drawn from a supplemental educational resource book—artistic representations from the period, a portion of the Muslim religious leader al-Harawi's speech in 1099 calling for a response to the First Crusade, excerpts of primary documents about the Crusades from Muslim perspectives, and excerpts of primary accounts of the Crusades by European crusaders (called "Franks" by Muslims at the time). His presentation concluded by bringing discussion back to President Bush's 2001 quote, arguing that the Crusades may be a problematic historical comparison to the war on terrorism today but that the comment may reflect an ongoing clash of cultures and the continuing role of religion in world affairs.

Days 6–7

Owing to school scheduling issues, Mr. Jackson combined these lessons originally planned for two days mostly into a single session. Previously students examined period accounts of Saladin that reflected his honorable conduct and generosity, praised even by his Christian enemies, and of Richard that reflected the sometimes unfavorable opinion Christian rivals had of him. Students turned in a worksheet for which they had to compile a list of adjectives based on the primary documents to describe Richard and Saladin (Table 8.3), and in the first several minutes Mr. Jackson went over and discussed student responses.

Next, Mr. Jackson distributed a worksheet to guide students in examining how *Kingdom of Heaven* depicts Saladin (Table 8.4). He showed four scenes from the movie, had students take notes to answer a question about the scene, and then discussed student responses after each scene. Aware that these scenes taken out of context may be confusing, he instructed students to keep track of any questions about what is happening and ask the questions afterward. A closer look at the questions he asked and how students responded illustrates both the educational potential of a history movie as well as some particular challenges.

Students were confused by the first clip, in which the two armies face off and negotiate withdrawal rather than fight. Mr. Jackson patiently explained that King Baldwin and

Table 8.3 Excerpts from Mr. Jackson's Worksheet on Richard and Saladin

Salah al-Din and Richard the Lionheart

Now that you have studied both Salah al-Din and Richard the Lionheart, make a list of adjectives which appropriately describe each man:

Salah al-Din:

Richard the Lionheart:

Brainstorm: In your opinion, do either of these historical figures fit the definition of a "good leader?" Use the criteria you came up with at the beginning of class to support your decision.

Saladin both felt it was more advantageous for them to negotiate than risk a battle and then turned to questions on his worksheet. One student responded that "the king [Baldwin] respected him [Saladin]" and noted Baldwin even greeted Saladin in Arabic. Mr. Jackson then observed that Saladin offered to send his own physician, probably more advanced than any among the Europeans at the time, to help the ailing king.

After the second clip he asked students, "According to this other warrior, who determines that outcome of battles?" Some students replied, "God." Mr. Jackson pressed them further on Saladin's reaction ("How many battles did Islam win before me?") that stressed the role of military preparations. "What does the warrior remind him of?" Mr. Jackson asked. He emphasized a particular quote from the film: "You promised us the return of Jerusalem." One young woman asked why the visiting warrior was so angry, if it was because Saladin was a liar? Mr. Jackson explained that the warrior wanted a battle and felt that Saladin was avoiding it unnecessarily.

When showing the third clip depicting the aftermath of the Battle of Hattin, Mr. Jackson warned students that this scene is more violent than the others. Students reacted with audible surprise when Saladin decapitates the captive Reynauld. Mr. Jackson explained that Saladin showed respect by offering iced water to King Guy, who refused it and handed it off to Reynauld, who drank it rudely. He added that Saladin had cause to want to kill Reynauld, who had slaughtered many Muslims on his raids. "I think they are all idiots," one student said. "Why are they killing each other?" Another student responded, "They're fighting over what religion is right." A third student disagreed: "No, they're fighting over the Holy Land." Mr. Jackson intervened by stating that they are fighting over which religion will control Jerusalem and told them "you've got to transport yourself back in their time, understand why they felt the city was important."

The final clip showing the aftermath of the battle at Jerusalem also provoked quite a few questions from students about who the characters were or what happened in the scene. Mr. Jackson explained that Balian is desperate to negotiate a surrender that

Table 8.4 Excerpts from Mr. Jackson's Worksheet on How the Film Depicts Saladin

Kingdom of Heaven:
Hollywood and Salah al-Din

Directions: As we watch the clips from *Kingdom of Heaven*, answer the questions below.

Scene 24: Jerusalem Has Come
King Baldwin and Salah al-Din meet and negotiate terms for the withdrawal of their forces from the battlefield.
What does this scene illustrate about Salah al-Din?

Scene 26: I Quake for Islam
Salah al-Din and a mujahid warrior discuss the terms.
What does the warrior remind Salah al-Din of?

Scene 33: A King's Example
Salah al-Din meets with Guy de Lusignan and Reynauld de Chatillon following the disastrous Battle of Hattin.
What role does the concept of respect play in this scene?

Scene 42: Nothing and Everything
Salah al-Din meets with Balian after the Battle for Jerusalem to discuss terms for surrender.
Why is Balian surprised by Salah al-Din's offer? What does this say about his character?

Part II: After Viewing

In your opinion, what is the perspective of the filmmakers toward Salah al-Din? Do they portray him as cruel or merciful?

Is Salah al-Din portrayed as a good leader?

Keeping in mind the idea of multiple perspectives, what could the film have done differently to be more balanced?

will spare their lives. He emphasized that Balian finds Saladin's offer "mind-blowing" because Saladin offers safe conduct for citizens to leave Jerusalem, even though in 1099 Christian conquerors butchered all the Muslims in the city.

With time running short, Mr. Jackson turned student attention briefly to the final questions on the worksheet. He said he believes the movie does a good job of being balanced. There is no clear good guy or bad guy. "What's the point then?" complained one student. "I'm so confused." Mr. Jackson responded by guiding the students instead to consider why Saladin in the movie describes Jerusalem as worth "nothing and everything." Another student answered that the damaged city itself isn't worth anything but symbolically it is worth everything to the people fighting. The special education teacher

Table 8.5 Excerpts from Mr. Jackson's Character Shadow Handout

Kingdom of Heaven Assignment

Character Shadow

Each of you will be assigned one of the below characters to shadow, or take the role of, as we watch the film. Using the film, daily prompts, and additional resources, we will work to achieve several objectives:

- Develop empathy for those involved in the Crusades
- Identify the role of both Europeans and Muslims
- Evaluate the historical reliability of the film
- Analyze the effectiveness the film has in shaping our knowledge of this event

Characters to be shadowed:
Balian of Ibelin   Guy de Lusignan   Sibylla
Salah al-Din   Reynauld de Chatillon   King Baldwin IV

Directions:
First, set up your notebook like this:

Scene: What is happening?	What is your character doing?	How does this relate to what we have learned in class?

As we watch the film each day, continue to make notes either during or after we view the film in the format above.

then pointed out that this is a Holy Land, everybody wants a piece, and people today are still fighting over it. Mr. Jackson briefly discussed with students whether Saladin's depiction in the movie matched what they read in the primary documents. Student responses mostly revolved around "respect" and being "peaceful." Mr. Jackson questioned whether Saladin should be considered "peaceful" since he was willing to order sieges and kill Reynauld.

In the last few minutes, Mr. Jackson previewed the Character Shadow assignment (Table 8.5) to go along with watching the whole movie. Mr. Jackson used a short computerized slideshow presentation (with graphics from the film) to identify the six characters (all of them actual historical figures) and foreshadow each character's role in the movie. Afterward, Mr. Jackson noted that he was very pleased by student involvement. Many of the students who responded during this lesson did not normally choose to speak in class.

Days 8–10

Over the next three class periods the class watched *Kingdom of Heaven* in its entirety. Mr. Jackson began by giving students a handout explaining the character shadow activity and assigning each student one of six characters in the film to take notes on while watching. He explained that these notes were "intended as a guide to help you remember" what the characters are doing throughout this long film as well as to get students to consider how the scenes relate to what was previously learned in class about crusades and why people went on them. He also asked for students to hold their questions for discussion at the end of each period rather than shouting them out during the film.

In addition to the character shadow assignment, Mr. Jackson gave students another writing prompt (Table 8.6) each day to go along with the film and its historical content. He explained that it was his preference for students not to try to write answers while watching but instead to write afterward.

Table 8.6 Excerpts from Mr. Jackson's Daily Writing Prompts for *Kingdom of Heaven*

Day 1

- Based on Godfrey's beliefs in the movie: What lies ahead in the Holy Land?
- Why is Balian going to the Holy Land?
- How does this compare with Pope Urban's description of the Holy Land in his speech at Claremont?
- How is Jerusalem portrayed in *Kingdom of Heaven*? Does this match the descriptions of Godfrey and Pope Urban II? Why might there be a conflict?

Day 2

- What is [your shadowed character's] purpose/role on the "Crusade"?
- What is your first impression of [the six characters to be shadowed]?

Day 3

Account of the Battle of Hattin, 1187
By a local Frank, "Ernoul", written soon after

[the text of the account describing the battle followed]

- What is the subject of this quote? What are the time, place, and setting?
- Who is the audience? Whom is this statement directed towards?
- What is the purpose or reason this statement was made?
- Who won the Battle of Hattin? Why?

Day 4 – The Siege

- Identify defensive strategies used to protect Jerusalem:
- Identify offensive strategies used to attack the city:
- What was the outcome of the siege at Jerusalem?
- What was the significance of the Christian knights losing the city of Jerusalem?

The writing assignments did not always go smoothly. On the days observed, not all students came to class with their notes or with written responses to the prompts. Some students lost the handouts or claimed they never received a copy and needed replacements. Nonetheless, the viewing of the film went smoothly and was completed in the three class periods planned, with the last writing prompt carrying over to a fourth day. Students seemed very engaged with the film. Students mostly held their reactions and questions until the last few minutes of class each day. Mr. Jackson answered student questions but always concluded by asking them questions of his own. His purpose was to help students summarize the complex content in each day's portion of the film as well as to check for student understanding.

Days 11–12

In the last two periods of the unit, Mr. Jackson engaged his students in thinking about the film's historical content and messages about how the past and its connection to the world today. He began by showing select portions of a documentary from the History Channel about *Kingdom of Heaven* that examined its historical accuracy. Next, he divided students into small groups to read together an informational handout that contained sections on elements in the movie that are historically accurate, scenes "that simply aren't true to history," the movie's characters compared with their actual historical counterparts, and how attitudes in the film differed from historical attitudes. Mr. Jackson himself wrote the handout based on the research he did about the Crusades before showing the film in class. The group reading was followed up with discussion between the teacher and the whole class.

His goal behind having students discuss the historical accuracy of *Kingdom of Heaven* was to get them to consider why the movie is educationally useful in learning about the Crusades. Mr. Jackson finds the film to be largely historically accurate with only minor inaccuracies such as character details or exaggerated military special effects that can be addressed in class, as he did on his handout. He also wanted students to recognize that the movie makes some conclusions about history that are better attuned to attitudes today than how people in the past would have felt. For example, in his handout he wrote, "The cheers at Balian's surrender of Jerusalem are a 21st-century cheer for peace over what is depicted as pointless carnage. We all share those cheers. But 12th-century Westerners were devastated by Saladin's capture of Jerusalem." He also questioned the film's implication that crusaders were "fighting for wealth and land." In his response, "That is very much a modern suspicion, that American and European interests in the Middle East pertain to oil or some sort of colonial domination. Few [crusaders] got wealthy going to the eastern Mediterranean to fight for Christianity."

On the last period he reviewed the unit's major subject-matter knowledge with students and directed them to discuss the legacy of the Crusades. He distributed another handout of his own design that contained four quotes from President George W. Bush shortly after the attacks of September 11, 2001, and two quotes from remarks by Osama bin Laden on October 7, 2001. In pairs students read the quotes and answered a series of short reading-comprehension questions for each. Then, they responded to three questions in preparation for the whole class discussion (see Table 8.7). Mr. Jackson's goal was again to guide students to consider multiple perspectives on the history of religious conflict between Christians and Muslims. He made few direct connections to *Kingdom of Heaven*, but he believed the film was useful in getting students to think about the issues involved. Chiefly, he wanted students to recognize that there were different experiences and views of the Crusades in the past. For the world today, by extension, he wanted students to consider that President Bush and bin Laden do not speak for all Christians or all Muslims.

Table 8.7 Excerpts from Mr. Jackson's Worksheet for the Last Period of the Unit

---

The Impact of the Crusades

Part I: Excerpts from George W. Bush's Address to Congress, September 20, 2001

"The terrorists practice a fringe form of Islamic extremism that has been rejected by Muslim scholars and the vast majority of Muslim clerics – a fringe movement that perverts the peaceful teachings of Islam."

[...]

"This crusade, this war on terrorism, is going to take a while."

[...]

Part II: Remarks by Usama bin Laden – October 7, 2001

"And with regard to you, Muslims, this is the day of question. This is a new (inaudible) against you, all against the Muslims and Medina. So be like the followers of the prophet, peace be upon him, and all countrymen, lovers of God and the prophet within, and a new battle, great battle, similar to the great battles of Islam, like the conqueror of Jerusalem. So, hurry up to the dignity of life and the eternity of death."

[...]

Questions to think about:

If historians were to study these documents in 200 years to learn about the War on Terrorism, what may be some problems with using documents from President Bush and Usama bin-Laden?

How do you think that the Crusades have influenced the present?

In your opinion, in what ways are the Crusades and the War on Terror similar? How are they different?

Mr. Jackson's unit on the Crusades using *Kingdom of Heaven* illustrates how a historical feature film, though dramatized and fictionalized in some details, can be used to teach about a controversial issue in history by helping students to identify and understand multiple perspectives from the past as well as different views about the legacy of the issue. He wanted students to learn about the Crusades, and to consider their impact, from both European and Muslim perspectives. His goal was to move student thinking beyond "good guys" and "bad guys" and to understand a wider range of motivations behind those who participated in the conflict. *Kingdom of Heaven* is a powerful resource for him because it dramatizes multiple perspectives from the Crusades and presents reasonable Muslims like Saladin in sympathetic light rather than as predictable villains. He also was very pleased that students who normally do not choose to speak in class responded to the questions and discussions for *Kingdom of Heaven*. Perhaps this is reflective of the approachability and special potential of movies to motivate student interest, particularly those who may not respond enthusiastically to traditional instruction.

There are several features of Mr. Jackson's approach that make it effective. First, he researched the historical background and conveyed some of this knowledge to students to help them better understand the content in the film. Second, he positioned the film within the unit so that it was supported by learning broader content knowledge and in turn supported student learning of multiple perspectives on the historical controversy. Third, he employed additional materials such as primary documents, supplemental publications (from the National Center for History in the Schools and the Council on Islamic Education), and documentary film segments to support his instructional use of the movie. Additionally, he created student handouts and activities to guide their viewing and engage them in critical thinking about the film.

Student activities were essential to the effectiveness of this film-based unit. They focused student attention on the content and themes in the movie that the teacher wanted to emphasize. The "character shadow" activity (Table 8.5) was Mr. Jackson's new addition to the unit this time. He said, "I think that this helped to overcome what used to be my number one concern when showing the film"—that students would be confounded "by the various characters, religious military orders, and a plot which can be confusing." As can be seen in his student handouts (Tables 8.3–8.7), Mr. Jackson engaged his students in a considerable volume of work revolving around the movie. Although perhaps this amount is not always necessary or desirable, the activities and daily questions did require students to watch the film in ways directed by the teacher and also reviewed important content in the film. Mr. Jackson plans on adding even more instructional support to his unit for future improvement. Next time he is thinking about "adding a vocabulary guide or glossary of some sort, as some of my students had difficulty keeping up with the dialogue" and incorporating "some of the vocabulary into a lesson prior to showing the film."

REFLECTION ON THE CASE

Mr. Jackson believes that *Kingdom of Heaven* makes an important contribution to his unit on the Crusades. Nonetheless, he is aware that there are some challenges and tensions. Whereas his intention was to present *Kingdom of Heaven* as a largely accurate and educationally useful film, he was surprised that many of his students reached the opposite conclusion. In the closing discussion as well as on an essay prompt on his unit exam, he asked students to reflect on what can be learned from the movie and whether it should be shown in schools to teach about the Crusades. He found that his students overwhelmingly focused on small details of inaccuracy rather than on the broader representations or perspectives. It is his hunch that students latched on to small but memorable details from the History Channel documentary or his informational handout and thought that this was what the teacher wanted them to do. Another possibility is that most history classes typically experienced by students emphasize the memorization and recitation of pieces of factual information. Mr. Jackson's students may have been more comfortable with this traditional student task than with the more intellectually demanding role he laid out for them. Mr. Jackson's observation raises an important caution: No matter how purposeful and intentional the planning for a film-based unit, there are limits to the teacher's control over the directions student thinking may take. There can be inadvertent consequences to instructional decisions that otherwise have good intentions. By devoting so much attention to inaccurate historical details in the film, he may have suppressed student attention to his broader goals in using the film. This is not to say that distinguishing fact and fiction is not important, only that any instructional purpose needs to be carefully and consciously balanced with other goals.

Another challenge that emerges from reflecting on Mr. Jackson's case is the risk that a movie can simplify student perceptions of a controversial historical issue. It should be noted that this concern is not unique to film (textbooks are open to similar critiques), but the special visual and emotional power of film may obscure important historical interpretations unless the teacher directly attends to them. The Crusades are an immensely complex series of historical events that played out over hundreds of years, that were very diverse in participants and their motivations, and that continued to influence European and Muslim identities and ideas about themselves and each other for centuries after (Tyerman, 2006). What makes this complex, controversial topic so difficult to teach is the multiplicity of possible interpretations and generalizations.

For example, consider the crusader lord Reynauld of Chatillon and Muslim sultan Saladin. *Kingdom of Heaven* depicts Reynauld as a ruthless warmonger eager to help Christian fanatics provoke war, and Saladin is depicted as a reasonable, often merciful, but determined ruler who balances the fanatics on his own side with the benefits of peace. This is one possible interpretation: The historical Reynauld was a vicious raider capable of great violence against even non-combatants, the historical Saladin was renowned even among his enemies for his compassion and honorable behavior, and the provocations of Reynauld's faction led to the disastrous battle of Hattin in 1187. Yet the collapse of the Crusader Kingdom of

Jerusalem suggests another possible interpretation. Saladin built his empire by gradually conquering the independent Arab and Turkish Muslim domains of the Middle East. Once this process was complete, his empire would have the crusader states completely surrounded and overpowered. Reynauld may have seen this danger more clearly than others and launched his raids and attacks as a way to disrupt Saladin's expansion and force a decisive battle while the crusader states still had at least a chance of winning. *Kingdom of Heaven* offers only the former possible interpretation, depicting Reynauld's faction as fanatical and pointlessly violent. Without direct involvement by the teacher, the complexity is lost.

The potential for disconnect between the themes and historical messages from the movie and discussion about how the historical controversy affects the world today is also visible in Mr. Jackson's unit. *Kingdom of Heaven* was focused on his goal of getting students to visualize multiple perspectives on the Crusades, and he wanted to connect the Crusades as a historical controversy to the contemporary global struggle against Islamist terrorism. However, the film was not really a part of his lesson on the legacy of the Crusades, which revolved around quotes from President Bush and Osama bin Laden. After showing the film in class he did want students to recognize the film's messages about multiculturalism and religious toleration in the Holy Land, but he framed these observations strictly as matters of historical accuracy (21st-century attitudes vs. 12th-century attitudes). *Kingdom of Heaven*, made for audiences in 2005, comments on the legacy of the Crusades for the modern world by bemoaning the violent religious hatred the Crusades represented and fanned, depicting Saladin as a moderate Muslim whose mercy should be a model, and constructing a hero (Balian) who reflects the values of multiculturalism and toleration. Addressing and critiquing these themes from the film would have directly informed the class discussion about the modern-day implications of the Crusades. This also would have provided a clearer channel for applying historical information learned from the film and from the class readings and lessons to the culminating question (see Figure 8.7) about whether or how the Crusades can be compared to the global war against terrorism. Otherwise, such a question risks remaining largely "in your opinion" rather than an evidence-based discussion of different interpretations.

Mr. Jackson's case also touches on the other themes in history education that are the focus of other chapters in this book. His use of *Kingdom of Heaven* to help students recognize different perspectives on how people at the time may have experienced the Crusades connects to historical empathy (see Chapters 3 and 4). Similarly, a major motivation for using the film in class was to help students visualize what medieval Jerusalem and crusader warfare may have really looked like (see Chapter 9). His emphasis on multiple perspectives has connections to using film as historical narrative (see Chapter 10). The film also was used as a secondary source (see Chapter 6) to provide students with a factual account of how the crusader states fell in the 1180s, with historical licenses or inaccuracies confronted in class readings and discussions. The film was even used as a primary source (see Chapter 5), in a sense, in class discussions that asked students to consider how the movie reflected 21st-century views of multiculturalism and religion. Overall, Mr. Jackson's unit demonstrates how film-based instruction can accomplish multiple goals.

Strategies for Using Film to Teach Controversial Issues in History

Mr. Jackson's case suggests four key strategies for using film to teach controversial issues in history. First, multiple perspectives are essential. Something that happened in the past remains controversial because there is uncertainty or disagreement about what it means, caused, or decided. History is experienced by different people in different ways, and a nuanced understanding of a historical controversy requires a consideration of these different viewpoints and interpretations. Mr. Jackson wanted students to look at the Crusades from the perspectives of both European Christians and Muslims from the Middle East— as well as to think about how Westerners and Muslims might think differently about conflicts in the Islamic world today based on the legacy of the Crusades. Connections to the present should encompass the reasons why the historical issue remains controversial and encourage students to evaluate alternate perspectives in drawing their own reasoned and informed conclusions.

Second, the teacher must frame the issue in alternative ways that make explicit the social values and identities at stake. Students may not be able to perceive these on their own from just watching a history movie as a compelling narrative story. Without Mr. Jackson's direct involvement, it is not clear how many of his students would have analyzed *Kingdom of Heaven* as a historical story about contemporary multiculturalism and religious toleration or would have reflected on how the film depicts Saladin sympathetically and why. That the Crusades have possible implications for religious violence or a "clash of cultures" between the West and Muslims in the Middle East today may not be clear to young learners on their own.

Third, teaching about a controversial issue in the past is, ultimately, a lesson in history. There certainly are connections to social and political debates in the present, but the desire to emphasize these connections should not be allowed to overshadow analyzing and understanding the controversial issue in the past in its own historical context. Mr. Jackson tried to attend to this in his unit by teaching about the different motivations medieval Europeans had for going on crusades. Throughout his unit he wanted students to recognize that 21st-century ways of thinking were not the same as medieval values and attitudes. Mr. Jackson's unit strayed from this important characteristic at the end when it focused heavily on the contemporary war against terrorism without rigorous connections to the historical context and perspectives that he used *Kingdom of Heaven* to teach to students.

Fourth, sufficient content knowledge preparation and activities supporting student learning are critical to understanding the complexities of a historical controversy. It would have been impossible for Mr. Jackson to help his students to compare different perspectives on the Crusades, to evaluate historical accuracy in *Kingdom of Heaven*, or to critique the film's themes and messages without the prior research he did. Doing outside reading or viewing informational documentaries can be time consuming, but Mr. Jackson demonstrates that this is possible even for a very busy teacher. The next step is to translate this knowledge in ways students can learn and use. The computerized slideshow presentation and student handouts represent Mr. Jackson's attempts to equip students with background subject-matter knowledge and structure activities in which students would apply this learning to understanding and evaluating the controversial issue in history.

Strategies for Selecting Films to Teach Controversial Issues in History

Reflecting on Mr. Jackson's case suggests three criteria to consider when choosing films to teach about controversial issues in the past. First, the film should provide or be used to introduce to students multiple perspectives on the controversy. Second, the film should include historically accurate information or provide the teacher the opportunity to help students apply content knowledge in identifying and refuting historical inaccuracies or examples of presentism in how the movie presents the historical controversy. Third, the film should be visually and emotionally engaging in its presentation of the controversy so that students will perceive the issue as immediate rather than distant, real rather than abstract.

In general, movies that are effective for teaching controversial issues in history have clear and powerful connections to our world today. They dramatize something contentious or ambiguous that happened in the past with implications for the present or future. Movies commonly illustrate one particular perspective strongly—so a teacher can use clips of several films to illustrate several perspectives, or might use one whole film to examine one perspective in depth and present other perspectives to students through other means or resources. When a film presents just one perspective or interpretation, it is essential for the teacher to recognize this and to structure the lesson or unit in ways that provide alternative frames on the controversy and get students to consider different viewpoints.

There are many other controversial issues in history that have received feature film treatments in recent years that can be appropriate and effective for use in secondary history classrooms. Edward Zwick's *The Last Samurai* (2003) tells a fictionalized story of the last samurai rebellion in Japan on the eve of Western-style modernization and industrialization. The spread of capitalism as it relates to imperialism is a controversial issue in history. Is the spread of capitalism the spread of Western culture at the expense of traditional native cultures? *The Last Samurai* implies that capitalism and the modernization of Japan represented the destruction of traditional Japanese culture and even put the country on the path toward war against the United States. Through the experience of its fictional

American protagonist (played by Tom Cruise), the film directly compares the suppression of the samurai during Japan's modernization to the subjugation of Native Americans during U.S. Westward Expansion.

A second possibility is Michael Apted's *Amazing Grace* (2006), which dramatizes the struggle of the British abolitionist William Wilberforce (Ioan Gruffudd) against the international slave trade in the early 19th century. Wilberforce was a passionate Christian reformer who used his political connections to powerful politicians such as Lord Fox and William Pitt to outmaneuver the business interests that supported the slave trade. The film also includes some slave viewpoints (18th-century former slave Olaudah Equiano is one of the characters) and depicts why the slave trade was so politically entrenched. Why the international slave trade lasted so long and how it was finally ended is a controversial issue in history. Were reforming individuals such as Wilberforce largely responsible for ending it, did it take pressure by radical abolitionists in many countries, or did the slave trade end only when modern capitalism and industrialization made slavery less profitable or efficient? *Amazing Grace* emphasizes the impact of committed individuals such as Wilberforce.

Finally, Clint Eastwood's *Letters from Iwo Jima* (2007) dramatizes the decisive World War II (WWII) battle in the Pacific exclusively from the Japanese perspective. The film depicts the suffering faced by the Japanese during the long, deadly battle. When atrocities are committed, they are inflicted by American soldiers (who try to shoot some Japanese prisoners because they are too bored to bother guarding them). Atrocities and war crimes in WWII are a controversial issue in history, especially in light of current debates over responsibility for causing the war. For example, when Japan recently made slight changes in its history curriculum that downplayed Japanese aggression in Asia, official and very public protests were issued by Asian targets of Japan's WWII expansion, particularly China and South Korea. Was the savagery and length of WWII in the Pacific due to Japanese militaristic expansionism or the American policy of unconditional surrender? Does Japanese suffering during WWII (including devastating casualties at Iwo Jima) mitigate responsibility for atrocities? Should U.S. actions or policies against Japan during WWII be considered atrocities today? *Letters from Iwo Jima* is ambiguous on these questions, but it presents a powerful, poignant Japanese perspective on WWII.

Teaching controversial issues in the past is an essential part of rigorous historical thinking. Historical controversies typically relate to significant episodes of tremendous change or turmoil that are important to understanding why the world is the way it is today. Critical thinking in history requires evaluating arguments and interpretations on contentious issues that are disputed or ambiguous in their meaning, conclusions, or legacy. Movies can be a very useful resource for raising and exploring multiple perspectives on controversial issues in history in the classroom.

PART V

Using Film to Visualize the Past and Film as Historical Narrative

Unlike the other sections in this book, the connections between the two cases in Chapters 9 and 10 are more incongruous. However, these cases work to juxtapose practices with film that provide for an intriguing conclusion to our book. First, we present one of the goals most often cited by teachers in using film to teach history—to help students visualize historic events, people, or periods. Aesthetic attributes in films, such as scenery, props, costumes, language, music, and special effects, can help students to "hear," "see," and "feel" the past. Although no film can completely recreate the past, they can imagine or reproduce the look and feel of the past based on historical evidence. It is easy to see why teachers often think of using film in history classes as a way to enhance students' understanding of historic events, people, and eras and to take advantage of their motivational and inspirational impact.

Second, we explore using film to interrogate common historical narratives—a use of film less common among history teachers. In other words, this case examines the use of film to challenge students' beliefs or understanding of how an event occurred or to challenge the most commonly accepted or portrayed perspective on an event. We hope the illustration of examining film narratives presented in Chapter 10 inspires teachers to think about using a different aspect of film—its constructed narrative—to engage students in authentic interpretation of the past and an examination of how it is constructed and represented.

FILM TO VISUALIZE THE PAST

The aesthetics of film and the ways in which teachers and students feel they can be transported to another time or place is often viewed as the "value added" benefit film can bring to a classroom; in some teachers' words, film used in this way helps to "bring the past alive" (Marcus & Stoddard, 2007). Films can "bring the past alive" to a degree, but there are severe limits to their ability to help us visualize the past. After all, we can never truly recreate the past. Films are constrained by the availability of evidence from the historical record and the subjectivities of how that evidence is interpreted. Films are also influenced by the views and biases of directors, writers, and producers and are reflections of the time period in which they were made. Therefore, any "recreation" of the past must be viewed and evaluated within these constraints. However, the powerful aesthetic attributes that film provides visually and emotionally, through elements such as sound and music, are hard to ignore and may well be used effectively to help students visualize what a historic event, group of people, or living conditions may have looked like. For example, *Master and Commander* (2003), adapted from Patrick O'Brian's historical-fiction novels, may help students to get a sense of what it might have been like to live and fight on a British warship in the 18th century for long periods of time in cramped quarters. Other films, such as Steven Spielberg's *Saving Private Ryan* (1998), went to great lengths and expense to "look" and "feel" as accurate as possible and take advantage of the aesthetics of carnage, arguably at the sacrifice of the historical narrative and details of the events being presented.

Unlike the use of film as a secondary source, a topic we explored in Chapter 6, here the focus is more on the ability of a film to present the aesthetics of an event, period, or place as opposed to how well a film may adhere to the historical record of how events occurred. Of course, some films may go to great lengths to do both. For example, *The Alamo*, the film used as a secondary source in Chapter 6, went to such great lengths to try to get both the aesthetics and story as accurate as possible that it could have lost its appeal to an audience interested purely in entertainment and was a financial flop at the box office. In fact it is often in these aesthetic details of film that cause teachers and students to view them as accurate overall—falling into the trap of if it looks real then the story being told must be accurate as well. When used explicitly as a medium for helping students to visualize and get a sense of what the experiences of those in the past may have looked and sounded like, for example, a glimpse into a Civil War or Revolutionary War battlefield, what it looked like to live in a frontier cabin, or what it would have been like to survive the voyage of the Middle Passage into slavery, it may help students better understand the history related to these representations. One critical facet to using films successfully in this way is that the teacher makes explicit the reason for the viewing—to help visualize what an event or life in this period might have looked like.

In addition to providing a glimpse into what life may have looked like, a film's aesthetics may also be able to provide a sense of the moods of the people involved or of the attitudes of American society or another society overall. We explored the idea of how the aesthetics of a film may provide evidence in using film as a primary or secondary source in Part III of this book, and to some degree explored how a film's aesthetics can help to engage students in historical empathy in Part II. Here, however, we examine how the aesthetics of making a historical event or period look and sound authentic, even if the story being told is far from accurate, can help students to visualize and understand the emotions and conflict that may have existed. For example, the film *Thirteen Days* (2000) provides a sense of the tension in the Oval Office of President John F. Kennedy during the Cuban Missile Crisis; *Amistad* (1997) goes to great length to introduce the language and culture of African characters and show how confusing and frightening it would have been to be captured into bondage and brought to a foreign culture; and *Iron Jawed Angels* (2004) and *The Long Walk Home* (1990) provide a glimpse into seeing and hearing the hatred and bigotry experienced by women suffragettes in the 1920s and blacks during the Civil Rights movement of the 1950s and 1960s, respectively. As we noted in earlier parts of this book, a teacher may want to use these powerful affective components of film to work toward different goals, ranging from empathy to simply a more in-depth understanding of why events they are examining in other sources happened the way they did. In Chapter 9, we explore how the film *Glory* can be used to help students visualize the experiences of African-American soldiers during the American Civil War.

FILM AS HISTORICAL NARRATIVE

In addition to favoring aesthetics over historical accuracy, the narratives filmmakers construct often reflect larger mainstream historical (and film) narratives that dominate society and American textbooks. For example, the narratives of American Westward Expansion often share many generic or thematic similarities to Western genre films. Both emphasize the rugged individualism and need to "civilize" the frontier made famous by Frederick Jackson's famous 1893 Frontier Thesis. These historic films and texts often also emphasize the dichotomous "good guys" versus "bad guys"—with white Anglo U.S. or immigrant settlers and U.S. Cavalry serving as the good, and with bandits, Latinos, and Native American tribes as the bad. These narratives in the above films and texts also present events and stories in U.S. history as part of a larger meta-narrative of progress and freedom, but leave out many of the complexities and marginalize many historical perspectives (Barton & Levstik, 2004; Ladson-Billings, 2003; Loewen, 1995). It is the narrative structures in popular film and "school" history, however, that also make these stories easy to understand and remember as people young and old use narrative templates to piece details together into a fluid story (Wertsch, 1998). It is because of these templates that one can turn on the television during the middle of a film and still easily make sense of the plot and quickly know which characters to root for and which to dislike.

Unfortunately, the narratives in films are often not examined or interrogated, especially for how they are often created for the largest portion of theater-goers, namely white middle-class males. Nor do teachers often select films based on their narrative structure and perspective. This is because popular film genres, much like the way history in the United States is told, tend to follow particular forms and rules that allow the audience to easily grasp the story. It is often only when a director breaks away from these genre forms that the audience notices that they exist at all, similarly to how teachers who attempt to challenge their students' common understandings of historical events tend to gain the attention of their students. In these cases the film narrative cannot easily be fitted into common narrative templates and an audience member is forced to renegotiate meaning. Many films, especially those that may not have been blockbusters or that promote non-mainstream perspectives, can be useful in challenging or interrupting students' common historical understandings and the narratives on which these understandings are based. For example, films such as *Bury my Heart at Wounded Knee* (2007) and *Dances with Wolves* (1990) countered the representations of many Western-genre films by presenting a more humanistic and positive view of native peoples and a more negative view of the United States' role in "settling" the West after the American Civil War.

This is not to say that the films are completely accurate or are even the most authentic representations of the native perspective, but the structures of the films' narratives represent a break from the common formulaic narrative templates common in historical and Western film narrative (Seixas, 1994). *Dances with Wolves* was successful at the box office because of the appeal of Kevin Costner and the fact that much of the story is still told through the perspective of a white male. For *Wounded Knee* (an HBO production) and other films produced for cable television or other outlets not as reliant on box-office success, they are allowed more freedom to create a story for a smaller and more sophisticated audience in terms of the complexity they present in their film. Although utilizing film as historical narrative is one of the least common pedagogical uses, there is great potential in what films can provide a classroom, especially to make the study of the past more complex and force students to examine the fluid and perspective-driven interpretive nature of history and historical film. In Chapter 10, we explore how *Ride with the Devil*, a film that examines the border wars between Kansas "Jayhawkers" and Missouri "Bushwhackers," challenges students' common understandings of the causes of the Civil War and their reading of a film that does not easily distinguish bad and good.

CHAPTER 9
Using Film to Visualize the Past

Figure 9.1 Glory (1989). Rawlins (Morgan Freeman) breaks up a scuffle between Tripp (Denzel Washington), a fellow soldier in the Massachusetts 54th during the Civil War, and white soldiers.

The case discussed in this chapter exemplifies using film to represent or visualize the past—to aesthetically present past events, people, and attitudes. Using film in this manner can both motivate students' interest in history as well as help them visualize the context of the events and people they are studying. A film's scenery, language, costumes, props, music, lighting, and other features, all contribute to, or can detract from, the reality of a recreated past. Helping students to "see" the past is very difficult to accomplish using textbooks and lectures. Primary sources often help, but can be equally as dense as a textbook. Films are potentially the most powerful mechanism for visualizing the past in ways that motivate students, enhance their understanding of the past, deepen their appreciation for the past, and connect the past to the present, but they also bring the potential drawback of being "too real" or of upsetting students emotionally, as with a film such as *Schindler's List* (1993). In addition, teachers must constantly remind their students and themselves that films are still interpretations and are not the actual events and/or people. Using film to visualize the past is not as simple as just exposing students to the film but, like other practices with film described earlier in the book, requires careful and thorough planning. The case for this segment of the book analyzes how Mr. Irwin uses *Glory* (1989) (described in Table 9.2) to visualize the past during his unit on the Civil War. *Glory* is an excellent example of a film that successfully visualizes the past.

Toplin (1996) postulates that even for directors, producers, and writers who are arduously committed to reliably and realistically presenting the past there are tremendous pressures to add fictional elements to films. In addition to these pressures—financial, creative, political, and social—the ability of films to visualize the past are hampered by the limits of evidence from the historical record and the influences of modern-day events. In addition, filmmakers may alter the historical record in order to create more powerful aesthetics or have the aesthetics connect to a modern audience. For example, in *Glory*, the final battle scene helps the audience to visualize the attack on Fort Wagner in remarkably evocative ways but, because of lighting and other filming issues, the soldiers are attacking in the wrong direction. Therefore, any "recreation" of the past must be viewed and evaluated within these constraints. A key question for both teachers and historians posed by Toplin is: "how much slack is acceptable in the rope of creative liberty [when making films]?" (1996, p. 2). In the case of *Glory*, it appears these constraints are present, but not in ways that alter the film's ability to powerfully visualize the past. According to historian James M. McPherson *Glory* is "one of the most powerful and historically accurate movies ever made about that [Civil] war" and has the "most realistic combat footage in any Civil War movie" (McPherson, 1996, p. 128).

In the case that follows Mr. Irwin showed *Glory* to help his students visualize the past. His teaching practices demonstrate several key features of using film in this way such as conducting research to carefully choose a film that could provide a relatively accurate portrayal of soldiers and battles during the Civil War and providing students with important background and contextual information to support their understanding of the film. Mr. Irwin's teaching was also effective because he used guiding questions and class discussion to focus students on important characteristics of the film. In addition, he and the students discussed the film every day at the end of viewing rather than waiting until the film was finished. Finally, Mr. Irwin informed students of the goals for viewing up front so they understood the focus for viewing. All of these effective practices with film to visualize the past focused on illustrating specific aspects of the Civil War including the living conditions of soldiers, racism against African Americans and other racial issues, the brutality of battle, and the role of African-American soldiers in the war—particularly the Massachusetts 54th.

VISUALIZING ASPECTS OF THE CIVIL WAR WITH GLORY

Case Description

The case focused on *Glory* takes place in the eighth grade classroom of Mr. Irwin at Monet Middle School in Northeast Connecticut. Monet M.S. has approximately 700 students in grades 5–8 and a student population that is 95% white. The school is located in a small town that is an outer-ring suburb of a mid-size city.

The class is a U.S. history course that covers from just before the Civil War through the 1950s in five large units. The case described and analyzed here was part of an 11-day Civil War mini-unit within the larger unit titled "Division and Reunion." The class meets every other day for 90-minute blocks. There are 23 students in the non-tracked class including three students of color and several students who receive special education services.

The small number of units covered over the course of the year promotes significant depth in each topic and allows for the use of multiple resources including films. Mr. Irwin's overall goals in the class are to "awaken the inquisitive nature of historical investigation" in his students and have them act as historical detectives. He also emphasizes how the world has changed including technology, social issues, and how the government functions—thus promoting connections between the present and the past. Mr. Irwin also focuses on the role of race in "the story of America." He believes that the issue of race is crucial to understanding the past and understanding today's world. In addition to *Glory*, Mr. Irwin shows *12 Angry Men* (1957), *All Quiet on the Western Front* (1930), *The Lost Battalion* (2001), and numerous documentary films during the school year. His primary rationale for showing films—both feature films and documentary films—is to "bring the past alive and provide a sense of the time period represented in the film," show perspectives not in other sources, and have students think about "humanity as a whole." He is concerned that the textbook often lacks depth and multiple perspectives. Mr. Irwin also discussed his objective of helping students learn to be more critical consumers of history-based films. He remarked that his students arrive in his class and often the only exposure they have to many past events and time periods is a feature film. Specifically, he cited having students who are still trying to figure out what is real or not real in *Forrest Gump* (1994) as an example of their inability to evaluate films.

Mr. Irwin has been teaching for 10 years, nine at Monet Middle School. One year prior to teaching this unit he participated in a summer workshop on using film to teach history and it is clear his practices with film are thoughtful and aimed at developing students' ability to investigate the past using the skills of history scholars. For example, he asks students to evaluate the accuracy of films by comparing them with other historical documents.

Unit Overview

Mr. Irwin's goals for his civil war unit included developing students' historical empathy and "bringing the past to life" or visualizing the past. These two goals also guided his use of *Glory*. Therefore, like many of the teachers discussed in this book he used a film

Table 9.1 Outline of Lessons: The Civil War and *Glory*

Day	Activity	Goals
1–4	Background of Civil War Readings. Presentation/discussion of causes and effects of Civil War. Readings and documentary on Stonewall Jackson and Ironclad technology. Group projects and presentations on civil war highlights.	
5	Introduction to *Glory*. Viewing of *Glory*. Film stopped at various points for brief discussion.	Analyze what life was like for an African-American soldier during the Civil War including training, battle, and African-American–White relations. Visualize the past in terms of battles, uniforms, tactics, etc. Evaluate film as a source of knowledge about the past.
6	Viewing of *Glory*. Film stopped at various points for brief discussion.	Analyze what life was like for an African-American soldier during the Civil War including training, battle, and African-American–White relations. Visualize the past in terms of battles, uniforms, tactics, etc. Evaluate film as a source of knowledge about the past.
7	Discussion of *Glory*. Read and discuss "Connecticut's Own Glory." Analyze and discuss primary sources about women in the Civil War.	Analyze what life was like for an African American soldier during the Civil War including training, battle, and African-American–White relations. Visualize the past in terms of battles, uniforms, tactics, etc. Evaluate film as a source of knowledge about the past.

Table 9.1 (continued)

Day	Activity	Goals
8–11	Read and discuss Andersonville Play and Emancipation Proclamation.	
	View Documentary on General Sherman and Sherman's march to the sea.	
	Primary Documents Activity on Lincoln conspiracy theory.	
	Read and discuss "O Captain My Captain" by Walt Whitman	

to achieve multiple objectives. His use of *Glory* to develop empathy will be touched on briefly, but the thrust of the chapter is devoted to discussing how *Glory* recreated the past for his students.

He believed it was important to "recreate" the past for the students—to help them visualize the past, particularly life for the soldiers. He uses *Glory* as a tool for visualizing life of Civil War soldiers with a focus on the African-American soldier. This focus was primarily a result of his belief that race and racial issues play a critical role throughout U.S. history, but also due to the paucity of inclusion on race in the textbook. Mr. Irwin completed several activities with students before they viewed the film in class to provide background and context for the film and for the larger Civil War unit. Students were provided guiding questions to answer during their viewing of the film that asked them to consider various aspects of soldiers' lives such as why they would enlist, how they were trained, the relationships between white and black soldiers, how they experienced battle, and how they changed over the course of the film. He wanted to help students not only "see" the recreated past in terms of uniforms and battle scenes, but recreate some of the "conditions" or "mood" of the past, such as race relations, that provide context for people and events. Mr. Irwin then led discussions of these elements and others to check for student understanding and elaborate on various aspects of the film. For example, why were they willing to fight and die?

Following the activities with *Glory* Mr. Irwin had students read about Connecticut's own black regiment during the Civil War, the Connecticut 29th, and compared their experience with those of the soldiers in the film (Massachusetts 54th). The unit concluded with several additional activities over four days building on, but not explicitly connected to, *Glory*.

Unit Outline

The Civil War unit in Mr. Irwin's class spanned 11 days, though only 3 of the 11 days focused on using *Glory*. Table 9.1 provides a brief description of activities prior to and after the use of *Glory* and more detailed descriptions of the three days revolving around *Glory*. The three days of the unit that use *Glory* will be the focus of this chapter. *Glory* was viewed on days 5 and 6 of the unit with day 7 focused on post-viewing activities, for a total of 270 minutes devoted to activities involving the film.

Films

Glory, the only feature film used for this case study, is briefly described in Table 9.2.

Table 9.2 Description of Film

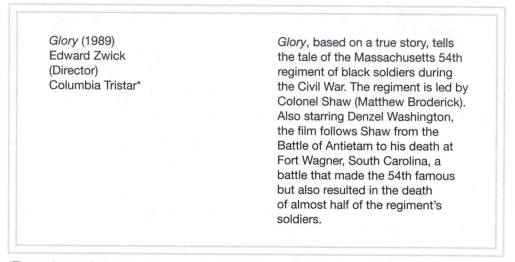

Glory (1989)
Edward Zwick
(Director)
Columbia Tristar*

Glory, based on a true story, tells the tale of the Massachusetts 54th regiment of black soldiers during the Civil War. The regiment is led by Colonel Shaw (Matthew Broderick). Also starring Denzel Washington, the film follows Shaw from the Battle of Antietam to his death at Fort Wagner, South Carolina, a battle that made the 54th famous but also resulted in the death of almost half of the regiment's soldiers.

*The version used is an educational version that deletes some of the language elements that might be inappropriate for eighth grade students

FILM ACTIVITIES

Days 1–4

During the first four days of the unit Mr. Irwin and his students explored the causes of the Civil War and other contextual information leading up to the Civil War (days 1 and 2) and studied an overview of the war's key events (days 3 and 4). The activities included background readings out of the textbook with guiding questions and follow-up discussion, viewing a documentary on Stonewall Jackson with guiding questions and follow-up discussion, and a teacher-led presentation/discussion on the causes and effects of the Civil War, North/South differences, Civil War geography, war strategy, important battles, key leaders, numerous photos to provide visual context, medical conditions for soldiers, and the role of women in the war. The students also completed a more in-depth activity on Ironclad ships in the war and on day 4 students had to present in small groups on topics they had researched (Strategies for Victory, Battle of Bull Run, Naval Action, Antietam, Confederate Victories, and War in the West). All of the activities in days 1–4 provided background and context for the viewing of *Glory*.

Day 5

Mr. Irwin spent the first 20 minutes of day 5 preparing students for the film. He provided a film viewing guide (Table 9.3), and using the guide, reviewed the film's seven main characters, information on the film, and background about the Massachusetts 54th. Mr. Irwin also briefly highlighted some of the questions on the film guide and reminded students about expectations for completing their work. The film guide contained 19 questions including several asking for information that Mr. Irwin believes is important for students to know to understand the film (e.g., Who is Frederick Douglas?) as well as questions that ask students to infer or make judgments (e.g., Why do you think Trip hates Thomas so much? How has Shaw changed from Antietam to Fort Wagner?). Many of the questions focused on the issue of race as a way to help students understand the mood recreated by the film and to support the development of historical empathy (e.g., 5. What does the Confederate proclamation state? What does this mean to members of the 54th?) Finally, Mr. Irwin focused students' viewing by presenting three themes to pay attention to and take notes on for post-film discussion: (1) What made soldiers enlist or sign-up for the military (and how is that the same or different today)? (2) What are the issues of race that emerge during the Civil War and specifically for the Massachusetts 54th? (3) What is real in the film versus what is "Hollywood" or made up and how does the film recreate the past?

The majority of class time was spent viewing the film. Mr. Irwin periodically stopped the film or spoke over a quiet moment in the film to point out a key scene or idea or to provide a clarification. For example, he highlighted the soldiers in the film playing baseball to make a connection to today, pointed out characters when they first appeared on screen, and discussed racial issues such as former/runaway slaves joining the military.

The final 15 minutes of class were used by Mr. Irwin to review key aspects of the film viewed so far and to review the first six questions from the viewing guide as a way to assess student understanding and to scaffold learning from the film. For example, he led a discussion about what happened at the battle of Antietam, connecting previous material to the film, and asked students to talk about what they "saw" in terms of battles and other ways the Civil War could be visualized. Students actively participated in a discussion of answers to the questions with a majority of the students volunteering to provide answers. Several students were confused about the names of characters so Mr. Irwin reviewed that again. He also had to explain what "fraternizing" meant and provided additional details about the impact of what students saw in the film on African Americans enlisting in the military and other issues of race. Finally, students struggled to answer question 6 about why Shaw distanced himself from his troops and Mr. Irwin provided a detailed explanation.

Day 6

At the beginning of day 6 Mr. Irwin and the students reviewed answers to questions 7 and 8, which had been covered the day before. He then provided a preview of key events the students would view in the film including the 54th regiment's first battle (in South Carolina) as well as their activities in Georgia. He specifically guided students to pay attention to scenes where *Glory* was effectively recreating the past and could help

Table 9.3 Glory Viewing Guide

Civil War – *Glory*
Main Characters
Robert Gould Shaw (Matthew Broderick); Trip (Denzel Washington); Cabot Forbes (Cary Elwes); Rawlins (Morgan Freeman); Jupiter Sharts (Jihmi Kennedy); Thomas Searles (Andre Braugher); Mulchahy (John Finn).
Note
This movie came out in 1989 and won 3 Academy Awards: Best Supporting Actor (Denzel Washington), Best Cinematography, and Best Sound.
Background
The movie *Glory* is based on the letters of Robert Gould Shaw, *Lay This Laurel* by Lincoln Kirstein, and *One Gallant Rush* by Peter Burchard. It is about the 54th regiment of MA under the command of Colonel Shaw. The regiment was first formed in November of 1862 and did not see any fighting until July of 1863 at James Island, SC. However, its reputation for bravery and courage was not established until later that summer at Fort Wagner in the Charleston Harbor.
Questions
1. Who is Frederick Douglas? What does Douglas, the governor and his dad want Robert to do?
2. What is the difference between Thomas Searles and Jupiter Sharts?
3. Why won't Shaw permit any fraternizing between the enlisted men and the officers?
4.   Why do you think the regiment learns so quickly?
5.   What does the Confederate proclamation state? What does this mean to members of the 54th?
6. Why do you think Shaw is distancing himself from the regiment?
7. What effect does the flogging have on Trip? Shaw?
8. What events or actions help build camaraderie amongst the officers and enlisted men?
9. Why is the experience in GA so negative for the men of the regiment?
10. Why do you think Trip hates Thomas so much?
11. Why does Rawlins not want the 'n' word used? How does Rawlins think they should behave?
12. What impact do you think the battle at James Island, SC had on the entire regiment?
13. Who is Trip fighting for? Why do you think he refuses to carry the flag into the battle at Fort Wagner?
14. Why do you think Shaw volunteers his regiment to be the first to charge into the Fort?
15. Do you think Shaw fully comprehends his decision? (explain or give examples)
16. What do you think Shaw meant when he said, "I will see you in the fort, Thomas?"
17. Why do you think these men were so willing to sacrifice their lives in the Civil War?
18. How has Shaw changed from Antietam (1st battle) to Fort Wagner (the last)?
19. How do you think you would have felt if you had been in the 54th regiment?

them visualize what the past may have looked like and felt like. Mr. Irwin again stopped the film intermittently to clarify moments in the film, answer students' questions, or focus students on an important aspect of the film. A particularly poignant pause revolved around a scene in the film when Colonel Shaw and his men are ordered to burn a Southern town. Another African-American regiment is already in the process of carrying out this order (and doing it gleefully), but Shaw and his men hesitate, communicating a message of the film that these acts were not appropriate even in a time of war. Mr. Irwin's students were especially disturbed by the war crimes in this scene and asked many questions.

At the conclusion of the film Mr. Irwin and the students continued to discuss answers to questions from the film guide. Questions 9–12 were answered. Students' responses and questions almost all revolved around issues of race. Students discussed the issue of former slaves vs. freemen fighting for the 54th, the challenges to being an all-black unit (including problems with Northern white soldiers), and the role of the 54th in opening the door for other African-American troops to fight. The film's focus on race was influencing students' questions and appeared to be positively impacting their learning.

Mr. Irwin also provided details about what aspects of the film were "real" and which were fictional. Students asked several questions about the reality of specific characters and about their behaviors. Mr. Irwin explained the concept of composite characters (one character in a film representing a much larger group such as Trip representing former slaves and Thomas representing free, educated blacks) and discussed which characters were "real" and whom the composite characters represented. He also clarified that the battle scenes were "real" and accurate in terms of what it was like (uniforms, importance of flags, noise, confusion, terror, communication, casualties, etc.), though the exact minute-by-minute action shown was not necessarily exactly as it was. Finally, he identified the idea of respect and self-respect that appears in the film as a reflection of when the film was made. For example in one scene Rawlins, an African-American soldier played by Morgan Freeman, restrains fellow members of the 54th who are being taunted by white soldiers. He tells them they need to have self-respect. In other scene he admonishes his peers for using the word *nigger*, again to promote the issues of self-respect. Mr. Irwin uses these scenes as an illustration of a "modern" issue that was in the film that is perhaps more a reflection of when the film was made than an accurate portrayal of how the soldiers would have thought and behaved.

Day 7

The first half of day 7 included Mr. Irwin and his students exploring answers to questions 13–19 of the film guide. Again students actively participated in discussing the film and asked numerous follow-up questions. The dialogue centered on the perspectives of the African-American soldiers and on the beliefs and actions of Colonel Shaw, supporting Mr. Irwin's empathy goals. After answering the film guide questions Mr. Irwin led a follow-up discussion of *Glory* as a Hollywood creation building on the previous day's work. He reflected on the film's final battle at Fort Wagner as a recreation of the past (e.g., the "feel" was accurate though they were charging the wrong direction) and asked students how the music in the film, particularly in the battle scenes, made the film more or less real and how it impacted how they reacted to the scenes. Finally, Mr. Irwin read excerpts from *The Civil War: The Complete Text of the Bestselling Narrative History of the Civil Wars* (Ward, Burns, & Burns, 1990) based on the Ken Burns documentary. The readings included information about the flag bearer at the Fort Wagner battle (he had four bullet wounds), an excerpt from a newspaper account of the battle that likened the Fort Wagner assault to an African-American Bunker Hill, and an excerpt from an interview with Colonel Shaw's father about Shaw being buried by the Confederates with his troops. These excerpts built on the final scene in *Glory* and reinforced the film's account of the Fort Wagner battle as "real."

The second component of class consisted of students reading and discussing a 1989 article from *The Hartford Courant* titled "Connecticut's Own Glory" (12/15/89, E1; E9) about Connecticut's 29th regiment, an all-African-American unit created during the Civil War. The students read the article and answered questions on their own (see Table 9.4 for the article guide). The first part of the article guide required students to glean information from the article about Connecticut's 29th regiment. The second component of the article guide asked students to compare and contrast the Massachusetts and Connecticut units.

Mr. Irwin then led a discussion of the article. Students consistently referred to *Glory* when discussing the article. The film helped to make the Connecticut soldiers more real to the students as if the students could imagine the soldiers and their experiences more easily. The students were also excited that they could connect the film to their home state. In addition, the article provided a nice contrast to the film. Whereas the film was heavily based on Shaw's perspective (using his letters) what is known about the 29th is based on the journals and autobiography of Alexander Newton, an African-American soldier.

Table 9.4 Questions for Article on Connecticut's Own Glory.

Questions for "Connecticut's Own Glory," *The Hartford Courant*, 1989

Part I
CT's own "Glory" was called what?
Who is Alexander Newton?
Why didn't Governor Buckingham allow black men to form regiments before 1863?
In New York, during the summer of 1863, why did the Irish Americans start a riot?
How does Newton compare his fellow soldiers during battle with white soldiers?
How did Lt. Col. Oliver T. Beard describe his soldiers during combat?
Describe Wooster's relationship with the enlisted men of the 29th regiment.
Even though the movie *Glory* is not one hundred percent accurate, why does historian James M. McPherson feel it can be used in social studies classes?

Part II
"Because I kept a diary during the Civil War the history of the 29th Regiment is known. Who am I?"
"I was Colonel Shaw's counterpart of the 29th Regiment. Who am I?"
What prompted the forming of the 29th Regiment from CT?
Name three similarities shared by Colonels Shaw and Wooster (excluding skin color).
What act showed how much Colonel Wooster cared for his men?
According to the article, what did the men of the 29th and 54th Regiments achieve by fighting?
You are a reporter from *Harpers Weekly* Magazine who witnessed the charge by the 54th Regiment against Fort Wagner. Write an account of what you saw and felt during the battle.

Days 8–11

Mr. Irwin followed up *Glory* with several activities that built on the background information and examination of the Civil War during the first seven days of the unit and added new layers of analysis. First, Mr. Irwin and the students analyzed and discussed several primary sources about women in the Civil War. Next, the students read and discussed a play about Andersonville (the South's prisoner of war camp for Union soldiers) as another way to "make the past come alive." The students also read and discussed the Emancipation Proclamation and viewed a documentary on General Sherman and his destructive march to the sea. The unit concluded with an activity that used primary source documents to explore a conspiracy theory about Lincoln's assassination, and with a reading and discussion of the poem "O Captain, My Captain" by Walt Whitman.

Mr. Irwin used the film *Glory* to help his students visualize the past, relying on the film's relatively accurate portrayal of soldiers and battles during the Civil War. The students embraced the film, illustrated by their enthusiasm during discussions of the film and through demonstrating an awareness of various aspects of the Civil War. Earlier parts of the Civil War unit studied were made more vivid through *Glory*, and subsequent activities built on understandings developed from the film.

Mr. Irwin's practices with *Glory* were especially effective because he provided appropriate and necessary context for the film prior to viewing, focused students on select aspects of the film through guiding questions and discourse, held discussions of the film each day of viewing, not just at the end of the film, conducted research in order to choose an appropriate film, and explicitly discussed his goals with students and used these goals to generate discussion of the film.

One of the most important aspects of the unit was the pre-film viewing activities. Providing context for the film helped students to understand why events occurred in the film and where they were occurring. For example, students knew background information about battles shown in the film, had a sense of the attitudes faced by African Americans, and understood, at least in terms of statistics, the dangers of battle.

Mr. Irwin's guiding questions were effective at helping students focus on and comprehend the mood recreated by the film, particularly around issues of race and attitudes toward African-American soldiers. This was reinforced by holding discussions each day rather than waiting until the end of the film so that the film was fresh in the students' minds and so that he could quickly dispel any misconceptions.

Because Mr. Irwin was explicit about his goals and about the film not being a perfect representation of the past the students could focus on how the film

REFLECTION ON THE CASE

was a recreation and do so with a more critical analysis. He helped students to interpret the film rather than letting the film stand on its own without the evaluation required by good historical inquiry. The research he did prior to the unit supported these activities, though Mr. Irwin reflected that he "doesn't know it all" but wants to be sure he shares what he does know about the film.

Student response to the film was very positive in terms of engagement and appeared to influence their learning. Mr. Irwin emphasized how well he believed *Glory* recreated the past in ways that other sources such as readings could not, especially in illustrating the living conditions of soldiers, racism against African Americans, and the brutality of battle, especially little details such as what it is like to use muskets, for instance the difficulty of reloading and what happens when you run out of time and use bayonets.

In a follow-up interview Mr. Irwin recounted the impact he believes *Glory* had on how students remembered the Civil War. Students repeatedly brought up issues from *Glory* in class activities and related them to other events or ideas discussed. Emotionally powerful moments in the film were brought up the most often, such as Trip being whipped for leaving camp and the burning of civilian homes by troops. Mr. Irwin planned to draw on the visualized past in *Glory* later in the year by comparing the life of a soldier and the nature of battle with similar aspects of World War I (with WWI being visualized by *All Quiet on the Western Front* (1930) and *The Lost Battalion* (2001)).

The use of *Glory* in this case is a good example of using film to recreate the past. Mr. Irwin's one regret was that, although he did extensive research on the film, he wishes he had even more time to study the film. He expects to add to his own background knowledge each year, particularly on Colonel Shaw and on Connecticut's 29th, and hopes to locate additional analysis of the film by historians.

Another aspect of the unit that could be tweaked is the way students analyzed the film. Mr. Irwin provided the relevant information about what was accurate and how the film successfully (and unsuccessfully) recreated the past. In this case he was limited in what he could with the eighth grade and by time constraints. However, with additional time and students with more sophisticated historical research skills, the students could do more of the work of investigating and evaluation the film. For example, rather than just using short primary source excerpts, a teacher could ask students to read actual letters from Colonel Shaw, *Lay this Laurel* (1973) by Lincoln Kirstein, and *One Gallant Rush* (1965) by Peter Burchard (the documents the film was based on) as well as other primary and secondary source documents, thus reviewing the accuracy of the film based on the historical record. Students could be asked to focus on various aspects of the film such as the life of a soldier, the nature of battles, and the attack on Fort Wagner, meet in small groups to discuss, and then write a review of the film from the perspective of a historian. In this way students would have to make their own judgments and come to their own conclusions and would be better prepared to evaluate other history films.

Finally, the use of primary source excerpts worked well to *reinforce* the accuracy of the film's recreation. However, at the same time it left the film unquestioned. Additional primary sources could be used—such as with the activity mentioned above—that could maintain the general integrity of the film, but challenge some of the film's representations as a means of considering how history is represented in film and to further explore the film's content.

Strategies for Using Film to Visualize the Past

There are several lessons about using film to recreate the past that emerge from this case and are important to consider when using film for this purpose. Perhaps the most crucial task for the teacher is to carefully research the film. Without this information a film may be a powerful learning tool, but provide students with recreations that do not adhere to the historical record or grossly distort reality. Mr. Irwin's research on the film allowed him to guide students' viewing of the film.

Another important pedagogical strategy is to focus students on what you want them to get out of the film and how they can do it. This includes having specific goals, providing guiding questions/themes, and explicitly discussing the film as a vehicle for understanding the past. Whereas these may be good practices in general, to utilize film to recreate the past students require a focus that helps them to see through a film's "entertainment" mechanisms (even while relying on them to visualize the past), and need support to develop the skills to analyze film, thus explicit and transparent discussions. Mr. Irwin provided specific goals and carefully raised issues directly about the film's representation of the past, supporting students' understanding of the Civil War, the film, and films about the past more broadly.

Also fundamental to using film well as a recreation of the past is providing the contextual background necessary for students to understand the why, when, and how of particular events and people. Students can truly understand a film's representation of the past only if they can place that representation in a broader context and within a greater understanding of people and events. The students in this case had readings, class activities, and formal presentations, all of which enhanced their understanding of the film.

Follow-up to the film is also important so that students can apply what they have learned and think about the content beyond the film. In this case students learned about the Connecticut 29th, which encouraged them to compare and contrast the two units while also making the content relevant to their lives as Connecticut citizens.

Glory was used in its entirety, but an important decision for a teacher to make is whether to show an entire film or to use smaller clips. Mr. Irwin's goals included developing student empathy. As a result it made pedagogical sense for him to show the entire film. However, in many cases teachers can use much smaller segments of the film in ways that focus the students solely on the recreated past relevant to the lesson. As discussed later, this could also help to home in on more accurate parts of a film while leaving out more fictionalized elements.

An additional feature of practice with film to consider is the use of other primary and secondary sources. The use of film to recreate the past will be more powerful when used in conjunction with other sources. As mentioned earlier, Mr. Irwin used primary sources that supported the film's representation of the past, but none that refuted it. Other sources can serve the purpose of providing context, supporting the film, and challenging the film. The use of other sources will help students to better understand the content as well as further develop their historical film literacy skills.

Finally, Mr. Irwin stopped the film periodically to discuss various elements. As discussed in previous chapters, stopping the film for discussion and clarification is a common and effective practice for teachers in our cases. However, it is important to consider when and how often to stop a film, particularly in attempting to visualize the past for students. In order to help recreate a mood or a set of event, it may be necessary to limit the number of interruptions. Although Mr. Irwin did pause the film numerous times, he never did so during the middle of a crucial segment such as a battle scene.

Strategies for Choosing Films to Visualize the Past

When choosing films to recreate the past for students there are a few criteria to keep in mind. Perhaps the most important, and the one cited by Mr. Irwin as his litmus test, is the accuracy of a film. Although general adherence to the historical record is important, even more critical is how well the film recreates the look and feel of a time period. In the case of *Glory* the film's creators worked hard to project realistic battle scenes as well as the feel, look, and mood of being an African-American soldier during the Civil War. Although this is perhaps one of the most tedious aspects of planning a lesson with film, there are ample resources available for teachers to research not just the accuracy but the "feel" of a film. If only clips are being shown there is less of a burden for the entire film to accurately recreate the past, though no less of a burden on the scenes being used. For example, a teacher might consider showing the opening scene from *Saving Private Ryan* (1998) as an accurate portrayal of the American perspective of the D-Day invasion during WWII. However, a choice may be made not to show the rest of the film, which is a fictional account of a group of soldiers.

A second consideration in choosing films for recreating the past is how well they work within the larger goals of the unit. Some films may recreate the past but do so without addressing the key objectives of the unit. This criterion is not necessarily unique to using film to recreate the past; however, it can be more tempting to use film in this manner even if disconnected from the rest of the unit. Films can be appealing because they often engage students, but if the scenes shown do not match other aspects of the unit their value and power will be undermined. For example, Mr. Irwin said one of his key reasons for choosing

Glory, in addition to its historical accuracy, was its focus on issues of race, a core theme in the unit and in the entire course. This made the use of *Glory* much more meaningful for the students and allowed them to connect aspects of the film to other units.

A related issue in choosing film is how well the film works as a document in conjunction with other documents in the unit. Since using film to recreate the past is only one small portion of how students will understand any particular event, it needs to complement other documents and both build on and help to support other documents.

There are many films that are effective at helping students visualize the past. For example, *Dances with Wolves* (1990) recreates life on the great plains for Native Americans and the incursion of white settlers. Although the narrative is fictional the film accurately recreates the scenery of the plains as well as the conditions of life, particularly for Native Americans. The film recreates not only the look but also the sounds, including Native Americans speaking in their native language, not English. The film is easily compared with other documents including written accounts of settlers, with photographs from the time—the film takes place during and after the Civil War—and with other films that portray Native American–white settler interaction.

Another example of a film that effectively recreates the past is *Gangs of New York* (2002). Like *Glory* and *Dances with Wolves*, this film recreates the past during the Civil War. *Gangs of New York* provides a fictional story, but accurately recreates life in New York in 1863, particularly for the poor and immigrants. The film can help students to understand conditions in a growing urban area during this era as well as the struggles of many immigrants through its visuals and sound. Within the film are "real" events such as the Civil War draft riots. There are numerous documents that can be used in lessons with the film including photographs, Ellis Island records, and newspaper accounts of the draft riots. *Gangs of New York* could also be used in conjunction with *Glory* and *Dances with Wolves* to demonstrate how, during the same time period, people lived in vastly different conditions and had enormously different experiences.

Finally, *Schindler's List* (1993) powerfully recreates life for Jewish victims of the Holocaust during WWII. The film's creators, including the director, Steven Spielberg, took enormous pains to accurately recreate the conditions, look, and feel of life and death in the ghettos and in work and concentration camps. The film relies heavily on first-hand accounts of survivors to authenticate its accuracy and the main characters and events are real, not fictional. The many documents that could be used in activities with *Schindler's List* include *Night* by Elie Wiesel, the numerous photographs and documentary footage films available, and survivor testimony recorded by the Shoah Foundation.

Films are extraordinary resources presenting unique challenges, but offering distinctive opportunities. Their ability to help students visualize the past through the visual and audio recreation of past people and events is unmatched by other sources and can be used powerfully by teachers.

CHAPTER 10

Using Film as Historical Narrative

Figure 10.1 Ride with the Devil (1999). Jack Bull (Simon Baker), Jake Roedel (Tobey Maguire), and Holt (Jeffrey Wright), riding to participate in the Raid on Lawrence by Bushwhacker forces.

"Why is the Black dude riding with the pro-slavery people?" This comment, made by a student watching *Ride with the Devil* (1999), captures the sort of questions posed during and after viewing the film as part of the following case set in a U.S. history survey course (see Table 10.2 for film details). The film tells the story of the Kansas–Missouri border war that occurred from the 1850s through the end of the American Civil War. The reactions of these students are illustrative of how film can be used to challenge students' beliefs about, and understandings of, one of the most commonly required and taught historical events in U.S. history classrooms: the American Civil War. This film-based lesson both challenged student beliefs that the American Civil War started at Fort Sumter, South Carolina, and forced them to look in a more complex way at the causes of the war and how it was fought. Although not originally a conscious goal for the lesson on the part of the teacher when selecting the film, the narrative structure of the film itself and the story it tells also interrupted and challenged students' often simplistic view of history and historical films as fitting a "good guys vs. bad guys" structure or providing an easy answer. In this way the teacher, Ms. Reed, used film both to confront the common historical narrative that exists about the causes of the Civil War, and also to challenge her students' ability to make sense of the film's lack of a standard film narrative structure.

The use of generic narratives (e.g., romantic comedy, biography, Western) by film production teams works to help in the efficient production of film and also to help audiences understand the stories being told. The common film narrative structures, or templates, have been long established for different genres—for example, for a Western, something is done to introduce the bad guys and good guys, pose the problem (e.g., murder, robbery, land infraction), lead up to a climactic event (e.g., shootout), and then end, usually in a happy way for the good guys. Films follow these templates so that audience members can easily understand the "relevant surroundings, positions and paths assumed by the story's agents" (Bruner, 1996, p. 49). For example, if it is a Western, the opening scene is usually signified by open terrain and a cowboy or frontiersman on a horse, so an audience can assume that it takes place somewhere in the western United States and is most likely set in the latter half of the 19th century. In addition, they can assume the protagonist, usually a soldier, cowboy, or sheriff, is attempting to resolve a problem with another group, generally American Indians, outlaws, or Mexican bandits. Because many audience members know what to expect from a Western genre film "schema," they can easily understand the narrative that is portrayed in the film.

The film studies expert David Bordwell (1985) argues that successful fiction films utilize narrative structures that are easily recognized and understood by a large audience, but often have some deviation from what the audience expects. Too close an adherence to the genre template makes a film unmemorable. This little twist or deviation from the formula is what makes a film memorable, and often successful. Too much deviation, however, may make a film unsuccessful at the box office even if it challenges the audience to think differently about the events or story portrayed. The film examined as part of this case, Ang Lee's *Ride with the Devil*, does exactly this in challenging students' common understandings of the Civil War and what caused it, and did poorly at the box office as a result of deviating too far from the formula. Films such as *Ride with the Devil* and the film examined in Chapter 9, *Glory*, are not likely to become big box-office successes if they are created for too small an audience, the history aficionado. When the story being presented becomes too complex or challenges the audience to think in complex ways, it tends to become less entertaining. However, this very disadvantage at the box office can work to a teacher's advantage in challenging students to think beyond common historical narratives, and can be especially potent when a film contests the notion of U.S. history as a narrative of inevitable progress and freedom (Barton & Levstik, 2004).

MS. REED'S CLASS: CHALLENGING COMMON (MIS)UNDERSTANDINGS OF THE CIVIL WAR

This chapter examines the use of film to challenge students common understandings of the U.S. Civil War, and also provides a case set in the context of a high-stakes testing environment in which teachers are allowed little freedom in the selection of topics they teach or ways in which those stories can be told. Ms. Reed, however, has found strategies to engage students in the material required by the test as well as challenge them to go deeper on important topics and discover certain analytical skills along the way. In the lesson described for this case, she utilized two long clips from *Ride with the Devil* to challenge students' notions that the Civil War started at Fort Sumter and their lack of understanding of what was happening in the West in the period leading up to the Civil War. She also asked students to make connections between the events in Kansas and Missouri and how they are used today as part of popular culture—in particular as part of college sports events and mascots. Although this is a short lesson and does not allow the time to go in as much depth as Ms. Reed would like, it shows how a film selected to challenge the historical understandings of her particular students can be effective in work toward more complex understandings of the past.

Case Description

This case focuses on a "Causes of the American Civil War" section of the North Carolina standardized U.S. history curriculum. Ms. Reed's junior-level U.S. history survey course was observed in the spring of 2009. The school, Jackson High School, is located in a major suburban district in North Carolina, where Ms. Reed's classes include honors and "regular" sections of primarily eleventh grade students. There were also a few seniors in her courses, as some students must retake the class if they were unsuccessful at passing the state test tied to the course. The honors designation is elective, and anyone can sign up, so Ms. Reed noted that often the classes were actually pretty similar, with the honors classes being sometimes more motivated to learn.

The high school where Ms. Reed works is relatively new, but the municipal area has grown so quickly that it was already over capacity by the time it was finished. Ms. Reed is one of a number of teachers in "temporary" classrooms behind the main building. The classroom is clean and bright and has 32 desks as well as a table where Ms. Reed places items related to her current unit. Ms. Reed noted that they are sometimes distracted in class because they can hear a family of foxes who are burrowing under their structure. The section of her U.S. history course described in this chapter is an honors section comprising 25 students on the days observed, including 15 white students, nine African-American students, and one Latino student (14 female, 11 male).

Ms. Reed has been teaching for five years. She had taught for three years in Wisconsin and was in her second year in North Carolina at the time of this observation. She graduated from a top teacher education program and also had a Bachelors degree in history. In addition to the eleventh grade U.S. history course, she also teaches an elective sociology course. She tries to incorporate a number of different strategies in her class and attempts to get students to do some writing, although she lamented that it is difficult given the tight timeline of the course.

> It is very high stakes. So that's why the emphasis on the regular [sections] is to try to do whatever you can with video, worksheets, projects, and what not to help them master the material. So you are almost forced to sacrifice some of those other skill sets . . . like their writing skills and analytical skills.

It is a semester-long course that meets in a block format (approximately 90 minutes) every day. She also discussed the difficult transition from her school in Wisconsin, which allowed teachers much more freedom in making curricular decisions than the highly standardized climate of her North Carolina school.

Ms. Reed is a film enthusiast. She uses some form of film almost every day, although generally her use includes very short clips to introduce a topic or to help students visualize some aspect of the past. She tries to make her class a story that is told through different perspectives, and she sees using film clips as way to help her do this. She also uses other media such as period music, images, and some documents or first-person accounts. Ms. Reed said it is easy to fall into the trap of just having students take notes from lecture, but explained that she feels the need to "diversify what we're doing on a daily basis to keep everyone's interests. It's hard though; the time constraints, the curriculum that I'm given makes it really hard to do." As some of the clips she uses come from films with R ratings, she includes a list of films as part of a letter to parents at the beginning of the semester and provides the opportunity for students and parents to opt out of the viewing. In the past, she has had parents who have requested their children do not view particular films and Ms. Reed has provided alternative activities on the same topic.

Unit Overview

The film activity in this case was part of Goal 3 in the North Carolina "standard course of study" U.S. history curriculum (see Table 10.1). As Ms. Reed's curriculum is driven largely by the state standards, and the Goals are aligned with the year-end test for this course, it is valuable to see how Ms. Reed includes this film activity within the context of a high-stakes testing environment.

The unit covers the above goal in roughly six instructional blocks (90 minutes per block). As part of the unit, students watched selected clips from *Ride with the Devil* and an educational film entitled *Causes of the Civil War* (2003), took some notes on the main causes of the war that align with the state curriculum, and did a timeline activity to help them organize all of the events and chronology. The class then studied the main battles, strategies, and turning points of the war using sources such as handouts, the textbook, and film clips. Finally, they finished the goal with a look at the Reconstruction period and its legacy in the South. Ms. Reed always tries to build in some geography work, usually in the form of map work, as part of her units. In this case, she had students map out the opposing sides and major battles. She believed this type of activity helps students to learn the content and prepare for the exam.

The film activity used with *Ride with the Devil* also addressed questions used as part of a school division-wide test that is meant to prepare students for the state exam and aligned with two Goal 3 objectives in particular (Table 10.2).

Table 10.1 North Carolina History Standard

> North Carolina Goal 3: Crisis, Civil War, and Reconstruction (1848–1877) – The learner will analyze the issues that led to the Civil War, the effects of the war, and the impact of Reconstruction on the nation.

Source: North Carolina Department of Public Instruction (2006).

Table 10.2 School Division Goal Objectives

> Objective 3.1: trace the economic, social and political events from the Mexican War to the outbreak of the Civil War.
>
> 1. How did the use of popular sovereignty (i.e., Kansas–Nebraska Act) and the compromise of 1850 create a greater regional and political crisis?
>
> 2. How did opponents of the institution of slavery use different methods to bring the issue to the attention of the American people (i.e., Stowe and Brown)?
>
> Objective 3.2: analyze and assess the cause of the Civil War.
>
> 6. What is the connection between territorial expansion and causes of the Civil War?

Ms. Reed identified four specific goals for the film-based lesson involving *Ride with the Devil*: (1) that students would gain an understanding of a major cause of the war, the Missouri–Kansas Border War (1854–1861) and its impact on popular culture today; (2) to "emphasize the importance of learning about lesser known historical events," such as the raid on Lawrence, which she notes is barely mentioned in the textbook but is shown vividly in the film; (3) to "encourage multiple perspectives in understanding historical events" as the film provides a complex history through the perspectives of the Missouri "Bushwhackers," Kansas "Jayhawks," the people caught in the middle of the fighting, and the U.S. Army; and (4) "Challenge the common historical narration of the Civil War as beginning with Fort Sumter (1861)."

For this unit, Ms. Reed explained she thought Goal 3 would take approximately 6–7 days including the school division-wide benchmark exam (Table 10.3). She would like more time to teach this important unit, but said it was difficult to take time from any other part of the curriculum. Further, tests were timed in a way that makes such changes difficult.

Table 10.3 Unit Outline

	Activity	Goal
Day 1	"Bleeding Kansas" film-based lesson (*Ride with the Devil*)	Understand role of border wars as one of the causes of Civil War
Day 2	Causes of the Civil War	Uses Schlesinger video on causes of the Civil War and timeline to help students understand main causes of the war
Day 3	Start of the war	To understand the final events that led to the beginning of the Civil War
Day 4	Fighting in the war and main strategies, also reading the Emancipation Proclamation	Uses clips from Ken Burns *Civil War* to help students identify main battles, strategies, and turning points in war
Day 5	Reconstruction	Understand major Reconstruction projects, the impact of 13th and 14th amendments, and the impact of reconstruction on the South and today
Day 6	Finish Reconstruction and exam	

Films

Ride with the Devil was directed by Ang Lee and released in 1999 to some critical acclaim, but to small audiences at the box office. The critic Roger Ebert (1999) praised the film for reflecting the local nature of the border wars, for what he claims is the first film on the Civil War that does not automatically show that the North will win, and for presenting characters such as Holt, the black man who rides with the Bushwhackers, without simplifying or even really explaining his complex motives. However, he also notes that some of the things that make the movie interesting are problematic when it comes to having a successful Hollywood film.

> "Ride With the Devil" does not have conventional rewards or payoffs, does not simplify a complex situation, doesn't punch up the action or the romance simply to entertain. But it is, sad to say, not a very entertaining movie; it's a long slog unless you're fascinated by the undercurrents. It's a film that would inspire useful discussion in a history class, but for ordinary moviegoers, it's slow and forbidding. (para. 9)

It is exactly this complex narrative that makes the film a powerful medium for engaging students in the events of Bleeding Kansas. As the unit went on, Ms. Reed also showed an educational video on the causes of the Civil War and clips from Ken Burns' documentary mini-series on the war to show some of the major events, strategies, and historical agents (see Table 10.4 for film descriptions and credits).

Table 10.4 Description of Films in Unit

Ride with the Devil (1999) Ang Lee (Director) Daniel Woodrell (Novel) James Schamus (Screenplay) Universal Pictures	This story of the Missouri–Kansas border wars of the 1850s and 1860s is told through the eyes of Jake Roedel, the son of German immigrants, who sides with his Missouri bushwhacker neighbors despite having few ties to the slaveholding South
Causes of the Civil War (2003) Volume 8, U.S. History series Henry Nevison (Director) Dana Palermo (Producer) Charles Hardy (Writer) Schlesinger Media production	Typical educational documentary style video with an anonymous narrator. Uses still images to cover the major causes of the American Civil War in this volume
The Civil War (1990) Ken Burns (Producer, Director) Public Broadcasting, Inc.	Ken Burn's epic miniseries on the U.S. Civil War – originally presented on PBS

FILM ACTIVITIES

On the day of the film activity, Ms. Reed has Civil War–era music playing as students enter the room and an array of University of Kansas memorabilia laid out on the table in the front of her classroom. These include a stuffed "Jayhawk" and logos promoting the "Border Wars" basketball game between the University of Missouri and the University of Kansas. Ms. Reed began by explaining the goals for the day—that the students were going to explore one of the lesser-known causes of the Civil War—and used the stuffed Jayhawk as part of her introduction for the lesson. She asked students to identify the creature. Students shouted out "blue bird," "Jayhawk," and "mascot." A student then identified it as the mascot for the University of Kansas. Ms. Reed then stated that "this Jayhawk mascot ties in nicely with one of the main causes of the war," to which one student remarked "did they ride with the devil?" Ms. Reed then explained who the Jayhawks were and provided some background on the history in Kansas and Missouri leading up to the Compromise of 1854 and the border wars. She also introduced the term "Bushwhacker," which caused a number of the students to giggle for the first half dozen times it was mentioned.

In order to go deeper into the background and set the class up for the film, Ms. Reed had students read a section of their textbook, *The Americans* (McDougall 2006, pp. 314–315), that explains the Missouri Compromise of 1854 and the opposing pro-slavery and anti-slavery sides. She then used the reading to introduce the idea that the border wars are largely forgotten as a cause of the Civil War and are often overlooked as a significant historical event. She explained that this omission in the textbook was a result of the event occurring in the West and that it was largely unorganized and complex because of the guerilla-style fighting and the pitting of neighbors against one another with no clear sides to the conflict.

Ms. Reed then prepared the students to view the first clip. She explained that they were not going to watch the whole thing because of time constraints, and because they do not need to see the love story portion of the film for the purposes of class. She also explained that it is an R rated movie, read the warning from the Motion Picture Advisory Board explaining why it received the rating, and then told her students that they could put their heads down during the violent portions if they wished, but that "this is not just Hollywood violence but because it really reflects the violence of the time." Students had a series of questions that they read through before viewing and were asked to identify answers while watching the clip (Table 10.5).

During the viewing Ms. Reed provided some help for students to identify the key points she wanted them to see, and the places in the film where an important answer to one of their questions was—"watching for number one right now" . . . "the answer for number two is coming up." She also answered student questions, such as when one student yelled out "who is Dutchy?" She quickly paused the film and explained that he is the character known as Jake, who is German or a Deutschmann, but whom some of the other Bushwhackers call "Dutchy" in a sort of derogatory fashion as they do not trust him. This kind of viewing intervention seemed to help students better follow what was going on. Students paid close attention to the film, although the detail of the questions at times seemed distracting as it caused the students to look up and down between the screen and the worksheet in an attempt to not miss an answer.

It was during this first clip that the impact of the film's narrative structure was evident to many students. The film does not present a clear "good guy" or "bad guy" as both sides

Table 10.5 Film Discussion Questions, Clip 1

Watch with the following questions in mind:

1. What is occurring at the start of the film? What does this tell you about people's daily life on the border? What do you notice about dress and social customs?
2. What are the men at the wedding meal conversing about? What are they worried about?
3. Who are the men that come in the middle of the night and kill Jack Bull's father?
4. How would you define guerilla fighting based on the scenes you saw?
5. What do you notice about the Bushwhacker clothing and style of dress? How does this tie into their belief system?
6. How are women and children treated in the film? What is their role amidst the violence on the border?
7. Who does Jake run into following the shoot out? What does this tell you about the conflict?
8. What happened to Jake's father?
9. What are the living conditions like for the Bushwhackers? How do they survive?
10. The introduction text explained that it was 'more dangerous to find oneself in the middle' of the fighting—what does this mean? How does this play out?

are seen undertaking horrific acts. Even the main character, played by Tobey McGuire of *Spiderman* (2002) fame, is somewhere in the middle fighting for the Bushwhackers but not believing in all that they do or stand for. One of the students finally yells out "are these good guys or bad guys?" when some of the Bushwhackers meet up with Union soldiers in a shootout. The film challenged their notions of who was bad and who was good, as the point of the film was not to provide an answer to that question but to let the audience decide.

The first clip Ms. Reed showed, the first 35 minutes of the film, helps establish what the conflict is about. It also provides some sense of who are on the two sides of the war, the Jayhawks and Bushwhackers, and also those who are stuck in the middle, German immigrants and pro-slavery and anti-slavery civilians. After they finished, the class went through and discussed the questions on the worksheet and the question raised previously by the student during the viewing regarding who the good guys and bad guys were. Some students weighed in on the matter, although most did not want to take a stance and remarked, "It is hard to see who is good and who is bad" or something similar, or to take the easy route and automatically say that the side for continuing slavery was bad. Then Ms. Reed tried to push them further to not just say that the anti-slavery forces were automatically good because of that position—"slavery is a horrible institution, so it is easy to say that the Bushwhackers are bad . . . but the Lawrence Jayhawkers are doing bad things . . . including killing Jake's father." Unfortunately, as Ms. Reed feels the time pressure to continue with the lesson, the discussion is cut off a bit prematurely and they move onto answering the remainder of the questions.

Students answered most of the questions directly and had obviously pulled from the film the information that Ms. Reed had envisioned. Questions that focused the class back on the good guys–bad guys debate and the complex motives of the characters seemed particularly powerful. For example, students picked up that the Bushwhackers would not hurt women, reflecting their Southern Gentlemen code of honor, but several noted that this was hypocritical as they were taking away the women's husbands by killing them and burning down their houses and businesses. One student argued "but they are basically leaving them to die—with no husband—no house." The conversation seemed to help students figure out the context for the film and also the complexities of the history being presented.

The second clip Ms. Reed showed depicted the Raid on Lawrence. She provided some context for the events and then had students read another section in their textbook (p. 316) that focused more explicitly on the massacre at Pottawattamie Creek and the Sack of Lawrence in 1856, but that left out any real detail of the much more brutal Raid on Lawrence that provided a segue into viewing the second clip. When the students read about the Pottawattamie Creek Massacre, including the way John Brown and his men would "hack off their hands when they were alive," some of the students responded to the brutality by gasping "oh my god" and "sweet Jesus." Ms. Reed again provided questions that were intended to help students make sense of what they were viewing and to help them focus on what she wanted them to take away from the film (Table 10.6).

It was during the viewing of this second clip, which focused on the Raid on Lawrence led by the Bushwhacker leader Quantrill and lasted for about 17 minutes (starting at scene 12), that students started to figure out who was on which side. It was as they showed the Bushwhackers making their way through the night to attack Lawrence that a student yelled out "Why is the Black dude riding with the pro-slavery people?" This

Table 10.6 Film Discussion Questions, Clip 2

Watch with the following questions in mind:

1. What is the tone of Quantrill's speech?
2. Why is Lawrence being targeted?
3. What is the crowd's reaction to Quantrill's speech?
4. What is the group planning to do in Lawrence?
5. What is symbolic about the destruction of the American flag?
6. How are the women in Lawrence treated during the raid? Why is this?
7. Why is Holt (an African American) riding with pro-slavery Quantrill and his raiders?

revealed the ways in which the film and its narrative structure defied students' common understandings of both the Civil War and the past in general. It also challenged what they expect from films in terms of easily definable problems and sides, especially knowing "which side to root for," as one student said. Students also discussed more fully who was caught in the middle, including civilians who were viewed as assisting one side or another, and the character of Jake (Tobey McGuire), whose family was not Southern and whose father wanted him to leave to the North. Jake did not fully believe in the Bushwhackers' cause but also did not want to turn his back on his friends. During both of these question and response sessions, the conversation went from comprehension-level recitation to true discussion in which students responded to each other, challenged each other's interpretations or built on each other's or Ms. Reed's comments.

Although the question was raised about why the African-American character, Holt, was riding with and fighting for the pro-slavery Bushwhackers, this topic was never fully discussed. Students were asked to respond, and they began to challenge each other's assertions, trying to work toward some kind of understanding of Holt's complex motivations. One student remarked "He was a slave; he didn't have a choice," to which another student responded "but he was armed and on a horse." A third student then interpreted the relationship between Holt and another character, George Clyde, whom he had grown up with and remarked, "[the other guy] saved his life—so now he is serving with him." Students showed the beginnings of deliberation and interpretation of the complex character Holt represented, but did not have the time to go to great depths. Holt's character is representative of a number of African Americans who are pictured riding with the Bushwhackers in photographs of the Raid on Lawrence.

As time was running short in the block, Ms. Reed moved along through the other questions in the discussion guide presented above and then helped the students connect the past with the popular culture remnants of these events in the form of the sports memorabilia. She asked students to examine two t-shirts worn by fans during the Missouri–Kansas basketball games from the perspective of what they knew about the events surrounding the border wars. A t-shirt for Missouri fans showed a famous watercolor of the "Raid on Lawrence" with the text "Scoreboard" beneath, and another for Kansas fans has a picture of John Brown, who was famous for the massacre of women and children from Missouri at Pottawatomie Creek, with the text "Keeping America Safe from Missouri since 1854" beneath.

During this part of the lesson, a number of the students made comments such as "that's disgusting" in response to what was represented on the shirts, although some other students also laughed at them and thought the shirt maker's use of history was clever. When asked by Ms. Reed to consider why people would wear these shirts, the students seemed to agree that they probably just did not really understand the violence that was represented in the images they were wearing. Ms. Reed then finished by talking about the seminar she had attended in Lawrence the previous summer and how there were small memorials all over town for the people that were killed in the raid and how it was still very much part of their history.

To finish out the period, students began to work on a timeline project that asked them to identify and record major events leading up to the Civil War, with the events in Kansas and Missouri being prominent. This timeline asked students to identify major causes of the war and was a way to collect and organize information that would be needed for the test, and a way to highlight again how the events in Kansas occurred long before Fort Sumter. This timeline project was continued the next day after students took notes and watched a video on the causes of the Civil War that focused on more traditional explanations, and that paid little attention to the events out West in Kansas and Missouri—a fact that Ms. Reed made abundantly clear for students. Throughout the first and second days of the unit, Ms. Reed also referred back to the important terms, such as "popular sovereignty," and to the geography of the places and regions they were discussing to reinforce both what she viewed as important (geography) and what students needed to know on the upcoming state exam (vocabulary).

The main goal for Ms. Reed in using *Ride with the Devil* was to challenge her students' understandings of the commonly accepted causes of the Civil War. This goal was clearly met as many students had not heard of Bleeding Kansas or even been aware that there was much going on west of the Appalachians before or during the war. The film was selected precisely because it presented the complexities of the Civil War overall, and the complexities of the particular microcosm of the war in Kansas and Missouri that did not necessarily reflect the same ideologies, values, or style of warfare seen in the East. What was not necessarily intended was the way in which the film's narrative structure also challenged students' beliefs about the past and their commonly held frameworks for making sense of the past and of films.

This unintended effect of the film activity was based on Ms. Reed's selection criteria for the film, although she did not realize the impact it had until after she used the film in class. After reflecting on the lesson, she realized how effective the film was in challenging students' beliefs about the Civil War and how film represents the past.

> I really liked when the kids in the first class asked, "who are the good guys, who are the bad guys?" "Who are we supposed to be cheering for?" . . . That's a major theme of the movie, but I just didn't think of a way of putting it out there.

REFLECTION ON THE CASE

So I loved how that was phrased and that was a question I wrote down. I definitely want to pose that question, because I think that that sums up a lot of the confusion about the time period.

As she reflected on the lesson, Ms. Reed also identified some instructional changes she would make next time using the film to make it more effective. She explained it might be more effective to make the characters' names explicit from the beginning, perhaps as a handout, as the story was so complex it was difficult to follow.

When it comes to identifying the characters, I want to put the character names [somewhere for students]. The two main characters [Jake and John Bull] that we see in the beginning of the film and actually throughout, put their names at the top of the sheet so the kids can see that and then make sure to point it out.

In addition to making the characters more explicit for students, Ms. Reed wished there was more time to discuss the complex aspects of the film. Unlike the luxury of time that Mr. Irwin was afforded in using *Glory* (see Chapter 9), Ms. Reed was under real time pressure. "I think more discussion would be great," she said. "I felt really rushed in that first class because again, I just wasn't sure exactly—Even knowing how long the clips were, you just never know how long it's going to take . . . Things like about the Holt character, and why would an African American be in this. And I think you could really pose some interesting debate questions . . . [or as] a short essay or response." She also wished some questions could have been explored further, such as "Why don't people know about this event? Or how did today's activity change your opinion of this event?"

The constraints of Ms. Reed's class in terms of the high-stakes environment and time limitations are obvious and becoming the status quo for social studies teachers in many states. Here, she was able to use film clips that get at the heart of what she wanted students to think about without losing the students completely. In part, she was successful because she selected specific clips that aligned with other aspects of the class—she used the first clip to introduce the mentalities of the two sides in the border conflict and provide context. She used the textbook to introduce these ideas and some guiding questions to help students make sense of the major points. Similarly, for the second film clip, students were introduced to the Raid on Lawrence through the textbook and Ms. Reed established the goal for viewing the event through identifying that this second and more vicious attack on Lawrence by the Bushwhackers is not even described beyond a mention in the text, but is of significance especially in that part of the United States as signified by its role in popular culture (as evident in the "Border Wars" t-shirt).

The main criticism of this unit is likely related to the time issue, over which Ms. Reed feels she has little control. It is easy to see how, given more time, the discussions around the major themes identified above could have led to powerful activities. One other question to consider, however, is the effectiveness of the list of questions for viewing. It seems based on the discussion that the questions that got at the big ideas related to how the film challenged students' notions of the past were most successful at helping students make sense of what they were seeing. Questions that asked students to consider why Holt, the African-American character, was riding with the Bushwhackers, who the good guys and bad guys were, seemed to be effective in forcing students to wrestle with what they saw in the film and helped them to relate it to the complex history of the Bleeding Kansas episode in U.S. history.

This discussion, had it gone deeper, would likely have gone further to challenge students' notions of U.S. history as a story of progress and freedom with clear good/bad, right/wrong dichotomies. The popular culture tie-in with the Jayhawk mascot and Border Wars theme of sporting contests made this point even more real and helped students to consider how historical events, even those that were brutal and violent, can be misunderstood and appropriated in our culture in seemingly odd ways.

Strategies for Using Film as Historical Narrative

Some key characteristics of practice for teachers to take from this case for using film as historical narrative are: (1) to find ways to help students make sense of a film that by design is difficult to make sense of and will challenge student assumptions and understandings; (2) to create a class environment in which students' understandings about the past are challenged and there are not finite correct or singular answers; and (3) to know your students' current understandings of historical events or issues so that you are selecting films that challenge their beliefs about the past that are commonly explained in textbook versions of history with a singular correct answer or are oversimplified, but for which there are multiple and competing answers or complex perspectives. Of course, the teacher needs to be successful in this latter characteristic without completely confusing her students.

In order to make the activity a success, it is important to frame the students' viewing in a way that will allow them to focus on the narrative aspects of the film as compared with how the event is normally taught in history classrooms. Focusing on big questions is a key, although the case above also illustrates how it is important to help prepare students for the viewing with some background, explicit goals for viewing the film, and pertinent details to help students successfully read the film, such as providing pictures and character names in advance to help them follow the film and be more specific in the discussion (see Chapter 5 for an example of this). Handouts such as Ms. Reed's with guiding questions can be successful, especially if the questions focus on the narrative disconnects and force students to make sense of them. As mentioned earlier, Ms. Reed's list of questions focused on some of the big ideas, such as "Why was Holt, an African American, riding with the Bushwhackers?", but also included detailed questions that were of little value to the overall goal. A shorter list of big questions to force students to examine the larger narrative of the film and how it challenges their understandings or some form of graphic organizer could also be effective—with students filling out part in advance with their take on an event and then comparing it with the film's narrative.

Another activity that could work toward these same goals is to adopt some of the practice identified in Chapter 4 to have students examine the events, and the narrative overall, through a character's perspective. This could be done through assigning students to shadow characters during the film and then join collectively to examine the larger narrative themes through the various perspectives that were represented.

Strategies for Selecting Films as Historical Narrative

Films that work well for this type of lesson, at least according to Bordwell (1985), will follow some genre characteristics so that students will be able to "read" it and identify the main ideas and actions, but will also diverge enough from the film and historical narrative to cause students to struggle with what they are seeing and what they "know" to be true. Like using film in some form of historical inquiry, as explored in earlier chapters, a film used to challenge students' narrative understandings would be most fitting for the types of historical events or questions that are open to interpretation or have multiple, competing answers; or, in the case of Ms. Reed's class, an event in history that is of great historical importance but for one reason or another has been cast into the dustbin of history during textbook and standards revisions.

Another key to successfully employing a film as historical narrative is the teacher's knowledge of her students and the context or curriculum that she is working with. Ms. Reed knew that the events of Bleeding Kansas and border wars were in the state standards and were briefly mentioned in the textbook. However, from her previous experience, she also knew that very few students knew anything about the events or saw them as particularly important, given that they were closer to the east coast and in the heart of the former Confederacy. It is important for a teacher to select a film that students will be able to relate to but that will counter or extend their understanding of a historic event or issue through the narrative presented in the film.

As mentioned above, in order to use a film to challenge students' narrative understanding of historical events, or challenge their notions of how films should be structured, it is important to select a film that diverges from the common structures and stories of the past but still follows enough genre rules to make it usable. There are a number of examples that would challenge students' narrative understandings of particularly important events. For example, a film such as the *Battle of Algiers* (1967) that is shot largely from the Algerian perspective but illustrates the violence on both sides of the conflict, challenges the concepts of terrorist versus freedom fighter or rebel versus patriot. This particular film was done in a style that also looks documentary in nature and was made so soon after the events in Algeria that many of the actors in the film were involved in the actual conflict. These characteristics accumulate into a film that challenges students to think about their own understandings of war and how messy it can be, especially as compared with a textbook rendition of France's brave fight to retain its colony in Algiers or a more progressive interpretation that it was just the natural time for the Algerians to begin self-rule.

In addition to *Battle for Algiers*, films that are a bit farcical in nature or break from history narrative norms can challenge students' notions of history and what it means to the present. For example, *Dr. Strangelove or: How I learned to Stop Worrying and Love the Bomb* (1964) is a classic critique of the Cold War social norms centered around fear and nuclear apocalypse. Similarly, *Little Big Man* (1970) presents a nonsensical plot that challenges students to think differently about American Westward Expansion during the latter half of the 19th century. Although both of these films could be used as primary sources, as they greatly reflect the social moods of their periods of production—an example is Mr. Briley's use of *Dr. Strangelove* in his 1960s unit (Chapter 5)—they can also be used to challenge students' understandings of society and events during the periods they represent. *Dr. Strangelove* actually presents an attempt to parody Cold War sentiments while presenting an exaggerated Cold War narrative. A third film that is more serious in presentation is *Sankofa* (1993). In this film the protagonist, a fashion model, is transported back in time to a plantation in the West Indies where she experiences the horrors of slavery and, eventually, the power of freedom as she becomes involved in a rebellion. *Sankofa* and an earlier film called *Burn!* (*Queimada*) (1969) both show empowered slaves of African heritage who fight for their freedom against their enslavers and could be used to challenge students' notions of slaves as passive or hapless victims.

As we note in the introductory section for Part V of this book, the use of film as a form of historical narrative as a way to challenge students' common assumptions and beliefs about the past is infrequently done. However, we hope the case of Ms. Reed and the powerful impact of *Ride with the Devil* on students' notions of the Civil War and of war as presented in film in general will help convince teachers to make use of this powerful strategy.

Figure Permissions and Credits

Figure 1.1
Forrest Gump (1994)
Directed by Robert Zemeckis
Shown: Tom Hanks (as Forrest Gump), President John F. Kennedy
Credit: Paramount Pictures/Photofest
© Paramount Pictures

Figure 2.1
Pearl Harbor (2001)
Directed by Michael Bay
Shown: poster art, Ben Affleck (as Capt. Rafe McCawley), Kate Beckinsale (as Nurse Lt. Evelyn Johnson), Josh Hartnett (as Capt. Danny Walker)
Credit: Touchstone Pictures/Buena Vista/Photofest
© Touchstone Pictures./Buena Vista Pictures

Figure 3.1
Gran Torino (2008)
Directed by Clint Eastwood
Shown from left: Clint Eastwood (as Walt Kowalski), Bee Vang (as Thao Vang Lor), Brook Chia (as Vu) Thao, Chee Thao (as Grandma), Ahney Her (as Sue Lor)
© Warner Bros
Photographer: Anthony Michael Rivetti
Credit: Warner Bros/Photofest

Figure 4.1
Swing Kids (1993)
Directed by Thomas Carter
Shown from left: Christian Bale (as Thomas Berger), Robert Sean Leonard (as Peter Muller), Jayce Bartok (as Otto), Frank Whaley (as Arvid)
Credit: Buena Vista Pictures/Photofest
© Buena Vista Pictures

Photographer: Frank Connor

Figure 5.1
Bonnie and Clyde (1967)
Directed by Arthur Penn
Shown: Gene Hackman (as Buck Barrow), Warren Beaty (as Clyde Barrow), Faye Dunaway (as Bonnie Parker)
Credit: Warner Bros/Photofest
© Warner Bros

Figure 6.1
The Alamo
Directed by John Lee Hancock
Shown: Thomas Joel Davidson (as Green Jameson), Billy Bob Thornton (as David Crockett), Patric Wilson (as William Travis), Kevin Page (as Micajah Autry)
© Buena Vista Pictures

Figure 7.1
The Jazz Singer (1927)
Directed by Alan Crosland
Shown at right: Al Jolson (as Jake Rabinowitz/Jack Robin)
Credit: Warner Bros Pictures/Photofest
© Warner Bros Pictures

Figure 8.1
Kingdom of Heaven (2005)
Directed by Ridley Scott
Shown: Orlando Bloom (as Balian of Ibelin)
© 20th Century Fox
Credit: 20th Century Fox/Photofest

Figure 9.1
Glory (1989)
Directed by Edward Zwick
Shown in foreground, from left: Jihmi Kennedy (as Private Jupiter Sharts), Denzel Washington (as Private Tripp), Morgan Freeman (as Sgt. Maj. John Rawlins)
Credit: TriStar Pictures/Photofest
© TriStar pictures
Photographer: Merrick Morton

Figure 10.1
Ride with the Devil (1999)
Directed by Ang Lee
Shown: Jonathan Brandis (as Cave Wyatt), Simon Baker (as George Clyde), Tobey Maguire (as Jake Roedel), Jeffrey Wright (as Daniel Holt)
© Universal Pictures
Photographer: John Clifford

Notes

4 Using Film to Develop Empathy as Perspective Recognition

1 Several quotes of Mrs. Johnson and her students are drawn from a previous publication on this case. For a more detailed analysis of the impact this unit had on students in Johnson's class, see Stoddard (2007).
2 The speech made by Adolf Hitler was given in 1940 to a group of munitions workers; Elie Wiesel's was his Nobel Peace Prize acceptance speech (1986).

References

Ashby, R., & Lee, P. (2001). Empathy, perspective taking, and rational understanding. In O. L. Davis, E. A. Yeager, & S. J. Foster (Eds.), *Historical empathy and perspective taking in the social studies* (pp. 21–50). Lanham, MD: Rowman & Littlefield.

Auster, A., & Quart, L. (1988). *How the war was remembered: Hollywood & Vietnam*. New York: Praeger.

Barton, K. C. (2005). Primary sources in history: Breaking through the myths. *Phi Delta Kappan, 86*(10), 745–753.

Barton, K. C., & Levstik, L. S. (2004). *Teaching history for the common good*. Mahwah, NJ: Lawrence Erlbaum Associates.

Bordwell, D. (1985). *Narration in the fiction film*. Madison, WI: University of Wisconsin Press.

Briley, R. (1990). Reel history: U.S. history, 1932–1972, as viewed through the lens of Hollywood. *The History Teacher, 23*(3), 215–236.

Briley, R. (2002). Teaching film and history. *Organization of American Historians Magazine of History, 16*(4), 5–6.

Briley, R. (2007). Doing the right thing by teaching film in the American History classroom: Spike Lee's *Do The Right Thing* as a case study. In A. S. Marcus (Ed.), *Celluloid blackboard: Teaching history with film* (pp. 217–234). Charlotte, NC: Information Age Publishing.

Bruner, J. (1996). *The culture of education*. Cambridge, MA: Harvard University Press.

Camicia, S. P. (2008). Deciding what is a controversial issue: A case study of social studies curriculum controversy. *Theory and Research in Social Education, 36*(4), 298–316.

Cornbleth, C., & Waugh, D. (1995). *The great speckled bird*. New York: St. Martin's Press.

Davis, N. Z. (2000). *Slaves on screen: Film and historical vision*. Cambridge, MA: Harvard University Press.

Davis, O. L. (2001). In pursuit of historical empathy. In O. L. Davis, E. A. Yeager, & S. J. Foster (Eds.), *Historical empathy and perspective taking in the social studies* (pp. 1–12). Lanham, MD: Rowman & Littlefield.

Dickinson, A. K., Gard, A., & Lee, P. J. (1978). Evidence in history and the classroom. In A. K. Dickinson, & P. J. Lee (Eds.), *History teaching and historical understanding* (pp. 1–20). London: Heinemann.

Dobbs, C. M. (1987). Hollywood movies from the golden age: An important resource for the classroom. *Teaching History: A Journal of Methods, 12*(1), 10–16.

Ebert, R. (1968, June 26). *The Green Berets. Rogerebert.com*. Retrieved June 10, 2009, from http://rogerebert.suntimes.com/apps/pbcs.dll/article?AID=/19680626/REVIEWS/806260301/1023

Ebert, R. (1999, December 17). *Ride with the Devil. Chicago Sun-Times*. Retrieved on March 21, 2009, from http://rogerebert.suntimes.com/apps/pbcs.dll/article?AID=/19991217/REVIEWS/912170305/1023

Epstein, T. (1998). Deconstructing differences in African-American and European-American adolescents' perspectives of U.S. History. *Curriculum Inquiry, 28*(4), 397–423.

Epstein, T., & Shiller, J. (2005). Perspective matters: Social identity and the teaching and learning of national history. *Social Education, 69*(4), 201–204.

Evans, R. (2004). *The social studies wars*. New York: Teachers College Press.

Hess, D. (2009). *Controversy in the classroom: The democratic power of discussion*. New York: Routledge.

Hobbs, R. (1999). *The uses (and misuses) of mass media resources in secondary schools*. Washington, DC: ERIC Clearinghouse (ERIC Document Number ED439452).

Hobbs, R. (2006). Non-optimal uses of video in the classroom, *Learning, media and technology, 31*(1), 35–50.

Johnson, J., & Vargas, C. (1994). The smell of celluloid in the classroom: Five great movies that teach. *Social Education, 58*(2), 109–113.

Kraig, B. (1983). Visions of the past: History in the movies. *Georgia Social Science Journal, 14*(1), 1–6.

LaCapra, D. (1985). *History & criticism*. Ithaca, NY: Cornell University Press.

Ladson-Billings, G. (2003). Lies my teacher still tells: Developing a critical race perspective toward the social studies. In G. Ladson-Billings (Ed.), *Critical race theory perspectives on the social studies* (pp. 1–11). Greenwich, CT: Information Age Publishing.

Loewen, J. (1995). *Lies my teacher told me: Everything your American History textbook got wrong*. New York: Simon & Schuster.

Marcus, A. S. (2005). "It was as it is": Feature film in the history classroom. *The Social Studies, 96*(2), 61–67.

Marcus, A. S. (2007). Students making sense of the past: "It's almost like living the event." In A. S. Marcus (Ed.), *Celluloid blackboard: Teaching history with film* (pp. 121–66). Charlotte, NC: Information Age Publishing.

Marcus, A. S., Paxton, R. J., & Meyerson, P. (2006). "The reality of it all": History students read the movies. *Theory and Research in Social Education, 34*(3), 516–552.

Marcus, A. S., & Stoddard, J. D. (2007). Tinsel town as teacher: Hollywood film in the high school history classroom. *The History Teacher, 40*(3), 303–330.

Marcus A. S., & Stoddard, J. D. (in press). The inconvenient truth about teaching history with documentary film: Strategies for presenting multiple perspectives and teaching controversial issues. *The Social Studies*.

Maynard, R. A. (1971). *The celluloid curriculum: How to use movies in the classroom*. New York: Hayden Book Company.

McDougall, L. (2006). *The Americans*. Evanston, IL: McDougall Littell, a division of Houghton Mifflin Company.

McPherson, J. M. (1996). Glory. In M. C. Carnes (Ed.), *Past imperfect: History according to the movies* (pp. 128–131). New York: Henry Holt and Company.

Metzger, S. A. (2005). The *Kingdom of Heaven*: Teaching the Crusades. *Social Education, 69*(5), 256–262.

Metzger, S. A. (2007a). Evaluating the educational potential of Hollywood history movies. In A. S. Marcus (Ed.), *Celluloid blackboard: Teaching history with film* (pp. 63–95). Charlotte, NC: Information Age Publishing.

Metzger, S. A. (2007b). Pedagogy and the historical feature film: Toward historical literacy. *Film & History, 37*(2), 67–75.

Metzger, S. A. (in press). Maximizing the educational power of history movies in the classroom. *The Social Studies*.

Metzger, S. A., & Suh, Y. (2008). Significant or safe? Two cases of instructional uses of history feature films. *Theory and Research in Social Education, 36*(1), 88–109.

Nash, G. B., Crabtree, C., & Dunn, R. E. (1997). *History on trial: Culture wars and the teaching of the past*. New York: Alfred A. Knopf.

North Carolina Department of Public Instruction (2006). Standard course of study: Eleventh grade United States History. Retrieved on March 21, 2009, from http://www.dpi.state.nc.us/curriculum/socialstudies/scos/2003–04/067eleventhgrade

O'Connor, J. (2007). Murrow confronts McCarthy: Two stages of historical analysis for film and television. In A. S. Marcus (Ed.), *Celluloid blackboard: Teaching history with film* (pp. 17–39). Charlotte, NC: Information Age Publishing.

Paris, M. J. (1997). *Integrating film and television into social studies instruction*. Bloomington, IN: ERIC Clearinghouse for Social Studies/Social Science Education (ERIC Document Number 415177).

Parker, W. C. (2003). *Teaching democracy: Unity and diversity in public life*. New York: Teachers College Press.

Paxton, R. J. (1999). A deafening silence: History textbooks and the students who read them. *Review of Educational Research, 69*, 315–339.

Pultorak, D. (1992). Problems of perception of audio-visual information in studying history. *History Teacher, 25*(3), 313–319.

Rosenstone, R. A. (1995). *Visions of the past: The challenge of film to our idea of history*. Cambridge, MA: Harvard University Press.

Rosenstone, R. A. (2002). The visual media and historical knowledge. In L. Kramer & S. Maza (Eds.), *A companion to western historical thought* (pp. 466–481). Malden, MA: Blackwell.

Rosenstone, R. A. (2004). Inventing historical truth on the silver screen. *Cineaste, 29*(2), 29–33.

Rouet, J. F., Mason, R. A., Perfetti, C. A., & Britt, M. A. (1996). Using multiple sources of evidence to reason about history. *Journal of Educational Psychology, 88*(3), 478–493.

Sabato, G. (1992). Movies bring history to life: Take it from experience. *Social Studies Review, 32*, 83–88.

Seixas, P. (1994). Confronting the moral frames of popular film: Young people respond to historical revisionism. *American Journal of Education, 102*(3), 261–285.

Seixas, P. (1996). Conceptualizing growth in historical understanding. In D. Olson & N. Torrance (Eds.), *Education and human development*. London: Blackwell.

Smith, M. (1995). *Engaging characters: Fiction, emotion, and the cinema*. New York: Oxford University Press.

Stoddard, J. (2007). Attempting to understand the lives of others: Film as a tool for developing historical empathy. In A. Marcus (Ed.) *Celluloid blackboard: Teaching history with film* (pp. 187–214). Charlotte, NC: Information Age Publishing.

Stoddard, J. (2009). The ideological implications of using "educational" film to teach controversial events. *Curriculum Inquiry, 39*(3), 407–433.

Toplin, R. B. (1996). *History by Hollywood: The use and abuse of the American past.* Urbana: University of Illinois Press.

Toplin, R. B. (2002). Invigorating history: Using film in the classroom. *Magazine of History, 16*(4), 5–6.

Toplin, R. B. (2007). In defense of the filmmakers. In R. Francaviglia & J. Rodnitzky (Eds.), *Lights, camera, history: Portraying the past in film* (pp. 113–135). College Station: Texas A&M University Press.

Tyerman, C. (2006). *God's war: A new history of the Crusades.* Cambridge, MA: Harvard University Press.

Ward, G. C., Burns, K., & Burns, R. (1990). *The Civil War: The complete text of the bestselling narrative history of the Civil War.* New York: Vintage Books.

Weidhorn, M. (2005). *High Noon:* Liberal classic? Conservative screed? *Bright Lights Film Journal, 47.* Retrieved on June 12, 2009, from http://www.brightlightsfilm.com/47/index.html

Wertsch, J. (1998). *Mind as action.* New York: Oxford University Press.

Wineburg, S. (2000). What can *Forrest Gump* tell us about students' historical understanding? *Social Education, 65*(1), 55–58.

Wineburg, S. (2001). *Historical thinking and other unnatural acts: Charting the future of teaching the past.* Philadelphia, PA: Temple University Press.

Wineburg, S., Mosborg, S., Porat, D., & Duncan, A. (2007). Common belief and the cultural curriculum: An intergenerational study of historical consciousness. *American Educational Research Journal, 44*(1), 40–76.

Yeager, E., & Foster, S. (2001). The role of empathy in development of historical understanding. In O. L. Davis, E. A. Yeager, & S. J. Foster (Eds.), *Historical empathy and perspective taking in the social studies* (pp. 13–20). Lanham, MD: Rowman & Littlefield.

Index

12 Angry Men (1957) 161
300 (2007) 7–8, 74, 111

Adventures of Huckleberry Finn, The 12, 115, 117, 129–30
African American 12–13, 22, 33, 52, 93, 115–18, 120, 123–4, 126–9, 133, 157, 160–3, 165, 167–70, 172, 177, 184, 186–7
aesthetics 156–7, 160
Age of Ballyhoo, The (1986) 122, 123
Alamo, The (2004) 6, 7, 11, 21, 23, 71, 91, 93–8, 102–3, 105, 156
Alamo 11, 91, 95–106
Alexander (2004) 6
All Quiet on the Western Front (1930) 161, 171
All the President's Men (1976) 74, 85
Amazing Grace (2006) 154
America and the Holocaust: Deceit and Indifference (1994) 10, 54, 56, 62, 65–6
America beyond the Color Line: Black in Hollywood (2002) 122, 128
American colonists 98
American Experience: New York, A Documentary Film (1999) 123
American Experience: Stephen Foster (2000) 121–2
Amistad (1997) 67, 157
Amos 'n' Andy 120, 128
Andersonville 163, 169
Anglo settlers 98
Antietam, battle of 164, 165
Apocalypse Now (1979) 88
Atanarjuat: The Fast Runner (2001) 49
Asian 33, 34, 35, 37–8, 44, 127, 154
atomic bomb 107
Aunt Jemima 123
Austin, Stephen 98

baseball 123, 165
Battle for Algiers (1964) 189
Bury my Heart at Wounded Knee (2007) 158
Between Two Worlds: The Hmong Shaman in America (1984) 35–6
blackface 12, 111, 113, 116, 117–21, 124–30
Bonnie and Clyde (1968) 11, 71, 73, 74, 75, 76, 77–8, 80–3, 85–8
Bowie, Jim 97, 98, 99–100
Broadway 120, 123, 125
Bull Run, Battle of 164
Bunker Hill 168
Burchard, Peter 166, 170
Burn! (Queimada) (1969) 189
Burns, Lucy 107

California Gold Rush 94
Catholic 99
Causes of the Civil War (2003) 178, 180–1
Chinatown (1974) 85
Civil War 13, 22, 52, 93, 156–7, 158, 159, 160, 161–5, 166, 168–70, 171–3, 175–6, 177, 179–81, 184–5, 189
Cleveland Indians 123
Clooney, George 93
Coming Home (1978) 88
Confederate 164–5, 166, 168
Connecticut 13, 93, 115, 138, 161, 162, 163, 168, 171
Connecticut 29th 163, 171
content knowledge 17, 18, 20–1, 22, 47, 94, 99, 108, 110, 137, 139, 149, 152–3
Cool Hand Luke (1967) 76, 88
Crockett, Davy 91, 97, 98–9, 103–4
Crossing, The (2000) 94

D-Day 25, 52, 172
Dances with Wolves (1990) 28, 94, 104, 158, 173
Deer Hunter, The (1978) 88
Divine Horsemen: The Living Gods of Haiti (1985) 49
Do the Right Thing (1989) 76, 193
documentary films 10, 21, 32, 34, 53, 65, 69, 91–2, 94–5, 105, 129, 161
Douglas, Frederick 165–6
Dr. Strangelove or: How I learned to Stop Worrying and Love the Bomb (1964) 75, 189

Easy Rider (1969) 11, 76, 77, 78, 83–5, 87
El Norte (1983) 49
Eminem 126
Enemy at the Gates (2001) 52

Fat Man and Little Boy (1989) 107–8
feature films 4–5, 10, 71, 91, 95, 105, 129, 131, 137, 161
film as entertainment 116
film as historical narrative 151, 155, 158, 175, 187–8
film to visualize the past 12, 155, 159–60, 171
films as texts 75
Flags of Our Fathers (2006) 34, 45
Footloose (1984) 116
Forrest Gump (1994) 3, 9, 71, 161
Fort Wagner 160, 164, 165, 166, 167–8, 170
Freeman, Morgan 159, 166, 167
Frontier House (2002) 67
Full Metal Jacket (1987) 88

Gallant Hours, The (1960) 52
Gangs of New York (2002) 173
Gates, Henry Louis, Jr. 122, 128
Georgia 165
"Gimme a Pig Foot and a Bottle of Beer" 123
Gladiator (2000) 6, 21
Glory (1989) 13, 22–3, 52, 93, 94, 157, 159–60, 161–73, 176, 186
Good Morning Vietnam (1987) 48
Good Night and Good Luck (2005) 93, 133
Graduate, The (1967) 11, 76, 77, 78, 83, 85, 87
Gran Torino (2008) 10, 31, 34, 35–6, 37, 39, 45–6, 48–9
Grapes of Wrath, The (1940) 52, 53
Great Migration 12, 118, 123, 124
Green Berets, The (1968) 11, 74, 76, 77, 78, 79–80, 84, 87
Groves, General 107

Hair (1978) 88
Harlem Renaissance 12, 116, 118, 123, 124
Hartford Courant, The 126, 168
Hearts and Minds (1974) 88
Hess, Diana 109, 114
High Noon (1952) 74
History Channel 4, 21, 147, 150
historical controversies 9, 111, 136–7, 154
historical empathy i, 9, 10, 15, 25, 27–8, 47, 51, 53, 64–66, 93, 95, 102, 107, 151, 156, 161, 165; for

caring 10, 27–8; as perspective recognition 10, 27–8, 64
historical film literacy i, 6, 7–9, 15, 32, 71, 81, 92, 104–5, 108, 115, 171
historical thinking 5, 6, 9, 18–19, 22, 25, 136, 154
Holocaust 10, 29, 30, 32, 51, 53, 54, 55, 56, 57, 59, 60, 62–3, 64–6, 173
Holocaust: In Memory of Millions, The (1994) 54, 56, 59
Hotel Rwanda (2004) 32, 67, 133

In Memory of Millions (1994) 10, 55, 60–63, 65–6
Iraq 7, 46, 111, 133–4, 139
Iron Jawed Angels (2004) 93, 94, 107, 157

Jackson, Stonewall 162, 164
Jazz Singer, The (1927) 11–12, 111, 113, 115–20, 123–6, 128–32
Jefferson, President 98
Jeremiah Johnson (1972) 67
Jews 6, 29, 32, 55–6, 59–64, 125, 136, 139, 141
JFK (1991) 75
Joplin, Scott 125
Journals of Knud Rasmussen, The (2006) 49

Killing Fields, The (1984) 34, 35–36, 38–39, 76, 88
Kingdom of Heaven (2005) 6, 12, 23, 111, 135, 136–7, 138–9, 140–153
Kirstein, Lincoln 166, 170

La Bamba (1987) 116
Last Samurai, The (2003) 6, 111, 153
Latino/a 115
Lay This Laurel (1973) 166, 170
Lee, Spike 7, 93
Letters from Iwo Jima (2007) 34, 45–6, 154
Liberty Bell 99
Liquor, Shirley Q. 126–7
Little Big Man (1970) 189
Long Walk Home, The (1990) 157
Lost Battalion, The (2001) 161, 170
Louisiana Purchase 94, 98

Malcolm X (1992) 76, 93
Manhattan Project 107
Marie Antoinette (2006) 6, 7
Massachusetts 54th 93, 159, 160, 163, 164, 165
Master and Commander (2003) 53, 156
Matewan (1987) 53
McCarthy, Senator Joseph 133
McCarthyism 75, 93
MC Hammer 116–17, 121, 126, 128
McPherson, James M. 160
media 4, 5, 12, 18, 19, 46, 84, 94, 114, 116, 122–3, 124, 128–9, 133, 178, 181
Midway (1976) 52
Mississippi Burning (1988) 76
Motion Picture Association of America (MPAA) 25
Mr. Smith Goes to Washington (1939) 53, 94
multiculturalism 151–2

multiple perspectives 5, 9, 12, 19, 29, 52, 54, 60, 66–7, 107, 109–11, 114, 132, 134, 136–7, 139, 140, 144, 147, 149, 151–4, 161, 179
Murphy, Eddie 121, 127
Murrow, Edward R. 133

narrative 4, 6, 12–13, 18, 21, 25, 29, 32–4, 38–9, 41–3, 46, 48, 52, 61, 71, 77, 84, 91–3, 103, 105–7, 110, 129, 133, 137, 151–2, 155–8, 168, 172, 175–6, 180, 182, 184–5, 187–9
Native Americans 32, 104, 111, 124, 136, 154, 173
Neill, Colonel 100
Newton, Alexander 168
Night 173
Norbit (2007) 11, 116–17, 121, 126–7, 128
Nutty Professor, The (1996) 128
Nutty Professor II: The Klumps, The (2000) 128

O Brother, Where Art Thou? (2000) 116
"O Captain, My Captain" 163, 169
"O, Susannah" 122
One Gallant Rush (1965) 166, 170
Oppenheimer, Robert 107
Oregon Trail 94

Patriot, The (2000) 6, 23
Paul, Alice 107
PBS 4, 44, 63, 121, 122–3, 181
PBS: American Experience 56, 63, 121–3
Pearl Harbor (2001) 17, 22, 52, 93
People Like Us: Social Class in America (2001) 122, 128
Platoon (1986) 11, 76–80, 87
popular culture 5, 9, 11–12, 18, 71, 86, 115, 119, 127–9, 177, 179, 184, 186–7
presentism 6, 32, 79, 136–8, 153
primary documents 5, 11, 24, 53, 73, 88–9, 142, 145, 149, 163
primary sources 11, 70, 74, 86–8, 92, 94, 101, 103–4, 106–7, 140, 159, 162, 168, 170–2, 189
Prohibition 123–4

Rabbit-Proof Fence (2002) 49
Redacted (2007) 133
reflective planning 20
Ride with the Devil (1999) 13, 29, 158, 175–81, 185, 189
Roots (1977) 67
Rusesabagina, Paul 133
Rwanda 32, 67, 133

San Antonio 98
San Jacinto 101
Sankofa (1993) 189
Santa Anna 97, 98–9, 101, 104
Saving Private Ryan (1998) 25, 52, 156, 172
schema 176
Schindler's List (1993) 29, 60, 160, 173
Searchers, The (1956) 94, 104

secondary documents 75, 105
Seinfeld 133
Shake Hands with the Devil: The Journey of Roméo Dallaire (2004) 67
Shaw, Colonel 22, 164, 166, 167–8, 170
Shoah Foundation 173
Smith, Bessie 117, 123
Smoke Signals (1998) 29, 49
slaves 23, 52, 93, 98, 165, 167, 189
Sometimes in April (2005) 67
Soulman (1986) 11
South Carolina 23, 164–5, 176
Spain 98
special education 93–4, 138, 144, 161
Split Horn, The: Life of a Hmong Shaman in America (2001) 35–6, 43–6
Sponge Bob Square Pants 117, 121, 128
standardized curriculum 177–8
suffrage 107
suffragettes 157
Swing Kids (1993) 10, 51, 52, 54, 55, 56, 61–2, 64–5

Tejanos 99
Ten Canoes (2006) 49
Texan 99
Texas 83, 86, 93, 95–104
Texians 95–7, 99, 102
textbooks 3, 4, 5, 7, 13, 23–4, 32, 37, 46, 47, 69, 71, 74, 76, 79, 91, 105, 107, 114, 131, 133, 150, 157, 159
Thirteen Days (2000) 157
Titanic (1997) 93
Toplin, Robert Brent 5–6, 160
Tora! Tora! Tora! (1970) 52
totalitarianism 10, 51, 53, 54, 55, 57, 58
Tracker, The (2002) 49
Travis, William 91, 97, 98, 99, 100, 101–2
Twain, Mark 12, 117, 129

U.S.–Mexican War 94, 103

Vietnam: The Ten Thousand Day War (1980) 35–6, 43

Wave, The (1981) 10, 54, 55, 56, 57–61, 64–7
Washington, DC 107
Washington Redskins 123
"We Gather Together" 122
Westward Expansion 11, 23, 71, 91, 94–5, 98, 102–3, 122, 154, 157, 189
White Chicks (2004) 128
White House 107
"Whiskey in the Jar" 122
Whitman, Walt 163, 169
Wiesel, Elie 54, 59–60, 173
women's movement 107
World War II 17, 25, 29, 34, 52, 54, 55, 56, 62–4, 79, 85, 107, 154

Yom Kippur 125